CALL ME
TED

CALL ME
TED

TED TURNER
with Bill Burke

Doubleday Large Print
Home Library Edition

GRAND CENTRAL
PUBLISHING

NEW YORK   BOSTON

Grand Central Publishing
Hachette Book Group
237 Park Avenue
New York, NY 10017

Grand Central Publishing is a division of Hachette Book Group, Inc.

The Grand Central Publishing name and logo is a
trademark of Hachette Book Group, Inc.

Printed in the United States of America

ISBN 978-1-60751-287-5

**This Large Print Book carries the
Seal of Approval of N.A.V.H.**

This book is dedicated to my children. Of all my accomplishments, they're still the ones of which I'm most proud.

Contents

x   Contents

Preface

People have been after me for years to tell my story, but I was always too busy living my life to consider stopping to write about it. I've also resisted because I don't spend a lot of time dwelling on the past or thinking about myself. In fact, one of the reasons I think I've been able to accomplish as much as I have is because I prefer to live in the present while spending my spare moments thinking about the future. But since stepping away from my company I've had the opportunity to reflect. I realize that my life has been an amazing ride and that now might be a good time to finally work on a book about it.

What follows are my best recollections of the full scope of my life, from my childhood to my business career, my time in competitive sailing, my ongoing efforts in philanthropy, and, of course, my family life. Some friends, family members, and colleagues have also been kind enough to contribute some anecdotes of their own. I've tried to tell my story in a way that you'll find interesting, entertaining, and maybe even a little inspiring.

I've accomplished a lot, but nothing was ever handed to me and I've had to bounce back from numerous setbacks. My childhood wasn't easy, and I lost my father and my sister tragically and too young. When I began sailing I lost race after race and nearly died at sea a few times, but I stayed with it long enough and hard enough to become a world-class champion skipper. After buying the Atlanta Braves, I suffered through a dismal string of losing seasons before we turned it around and eventually won the World Series. Through a lot of hard work and a little bit of luck I built a successful media company and a large fortune, only to get pushed aside and lose 80 percent of my wealth, all within a two-year period. (Don't worry about me, though—I'm figuring out how to get by on just a couple of billion dollars!)

As I built my wealth I grew more active in land conservation and philanthropy, and trying to solve some of the more serious challenges facing our planet has given me more satisfaction than I ever experienced in business. While I've struggled unsuccessfully to maintain my marriages, I'm pleased to have raised five terrific children, and as I approach my seventieth birthday, I'm happy to have my health, lots of energy, and plenty of challenges I plan to tackle before I'm through.

Going back through it all has reminded me that my life really has been pretty interesting. I hope you have as much fun reading about it as I've had living it.

CALL ME
TED

Early Years

My first word was "pretty." At least that's what my parents told me. As the story goes, I was looking at a butterfly and out popped, "pretty!" Other parents might have wished for "Mommy" or "Daddy," but by all accounts, mine were thrilled to hear my first word express an appreciation for nature.

My parents would probably never have met and I would never have been born had it not been for the tragic death of my mother's first fiancé—from complications of a burst appendix—the very day before their proposed wedding. Throughout her grieving, my mom remained very close to her fiancé's family and for the next several years did little if any dating.

It was toward the end of my mother's grieving period that Ed Turner (my father) made his way from his home in Mississippi to Cincinnati, Ohio. He was by all accounts a very enterprising young man and moved north after accepting a promising position in the sales department of a local Chevrolet dealer. In addition to responding to the appeal of a job in the automobile business, it's also likely that my father was eager to leave his home state. His parents had lost nearly everything after the stock market crash. They were living in near-poverty conditions as Mississippi sharecroppers, and opportunities in their area were slim. In high school my father had won acceptance to Duke University but hard times prevented his parents from being able to send him. He wound up going to Millsaps College, a less expensive Methodist school in Jackson, Mississippi. But even at the less pricey school, paying tuition was a hardship for my grandparents, and with a job opportunity up north he left school early, before ever earning his degree.

When my father reached Ohio the arrival of this gregarious and charming southerner did not go unnoticed. One Cincinnatian who took an instant liking to my dad was young George Rooney, my mom's brother. Hopeful that his sister might emerge from her grieving and find a new beau, George insisted that the two should meet. My mother, Florence Rooney, was a bright, beautiful, and elegant woman with a terrific personality. She stood about five foot eight, and my father, who was six feet tall, always liked tall women. My dad was smitten from the moment they met and he courted her aggressively. His extra effort was justified, as their differences were significant. In addition to being a southerner, my father was raised Protestant, and for the Rooneys, who were Catholic, marrying outside the church was no small matter. I've been told that it was only after he agreed to raise his children in the Catholic faith that my mom accepted his proposal for marriage. They were wed in a Catholic ceremony in the Rooneys' home on August 14, 1937.

I came along on November 19, 1938, the first Turner born north of the Mason-Dixon line, and as the first grandchild on either side of the family I was showered with lots of love from my parents and extended family. Some of my earliest memories are of holding the screen door open for my great-grandmother on my mom's side. She lived until she was ninety-one and used to call me "a little dickens." We would visit my father's Mississippi relatives on occasion but living my early years in Cincinnati exposed me more to my mother's side of the family. My grandfather George Rooney lived with two of his unmarried sisters—back then they were referred to as "old maids"—and I got along great with all three of them.

But despite being surrounded by loving family, my parents' marriage had its challenges from the very start and their differences over their parenting especially added to the tension. Regardless of his courtship assurances, after I was born my father let my mother know that he would not allow his children to be brought up Catholic. This was no small issue for my mom and the Rooneys. I'll never know exactly how those conversations went, but although I did attend a Catholic church occasionally, I was not raised Catholic. My mother never spoke of the issue in front of me but I'm sure she wasn't happy about it.

My earliest memories of our Cincinnati home are mostly pleasant. I was an energetic child and spent much of my time in the backyard and at the creek that ran through a little vacant lot down the street. I'd turn over rocks to find little bugs and crayfish and take them home to put in a jar. I was the center of my parents' attention for nearly three years, before the birth of my sister, Mary Jean. A beautiful baby, Mary Jean came along in September of 1941 and was the apple of my parents' eye. That date was significant because when the Japanese attacked Pearl Harbor just a few months later, my father joined the Navy. When it came time to head out for basic training, my parents also decided that military barracks and Quonset huts were no place for a little boy. They took their infant daughter, Mary Jean, but left me behind to attend a Cincinnati boarding school. I was four years old.

I don't recall the name of that school but

I sure do remember that I didn't like it. I went from living with my family in a nice home with a grass yard and a creek hollow down the street to a cold, concrete dorm room and a gray gravel courtyard framed by a chain-link fence. The place felt like a prison, and as a four-year-old, it was hard for me to understand why my parents took my sister and left me behind.

The school allowed me to spend Sunday afternoons with my grandparents but the other six and a half days and nights were extremely lonely. I don't recall feelings of anger toward my parents for leaving me behind, but I do know that I was unhappy a lot of the time. There was one woman there who served as a floor proctor and I have vague memories of her helping me fall asleep at night when I was feeling especially sad and lonely. The age of four is a very impressionable time and psychiatrists I've seen later in my life have attributed a number of insecurities I've had ever since to being left alone at such a young age. For example, to this day, I have a significant problem being by myself. I don't like to be isolated from other people and I also don't like to feel fenced in. Looking back, that boarding school even had an impact on my eating habits; they served us oatmeal every morning and sixty-five years later I still don't like it!

My unhappiness must have been obvious, as my parents decided from afar that I should spend the following school year with my Turner grandparents in rural Mississippi. They lived in a small town of about two hundred named Sumner (which later gained infamy as the site of the murder of Emmett Till, the tragic event that helped trigger the civil rights movement). Moving to Sumner meant more transition for me and while it was hard to leave Ohio, I was thrilled to get out of that awful school and was happy to be back with loving family members on a full-time basis.

My time in Mississippi provided constant exposure to nature. Living with my grandparents on the edge of town I observed all kinds of animals and birds and insects and they fascinated me. I spent hours fishing off a nearby bridge with a piece of bacon hanging at the end of a string and had fun catching turtles. While I was still isolated from my immediate family and I had plenty of lonely moments, I enjoyed spending so much time in nature and my memories of this time are mostly positive.

My father returned from the war the following year and our family was finally reunited in Cincinnati. After sending me to public kindergarten in Sumner, for first grade my parents enrolled me in a private school named Lotspeich. I was a restless kid and got in trouble a lot. I didn't do anything really bad, just a lot of little mischievous things like putting pebbles in the other kids' galoshes. Today's schools would probably jump to the conclusion that I had Attention Deficit Disorder, but that wasn't the case. After being isolated and alone for so long I was simply craving attention. My teachers became exasperated and after just one year they made it clear to my mom and dad that they didn't want me back for a second.

My parents didn't have a lot of money back then and while it may have been a financial relief to send me to public school, I'm sure they were disappointed to have to do it. For the next couple of years I attended Avondale, a local public school, and my behavior in this new setting was pretty much the same. I caused plenty of mischief but it was a lot harder to get kicked out of public school than private and I managed to stay there from my second grade year through the first part of my fifth grade.

After all the moves and separation of my earlier years, this was a time of relative stability for me. But that didn't mean that our home life was always smooth sailing. My dad was a complicated man. He was a perfectionist in every aspect of his life—from his dress and overall appearance to the way he conducted his business and raised his family. He was also a deep thinker. He wanted to do the right thing and he read a lot, including books about parenting. Putting into practice all the different approaches he learned about meant that his style was often unpredictable.

One constant in his parenting, however, was strict discipline and a firm belief in the value of hard work. I was only eight or nine years old when my father started making me work during summer vacation. I began at about four hours a day, and in those earlier years my chief responsibility was working in our yard. We had a man-powered push mower and if you've ever used one you know how tough they can be. Every little stick or acorn you'd hit would jam the thing up. And all these ants and chiggers would get you while you were down on your hands and knees pulling weeds. I'd be bent over, sweating up a storm, and my friends would come skipping by and say, "Ted, you want to go fishing?" I hated having to tell them I still had three hours more work to do. It was such drudgery that to this day I don't like to do yard work. I might have been out of school, but summertime for me was not a vacation.

My father was also an alcoholic and a heavy smoker. I don't know how much of a problem he had with these addictions before the war but I'm sure his experiences in the Pacific had an impact on him. He told me that he loved his time in the Navy, but while he appreciated the opportunity to see places like Australia and the Philippines, he also saw combat. He told me that he once killed a Japanese sailor at close range with a pistol. My father and some other guys were looking for souvenirs on a Japanese ship that was half sunk in shallow water in Manila Bay. Out of no-where, a starving, crazed man came run-ning out at them. He was screaming and hollering in Japanese and continued to charge my father so Dad shot him in self-defense.

But regardless of the reasons, my dad was a volatile man with a quick temper. When he drank, his temper got worse, and when I acted up, he'd spank me. This up-set my mother and I can remember times when I was getting a spanking and my mother stood outside my door, begging my father to stop. Dad would have me across his knee and say things like "I'm doing this to help you learn to do the right thing and to grow up to be someone we can both be proud of." Oftentimes he'd use a razor strap and he would say that it hurt him more to beat me than it would if I were hitting him.

I had no way of knowing if this was true but one time when I was only about six or seven years old he decided he'd prove it to me. I'll never forget it. He handed me the razor strap, lay face down on the bed, and told me to spank *him.* I tried to obey him but I couldn't. I loved him so much that I dropped the strap and broke down and cried.

Looking back, some of the biggest arguments my parents had concerned his treatment of me, but my dad ran an old-fashioned household and he insisted that pretty much everything had to be his way.

━━━━━━━ A TED STORY ━━━━━━━

"Dr. Jekyll and Mr. Hyde"
—Lucy Rooney

(LUCY ROONEY, TED'S AUNT, WAS MARRIED TO FLORENCE'S BROTHER GEORGE "BUD" ROONEY, WHO PASSED AWAY IN 1993. LUCY CONTINUES TO LIVE IN CINCINNATI, OHIO.)

During their courtship, Ed was very charming and he pursued Florence with everything he had. But their marriage ran into trouble early. His behavior was almost like a Dr. Jekyll and Mr. Hyde. He told Florence they could raise their children Catholic, but after Ted was born he said he'd sooner jump off the roof than do that and he wanted Florence to stop attending church herself. My sister-in-law was elegant and strong but Ed dominated that household. He also seemed to favor his daughter, Mary Jean. He could be brutal to young Teddy and the abuse began early. I recall one occasion when Ted was sick with a cold or flu. He was still just a little boy but when the doctor paid his house call, he found bruises on Teddy's body. Sometimes, when Ted was sitting in his high chair, Ed would come behind him and flick his ear with his fingers, hard. He said it would "toughen him up." Perhaps it did but it was certainly a difficult environment for a young boy to grow up in.

My father was not an easy man but I knew that he loved me and that he took a strong interest in my education and development. By the time I finished the fourth grade, he and my mother were concerned about the quality of the education I was getting in public school. At this same time— the summer of 1947—my parents were preparing to leave Cincinnati to move to Georgia. By this time, my dad had decided to make his career in the outdoor advertising business and had acquired a small billboard company in Savannah. The opportunity was a good one and I'm sure he was pleased to be moving back south. Had the decision been left to my mother, I imagine she would have tried to find a Catholic school or some other private institution but my father insisted that he made the money, so he made the rules. He was a conservative man in every way. (At the height of the Cold War he used to tell me that "the commies" were going to defeat the United States and would shoot everyone who had more than $50. For years I never walked around with more than $49 in my wallet!) My dad also placed a high value on his experience in the Navy and he believed that a military-style education would be good for me. When we moved to Savannah in October of 1947 I attended fifth grade at Georgia Military Academy, or GMA, located just south of Atlanta (the school exists today as Woodward Academy).

As a nine-year-old with a November

birthday I was one of the youngest kids in my grade and by arriving in October, I was joining my classmates a full month late. These factors alone would have been hard enough, but going to a southern military school as an Ohio transplant was a real recipe for disaster. It was now the late 1940s but I'd swear some of those kids thought they were still fighting the Civil War. They wanted nothing more than to make a little "Yankee" like me miserable. Some of the boarding students had been there since the first grade and these were some of the toughest kids I had ever seen in my life—it was like *Lord of the Flies*.

I decided I needed to show them that I was tough, too. I shared a bunk room with three other kids and on my first night there I announced to my roommates that I was going to be "the boss." They seemed to be okay with my plan but what I didn't consider was that there were four more kids on the other side of the bathroom that we shared. They were considered part of our group, and after sizing them up I figured I could handle them, too. When I let these guys know I would be their boss as well, they took the news a little differently. After looking at each other for an instant, all of a sudden they jumped me. Three of them held me down while the other one kicked me in the head. I thought they were going to kill me. My other three roommates stood by and watched, and my attempted dominance of the room group came to a swift, painful, and humiliating end.

It was a grim start and it was several months before things got any easier. One time, some kids spread a rumor that I had badmouthed General Robert E. Lee. It wasn't true but the news was enough to send a group of my classmates after me like a lynch mob. They chased me yelling, "Kill the Yankee!" I ran like hell until I got to a row of lockers and managed to squeeze inside one and pull the door closed. They came around the corner and guessed I was in one of those lockers but I stayed really quiet while they milled around outside like a swarm of bees. There had to be fifty of them and although I was really scared and short of breath, I stayed still until they gradually lost interest and drifted away. They didn't chase me much after that but they did make it a common practice to storm into my room and jump on top of me on my bed. Ten kids at a time would pile on and I'd nearly panic because I couldn't barely breathe.

I stayed as tough as I could, though, and by the end of the first semester I had become one of the guys. Some of the military training rubbed off on me and I suppose there were benefits to the overall experience. But my parents took some pity on me and the following year I was enrolled in Savannah public school where I spent my happiest year so far. It was great for me to be out of that confined military school environment and I enjoyed being able to spend more of my free time outside and in nature.

My dad's sporting magazines used to run ads for the Northwestern School of Taxidermy's correspondence course. For 50 cents a month they would send you a different how-to booklet and I was probably the first eleven-year-old who ever signed up. I used to find dead birds and squirrels, or on occasion I'd shoot them with my BB gun. The house we were living in had a garage with a little office-room inside. My parents never used it so that's where I did my taxidermy work. It was a pretty complicated process but I found it fascinating and I learned a lot about nature and biology.

Another bright spot during that time was the arrival of a twenty-one-year-old black man my father hired to take care of his new sailboat. His name was Jimmy Brown and little did I know that for the next fifty years Jimmy would be one of the most important men in my life.

Shortly after buying a fifty-foot schooner (which he renamed *Merry Jean,* a play on my sister's name), my dad realized that the boat was going to be a lot of work. He hired Jimmy after several friends recommended him as a capable handyman. Jimmy was raised by his mother and spoke with an accent typical of the kind of rural fishing village he was raised in, on a small island off the coast of Savannah. He learned a lot about fishing and fixing boats before being drafted into the Army and served with a medic division in the final stages of World War II.

As soon as Jimmy arrived, he and I started spending a lot of time together. He was like an older brother but we behaved more like two good friends. Eventually, he became like a second father to me. With my dad away or at work so much and my mom spending time with my sister, Jimmy and I would hang out—we'd fish, sail, go cast netting for shrimp, or just explore together. A birth defect left him with a slightly withered arm but Jimmy remained physically active and loved being outdoors. He taught me a lot about nature and a lot about life. I loved every minute of the time I spent with him and he became one of my best friends ever. Because of my love for him, and my father's color blindness, I grew up without a shred of prejudice. All in all it was great to be home, but consistent with the pattern of my childhood, that stability would be short-lived. Another change loomed.

2

McCallie

After just one relatively uneventful year of living at home, my dad then decided that for seventh grade it was time to send me away again, this time to McCallie, a well-regarded Christian military academy in Chattanooga, Tennessee. In truth, I was disappointed and my mom wasn't thrilled, either, but my father reminded her once again that he controlled the purse strings so he could make these decisions.

About half of McCallie's students were boarders, the other half were day students. There might have been four or five eighth graders living in the dorms but I was the only seventh grader so I was clearly the youngest, and also the smallest kid living on campus. This made me an easy target and the older guys picked on me from the start. It was a really tough time for me. At that age I hadn't gotten as much love as I would have liked and I was angry for having been sent away once again. I felt a need to create a stir and to draw attention to myself and I figured that if I couldn't be loved, I might as well be a hell-raiser. So, from the very beginning I set out to be one of the worst cadets in my class.

One of my first nights there, it was well past lights out but I was in my bunk reading. I loved books and enjoyed reading well into the night, but at McCallie, this was strictly against the rules. They had professors take turns as hall monitors and I could hear this one's footsteps approaching our door. With a lights-out violation, I knew I'd be up for demerits and that he would ask for my name to put it in the records. At military schools like McCallie they call you by your last name followed by your first initial. So, for example, with my formal name being "Robert," I'd be "Turner, R." It was too early in the year for him to know all our names, so I decided to have some fun with him. "Who's responsible for the light on in this room?" the professor barked outside my door. "Edison, T." was my wise-guy response.

Sure enough, when the demerits were posted the next morning on the bulletin board, my room had two demerits listed under "Edison, T"!

Bad as I was, I managed to make a few friends, mostly guys who were willing to join me doing all kinds of stupid things to pass the time and to stir up a little trouble. We'd put small containers of water on the top of an open door and leave it cracked so when someone came zipping in the water would fall on his head. We'd fold paper in a certain way so you could inflate it like a little balloon, fill it up with water, and throw it out a third story window at students heading home from the mess hall. By the time they figured out what had hit them you'd pull your head back in and run like the devil so they couldn't find you when they came tearing up the stairs.

When I noticed that one of the trees on campus was jammed full with a family of squirrels, I got an idea for some mischief

and found a willing accomplice in my roommate. I grabbed my laundry bag and shin-
nied up the side of the tree to a hole about
twenty feet up. Several minutes before, I'd
seen the squirrels enter the tree through
that hole, so I knew they were in there. I
covered the hole with the opening of the
bag while below my buddy knelt down with
a can of Kiwi shoe polish. We always had
plenty of Kiwi on hand and through some
previous foul play I'd discovered that it was
not only good for shining shoes, it also
burned well and put out thick black smoke
in the process. My accomplice slid the
lighted can into the hole toward the base
of the tree, and our plan worked.

Whiffs of smoke rose up the tree and
BAM! BAM! BAM!—three squirrels shot
into my bag at about ninety miles an hour—
they almost knocked me off the tree. Somehow I was able to hang on and tighten the
drawstring so I could lower it down to my
roommate. The squirrels inside were going crazy and it was funny watching them
try to punch their way out. We ran back to
the dorm with the bag of squirrels and let
them go on the third floor, where they took
off and ran around like mad. It took about

half an hour for our startled dorm-mates to get the windows open and shoo them out.

The mischief making was fun, but McCallie was a tough school whose administrators were determined to make gentlemen out of us. Their disciplinary system was elaborate but the bottom line was you got demerits for different offenses and were only allowed up to ten per week. These were very public, and as with my lights out violation, were posted next to everybody's name on the dormitory bulletin board. For anyone racking up more than ten, punishment was reserved for Saturdays. Students who steered clear of punishment were given four hours of freedom every Saturday afternoon from 1:00 to 5:00, and would often hitchhike downtown to hang out or go to the movies.

But if you had more than ten demerits by 1:00 on Saturday, you had to walk laps around the "bullring," our name for the track, and the punishment was one quarter mile lap for each demerit over ten. That doesn't sound like much but I got into trouble so frequently that it wasn't hard for me to rack up as many as fifty marks in a week. That's forty laps, or ten miles! The laps took forever because you couldn't run—they made you maintain a walk's pace. Needless to say, ten-mile walks kept me away from the movies and all the fun the other guys were having. But they were all part of my program and the price I'd have to pay for being one of McCallie's worst cadets.

You might wonder how one kid managed to get all those demerits, but in truth, for me it really wasn't very hard. First of all, they didn't just give them out for big stuff like setting squirrels loose in the dorm. They also put a lot of weight on your general attitude, which they measured by things like military drills and personal inspections. They figured they could tell how much you believed in their system by how well your shoes were shined. So if you really wanted to get ahead and were with the system 100 percent you'd have the best spit shine on your shoes that you could muster. In my case, not only did I not shine my shoes, I used them to show my disdain for the system. Right before inspection I'd take the heel of one shoe and grind down the tops of the other so that they were the scruffiest-looking things you ever saw. Every day like clockwork I'd get demerits for my shoes and every weekend I'd wear them for laps around the bullring. I wanted all of McCallie to know I was a rebel; heading to the track while they left for the movies was my way of driving the point home.

I was disruptive in class, too, and had to see the Discipline Committee about every two weeks. This group consisted of the headmaster and five or six professors. I'd have to walk in there and they'd tell me to grab my ankles and then they'd whack me hard on the backside with a paddle. It wasn't pleasant, but I could take it. I'd endured worse from my dad and I was so eager for attention that even this humiliating punishment couldn't deter me.

My first year at McCallie I was in front of the Discipline Committee about fifteen times out of a possible eighteen. They grew so tired of seeing me there that they even overhauled the system for the following school year. Among other changes, they made a rule that if you faced the discipline committee more than three times you'd be suspended. This got my attention and I was always careful to avoid crossing that line. Getting in trouble was one thing, but getting kicked out and being sent back home was *not* an option.

While my misbehavior continued, I never broke the school's code of military honor. We were not to lie, cheat, or steal nor tolerate that behavior in others. As difficult as I may have been regarding my personal appearance and disruptions around the campus, I was raised to be honorable and took the code seriously, even to the point of turning in classmates who fell short of its standards. We were required to attend church and Sunday school in two separate buildings and one time I saw a kid steal a magazine from a drugstore on the walk between the two buildings. It was against the code so I turned him in. They didn't throw you out for your first honor code violation, but you had to get up and apologize before the entire student body. After that, the Student Council tried your case. The council consisted of seniors elected by the student body. They took their jobs seriously and came up with some pretty severe punishments. For the first offense you'd get a lot of demerits and might be confined to campus for three weeks or so. The second time you might get suspended from school for three or four days and have to go home. It really was a very fair system. They believed in honor and I think it was good training for all of us to have to live up to those standards.

McCallie was a tough place and my summers at home weren't a whole lot easier. By the time I was twelve, during my summers my father had me working forty-two-and-a-half-hour weeks at his billboard company. Being the boss's son didn't get me special treatment—in fact, I did a lot of the toughest jobs. I spent a lot of the time with the construction crew, the bill posters, and the sign painters—the guys who had to go out in the Georgia summer sun to build the billboards and post the signs. The toughest assignments I got were cutting weeds in front of the billboards. They were planted right off the highway and the grass would grow high enough to hide rattlesnakes and all kinds of other critters. We'd have to slog through swampy water and we got bitten by mosquitoes and leeches.

I was the only kid and the only white person in the group. The entire team was black and they were great big bruisers. They could have stomped me into the ground but I followed their orders and worked hard. My dad had hired good people and as long as everyone did their job, we got along great. In later years I spent more time with the salespeople and traveled around town with a briefcase full of presentations. But in those earlier summers I got a sense for how the tough, physical side of the business got done.

The billboard work was always hard, but my toughest McCallie summer was the year my sister got sick. With big blue eyes and long brown curls, Mary Jean was a beautiful, sweet, charming girl. She made everyone smile and our family adored her. Her early schooling was all done from home and she attended local private schools in Cincinnati and Savannah. That meant most of the time I spent with her was during the summer. She loved horses and riding lessons were her favorite thing in the world. She idolized her big brother and I loved her dearly. She used to beg me to play chess with her, and I'd make her bet a quarter on every game. I almost always won, so soon she'd be broke, and I'd buy her whatever she would have spent her allowance on, mostly candy and ice cream. Her special place in our family made the news of her diagnosis particularly devastating.

Mary Jean was just twelve years old when she developed lupus erythematosus, an autoimmune disease. While turning a body's defenses against itself, the disease makes you vulnerable to other potential problems. In Mary Jean's case, we knew from the beginning that it was serious. Her condition deteriorated quickly. Shortly after the initial diagnosis, she then developed encephalitis, a swelling of her brain that put her in a coma. She didn't emerge for two months, and by the time she did she had experienced significant brain damage. My parents were also told that their precious twelve-year-old daughter might have as few as five years to live.

Needless to say, this put a tremendous strain on everyone. For the next several years, my parents tried to provide the best care possible. My father was practical and solution-oriented and brought her to all the finest specialists he could find. My mother played more of a nurturing role, making sure that Mary Jean was as comfortable and loved as she could be throughout her ordeal. It was incredibly hard to watch such a wonderful girl go through such agony and it was a situation that would have strained the strongest of marriages. For my mother and father, it was almost too much to bear.

It was hard for me, too. Because of the severe mental damage caused by her encephalitis, it became very difficult to interact or to communicate with Mary Jean. I remember sitting on the floor with my little sister and rolling a beach ball back and forth between us. That was the most we could play with each other. There were days when I would walk up to her and she'd say the most simple, childish thing like, "Teddy, you're my brother," then walk away and bang her head against the wall. It was heartbreaking.

Looking back, I don't know for sure if these events were linked, but shortly after the summer of the onset of Mary Jean's illness, my attitude at McCallie started to change. I was about halfway through the tenth grade and my mother had bought me new dress shoes (after I'd worn through the previous pair from laps around the bullring). Staring at those shoes, an idea struck me. Ted Turner was going to shock the daylights out of everyone by showing up at inspection with a spit shine. Not just any spit shine, but the very best I could muster. I'd spent three and a half years trying to be the worst cadet on campus, and now I was going to try a completely different approach.

I had never put any real effort into shining my own shoes, but after a year at Georgia Military Academy and my time at McCallie I'd seen enough to know how it was done and worked the leather on those shoes until they were absolutely perfect. Standing at attention in drill line, I waited for the inspecting officer to make his way down to me. When he looked up from my beautiful shoes to find them attached to my body, he nearly fell over backward!

From that point on I became completely

gung ho. I got good grades, I stayed out of the bullring, and I had a ball in the process. I had plenty of energy and since my dad had instilled a strong work ethic in me, instead of using mischief as my outlet, I now channeled my drive into being the best cadet I could be. I'd gone halfway through my sophomore year and was still at the level of private, but because of my turnaround they nominated me to be a corporal and I passed, managing to get back to the level of the other top classmates. By the end of my junior year, I was completely in high gear, winning the Linus Llewellyn Award for the school's neatest cadet.

The headmasters at McCallie were really pleased with what I had done. They never gave up on me and eventually their system had won me over. I fed off their positive reinforcement and started hitting my stride as never before.

My love of reading began at an early age and most of my intellectual energies went toward books. Students with a B average or worse—my early pattern—had to do four hours of mandatory study hall. I could get through my assignments in about two hours so that left about two more to use however I wanted. Reading was always my choice and I checked out nearly every book in McCallie's library that had anything to do with history—particularly naval history. At my reading pace of fifty pages an hour I could read 250-page books in just over two days so I finished about two books per week. Between academic years we had to read three or four books for school and my father made me read another book a week on top of that. So for the summer I figured I read a book a week and during the school year it was more like two and a half on top of my regular study load.

When it came to books, I couldn't get enough. In addition to military literature, I read a lot of the great classics—many for school but several just for fun. From Dante's *Inferno* to *War and Peace* and *Les Misérables*; you name it, I read it. I also got into memorizing sections of poetry, and I wrote and memorized some of my own poetry as well. I wrote one called "Indecision" for a school assignment and I can still recite it to this day:

While great Caesar lay yet dying
Brutus had the chance for the glory.
Had the future lain before him
His would be a different story.

At the feet of Hannibal
Like a ripe plum Rome once lay.
Oft he put the time of conquest
To a later, better day.

Hamlet's course was laid before him
All he had to do was act.
Yet he lacked the inner courage
To make his deep convictions fact.

Shortly after First Manassas
Fate knocked at the door of Lee
But he failed to take advantage
Or a different country this might be.

Many times through the ages
Like as not the chance appears
But because of indecision
Man's fond hopes are drowned in tears.

In addition to receiving an A+ grade, I'll never forget my teacher's comment. He wrote, simply, *"That's* a poem!"

This kind of feedback motivated me and I looked for other ways to excel and to be noticed. I joined the debate team and quickly became its star performer. My junior season, I had a memorable experience that would be a precursor to some of my future success in business.

Every year debate teams from all over Tennessee were given the same subject and there were affirmative and negative sides that you'd have to defend. The statement that year was "Resolved: Governmental subsidies should be granted according to need to high school students who qualify for additional training." At that time the government was contemplating whether it should have a role in providing financial aid to students, so everyone interpreted the question as asking if the government should grant aid to students according to the need *of the students*. After studying the statement long and hard and reading it back and forth, I concluded that the question could be interpreted differently; that the government should decide whether or not to grant subsidies based on the need *of the government*. Our team agreed to reinterpret the question completely, but to make sure we were on solid ground I consulted the head of the University of Chattanooga English Department, who agreed to state in writing that our interpretation of the terms was legitimate.

My team was on the affirmative side so we went first and established the terms of the debate. We established that aid should be provided to high-potential students to satisfy America's need for more scientists and engineers. That way we could compete with the communists. This was the 1950s and we were deep in the arms race and scared to death of the Russians. I began the presentation with one short sentence, delivered dramatically in Russian. "I greet you in the language of the future if our position is not accepted." I shifted back to English and then explained that if the government targeted promising scientists and engineers for scholarships, it would be no different than providing free tuition to train military officers at West Point or the Naval Academy. If we can do it for soldiers, why couldn't we do it for the students with the best abilities in engineering and science?

Nobody had looked at the issue this

way and we caught everyone completely unprepared. I remember one time after we defined the terms the two girls on the other team broke down and cried. We mowed down every school we faced and finished the season undefeated. Our team took McCallie's first state championship in thirty years and I won the school's oratory medal. Winning debate championships didn't bring me the same prestige as being a star football or basketball player, but this was my first and greatest award for academic achievement.

My training in debate would later provide a great foundation for my career, and looking back on the way we reinterpreted that resolution, I can now see the roots of the way I tackled many of my business challenges. Confronted with a problem I've always looked for an unconventional angle and approach. Nothing sneaky, nothing illegal or unethical, just turning the issue on its head and shifting the advantage to our side.

My time at McCallie was key to my development as a person and a leader. I gave them hell in those early years, and they gave me some back. Still, they never lost faith in me and when I finally decided to become a model cadet, the positive reinforcement they provided spurred me on to want to keep striving for more achievement. My turnaround there also gave me the credentials to apply to highly competitive colleges, something my father openly encouraged. To this day I've continued to stay involved with McCallie and several years ago pledged them a major gift.

───────── A TED STORY ─────────

"Sure, I'll Help You Out"
—Rody Sherrill

(RODY SHERRILL WAS A CLASSMATE OF TED'S AT MCCALLIE.)

Ted and I spent some time together as seniors when we were made captains of Companies E and F. The big guys who were leaders in the senior class were made captains of A, B, C, and D Companies and the littler captains were put in charge of the smaller kids in Companies E and F. We used to get our little guys together and Ted and I would march them around and teach them how to salute and do arms and all that stuff and he was good at it.

I really got to know Ted better many years later when I did fund-raising on behalf of the school. I'd usually call him about once a year and say, "Ted, we're a little short on our sustaining fund and we need about $10,000."

One year he might say, "Sure, no problem," and another year he'd say, "Rody, I'm too busy for this kind of thing!" and BAM—he'd hang up the phone. On those occasions, I'd just wait a few days and call him back and he'd respond with, "Hey, pal, how ya doing? Sure, I'll help you out, no problem!"

One year McCallie set off on an ambitious $30 million capital campaign. We had yet to contact Ted when I got a call from our headmaster. He said that Ted contacted him and wanted to see us that afternoon in Atlanta. So the headmaster, the head of fund-raising, and I got in the car and made the two-hour drive to

Atlanta. I'll never forget Ted's office—all those Academy Awards and other memorabilia all over the place. Anyway, before we could even mention a request—which at the very most might have been for a million dollars—he sat us down and told us he'd decided to give McCallie $25 million! It was an incredible thing—very generous and a total surprise.

3

College and the Coast Guard

During my senior year at McCallie I wasn't sure what to do about college. I'd grown accustomed to the discipline of a military-style education and considered applying to the service academies but my father ruled this out. His billboard company was growing and he made it very clear to me that he wanted me to take it over some-day. He was eager for me to get a college degree but didn't like the idea of the academies' mandatory service requirements keeping me away for so many more years.

While I had grown comfortable living in

the South and considered staying there for college, I'd become a product of an environment that stressed achievement and I definitely wanted to pursue as prestigious an institution as would accept me. With the military academies ruled out, I set my sights on the Ivy League. Unfortunately, my academic about-face at McCallie had come too late for me to graduate with as high a grade point average as these schools would have liked. Harvard, my first choice, rejected me but I did manage to get into the University of Pennsylvania and Brown University.

Brown was a school I might not have applied to had it not been for the influence of one of my father's business colleagues. His name was Miles Standish and he was a direct descendant of the famous *Mayflower* soldier. A loyal Brown alumnus, he owned a billboard company in Providence and he and my dad became good pals through industry functions and conventions. In addition to singing the school's praises, Standish assured my father that since he lived close by, he could keep an eye on me. Despite this support, my father still didn't have a preference between Brown and Penn.

As a result, this choice became one of the few decisions he ever let me make on my own, and it wasn't an easy one. On the one hand, I was drawn to the notion of getting the business education that Penn's Wharton School could provide, but downtown Philadelphia didn't hold much appeal for me back then. On the other hand, I was beginning to show promise as a competitive sailor (more on that later), and Providence was right there on the Narragansett Bay and Brown's sailing team was much better than Penn's.

Sailing became the deciding factor for me, but before I could commit to Brown, I felt the need for a serious conversation with my dad. My lifetime savings to that point amounted to about $2,000, so I'd be counting on him to pay my way. Given his concerns about a military commitment, I had to know that he was comfortable with me being away for four years and that he would be willing to support me financially. He assured me that he would.

It was now the fall of 1956, and nine

years after entering Georgia Military Academy as a scrawny "Yankee" from Ohio, I was now considered a "southerner," enrolling at one of the North's most elite institutions. As many of my classmates had graduated from prestigious New England prep schools like Exeter or Andover, coming to Brown fresh out of a Tennessee military academy cast me as a bit of an outsider once more. This perception probably wasn't helped by the fact that Jimmy Brown was the person who drove and dropped me off at school. I'm sure a lot of my classmates figured that this southern black man must have been my servant or something, but I didn't think anything of it. By then, Jimmy was a jack-of-all-trades for my parents and with my dad busy with work and my mom unable to leave Mary Jean, Jimmy had been taking me to McCallie for years, so the trip to New England seemed perfectly natural to both of us. But looking back, I can understand that it must have seemed a bit odd to my classmates.

—————— A TED STORY ——————

"We Didn't Know Shit"
—Peter Dames

(PETER DAMES WAS A CLASSMATE OF TED'S AT BROWN. HE WENT ON TO BECOME A CLOSE FRIEND AND BUSINESS COLLEAGUE.)

I met Ted very early on in our freshman year at Brown. I roomed in a dorm called Littlefield and there was a fire escape between that building and the next dormitory, Maxcy Hall. Several nights in a row there was this clatter of people running up that fire escape and every time they reached the top, Ted would give a loud rebel yell. They weren't drunk—they were just being loud. I was trying out for the football team and needed to get some sleep. One night I'd finally had enough and when Ted ran by my open window I reached out, grabbed him by the throat, and pulled him halfway into my room. I said, "Hey, what the hell's the matter with you?"

He said, "Don't hit me! Don't hit me!"

I said, "Well I'm trying to sleep here and every night you're out there clattering around. Don't they have a door in front of the dorm that you can use?"

And he said, "Yeah, but this is more fun."

We got to talking, and once it was established that I wasn't going to punch him out we became fast friends. It turned out that we had both gone to military high schools—mine was in upstate New York—and we were both fairly out of place at Brown. We didn't know much about women, and we didn't have all the social graces that the guys from Choate and Lawrenceville had learned. They all had a five-mile head start on us. They had their little leather patches on their elbows, the right jackets and the right ties, and we didn't know shit.

During my first several days there I really did feel like a fish out of water. After years of following a military dress code I wasn't even sure what to wear. The one place I felt like I fit in was out on a boat and, fortunately, trials for the freshman sailing team began right away. I had begun sailing after our move to Savannah. My father had joined the local yacht club and when they expanded to include a junior program, he signed me up. There were about fifteen dads involved and they bought a fleet of Penguin dinghies—one for each of us. I was about ten or eleven and was thrilled to have the boat but there was a catch. If I wanted to keep it I'd have to race it each and every weekend. I remember not liking the idea of *having* to do *anything* every weekend but it wasn't long before I fell in love with the sport and that commitment became a pleasure. Like most boys, I'd tried all the more popular sports like baseball, football, or track but I really wasn't good at any of them—I just didn't have that kind of athletic ability. At McCallie I was good at boxing, not because I had great reflexes but because I could take a lot of punishment. Unfortunately, I never earned a varsity letter since they eliminated boxing the year after a kid at one of the schools was badly injured in the ring.

Still, I hungered for athletic competition so sailing became my outlet. It didn't require physical skills like running or throwing a ball and I loved the outdoors and being out on the water. That's not to say I was good at it right from the start. In fact, I flipped my boat so many times that first year that the kids started calling me "Turn-over Turner" and "The Capsize Kid." But the teasing made me want to get better and I learned from each and every failure. At McCallie, one of my favorite teachers, Houston Patterson, used to take me out on a lake some weekends and he taught me a great deal, too. Through eight years there I never managed to win the Savannah club championship but I came closer every year.

Sailing also gave me some opportunities to spend some time with my dad and to have some pretty amazing adventures for a little kid. One particularly memorable time my father let me join him, Jimmy, and three other guys on a trip from Savannah to the Bahamas and back. We sailed down to Miami then went across the Gulf Stream. I used to get seasick back then and the ride back was so rough I stayed in my bunk for about thirty-six hours straight. I spent so much time hanging on to that bed that the rest of the guys called me "Sack Leech!" It was rough-going but an unforgettable experience.

By the time I entered Brown I had probably logged more hours on a sailboat than most of my classmates, and at freshman trials I won every single race, quickly earning the number one slot on the team. We had four regattas and a championship in the fall and another four more regattas and a championship in the spring. We won every regatta we entered and I did well enough to become one of only two sophomores to make the varsity the following year. Successful fall and spring sailing seasons provided bookends to a freshman year in which I really was "Mr. Straight Arrow." After the intense discipline of McCallie I didn't find the college workload very challenging. I studied hard and my grades were pretty good.

That first summer, however, was difficult as my parents' marriage ended in divorce. Their relationship was never easy. My parents were an unlikely pair to begin with, and my father's drinking and philandering were hard for my mother to tolerate. His harsh treatment of me was also a bone of contention. Still, my mom fully believed in "for better or for worse" and she did her best to stick it out and maintain some level of harmony.

Ultimately, it was my sister's worsening illness that took the greatest toll. Having emerged from that initial coma with significant brain damage, she could barely communicate and meaningful interaction with her became difficult. Along with her mental challenges, the increasing severity of her underlying lupus symptoms made matters worse. As often happens to people stricken with a severe case, Mary Jean's body literally started fighting itself. This caused extremely painful inflammation in her joints, and as her pain increased she would sometimes bang her head against the wall. The most difficult times for us were when she'd scream, "Please God, let me die!" As hard as it was for me seeing Mary Jean during the holidays and summer, for my parents, her illness was an everyday ordeal. My father was overwhelmed by her suffering and after visiting every medical expert he could find, wanted his daughter institutionalized. My mother refused, insisting that the best person to care for Mary Jean was her own mother and she'd make it her full-time responsibility. My dad had made most of the family's big decisions in the past but this was one where my mother drew the line. It was a breaking point for my father and they separated.

My mom moved back to Cincinnati to care for Mary Jean with the help of her extended family. They built a special room for my sister above the garage and had it specially padded and soundproofed. Taking care of Mary Jean was heartbreaking work but my mom was strong and stoic, and would have it no other way.

Up until this time I had been a religious person and I prayed for Mary Jean's recovery almost every day. In addition to its military structure, McCallie was a Christian academy and I absorbed this part of their teaching as much as any other. By the time I graduated I had been "saved" four times—once by Billy Graham himself when I attended one of his crusades—and I even considered becoming a missionary.

But seeing my kid sister ravaged by this disease challenged my beliefs. How could a just and loving God do this to someone so young and so innocent? To me it didn't make any sense and my faith was badly shaken.

By all accounts the terms of my parents' divorce settlement were fair but the custody arrangement was a little unusual. While Mary Jean would be in my mother's care, my dad insisted that he retain custody of me. I was eighteen years old and in college so this stipulation didn't make much practical difference, but it was further evidence of my father's intention to mold me to follow in his footsteps at the billboard company. All summer, I dutifully put in my forty-two-and-a-half-hour weeks at Turner Advertising.

After that tumultuous summer I was relieved to get back to Brown. As a sophomore, I was now in the second year of a bet my father had made with me before sending me off to college. If I didn't drink or smoke before turning twenty-one he'd give me $5,000. My dad was an alcoholic and smoked two packs a day and he didn't want his son to make the same mistakes.

Seeing what the booze and tobacco were doing to his health provided incentive enough, and $5,000 was a ton of money—probably more than a year's room and board back then—and I decided to go for it. He also agreed to send me a weekly allowance of $5 as long as I wrote a letter home every week. This was a woefully small stipend even then and being surrounded by guys with so much more money was tough. They'd go off on ski weekends and other adventures while I'd be stuck back at the dorm. Still, I counted on that $5 and never missed a week of letter writing my entire freshman year, but a month or so into my sophomore year I became distracted with academic and social commitments and missed one or two weeks. Always one to hold up his end of a bargain, my father let me know that my allowance was suspended. I was really upset. I felt like I'd been working so hard—on my school-work, my sailing, the billboard company in the summer, everything—and now he was cutting off my measly $5.

Making matters worse I was surrounded at Brown by guys who were constantly after me to drink. As best I can remember

I was the only guy in my entire fraternity who didn't drink and, as a result, if guys wanted to put a bottle somewhere for safe-keeping they'd leave it with me, knowing I wouldn't touch it. It so happened that right after I got the letter cutting off my allow-ance, somebody dropped a bottle off in my room. To the guy's surprise, I asked him if he minded if I had a drink and he said no. I had just turned nineteen and on that night I got drunk for the first time and I smoked my first cigar. I'd lost the bet with my dad.

I'm sure there were plenty of guys in my class who assured their parents that they were little angels and they wouldn't have dreamed of telling them the truth about their social activities. I, too, probably could have gone on with my new lifestyle and my father would have been none the wiser, but withholding that information from him would have been a breach of trust. I'd spent my formative school years following strict honor codes and I didn't think twice about what I needed to do.

The very next day, nursing my very first hangover, I let my dad know what I had done. He was already disappointed by my letter-writing lapse but now he kicked into a higher gear and got *really* mad. Not only could I forget the $5 allowance, I could kiss the $5,000 goodbye, too. I was disappointed by his response but not at all surprised.

During summers at the company my father had taught me basic principles of amortization and I decided to apply them here, doing some quick calculations. I figured that the first drink I took cost me $5,000. The second one brought my per drink cost down to $2,500. Applying that logic some more, five drinks would be $1,000, fifty drinks $100, but if I had five *thousand* drinks over the next couple of years they would only cost me $1 a drink. I could afford that, allowance or not!

My experience at Brown was just like it was at McCallie but in reverse order. Instead of going from bad to good, at Brown I went from good to bad, from being Mr. Straight Arrow to being a wild man. I fell in with the heaviest drinking crowd on campus and we'd stay up late and get into all sorts of trouble. Right before Christmas break and about a month into my new mode of behavior I went with a bunch of guys over to Wheaton, a women's college in nearby Massachusetts. We'd been drinking and we wound up throwing chairs out the windows of one of the dormitories there. After someone called the police and we got caught, I was suspended from Brown for the rest of that school year.

While stirring up trouble at Georgia Military Academy and McCallie, I'd been careful to stop short of suspension. Having crossed that line at Brown I dreaded my father's reaction as I headed home for Christmas. He was indeed upset—every bit as angry as I thought he'd be—but his response was tempered by the fact that there was a new woman in his life. Her name was Jane Dillard, and she was the divorced daughter of a prominent Savannah family (her father was president of the Central Georgia Railroad). After a whirlwind courtship they were already engaged to be married. I was pleased to see my father happy with a new woman, but like a lot of kids with divorced parents, I think I'd always hoped Mom and Dad would get back together. My dad's quick engagement was a surprise and while I would never share these feelings with my father, deep down I was really disappointed.

After sorting through his own wedding and honeymoon plans, my father finally discussed with me what I would do for the next nine months before the following school year. His inclination was to have me work for him full-time but I didn't like that idea. My peers were all in college and while it was one thing to be around home during the summer, it was quite another when school was in session. The draft was on, too, and as a suspended student there was an outside chance I'd receive notice. I decided to join the Coast Guard for six months as a reservist, figuring I could work hard, fulfill my military obligation, and head back to Brown in the fall. My father liked the idea of getting me back into a military environment and while he might have preferred that I stay home, he supported my decision to enlist in the Coast Guard.

After signing up at the recruiting station I headed to Cape May, New Jersey, for thirteen weeks of training. Most people consider boot camp to be a pain, but I

loved it. It was just like being back at Mc-
Callie. I embraced the discipline and structure and went right back to being Mr. Good
Guy. I became company commander and
led our team through Honor Company—a
weekly competition I was determined to
win. We were judged on military drill, clean-
est barracks, and so on—all the disciplines
I was used to from high school. Insisting
that we were going to outwork every other
company there, I put my leadership abilities to the test. As coxswain of our surf-
boat team, I decided we needed to hit the
water for practice an hour before everybody else. This meant we'd have to get up
at 5:30 A.M. every day instead of 6:30 like
the others. There was some grumbling but
the extra hours paid off and we started
winning.

I organized our competition like a business, delegating responsibilities to maximize our performance. For example, while
the rest of us headed out early, I had one of
our top guys hang back and supervise the
cleaning of the barracks. He didn't like being out on the water anyway so it worked
out best for everyone.

While we were beating the thirteen other

companies in most areas of the competition, we were still weak in military drill. We had thirty minutes off every night after dinner—our only free time of the day—and I decided that was a perfect chance for us to get in some extra practice. Not everyone in our company shared my enthusiasm for this idea, and things got so contentious that a big Italian guy from New York City even took a swing at me. Our fight was broken up quickly and when things settled down I sat everyone down as a group. I said, "Listen, if we're going to win Honor Company every week, we've got to do better on military drill. The only way we're going to do better is through extra practice, and the only time we have for extra practice is after dinner." I told them we'd vote on this plan as a team and the majority would rule.

Fortunately, morale was high and I managed to talk the majority into voting for the additional practice. As I led our team through after-hour drills, the guys from the other companies hooted and hollered at us while they relaxed in front of their barracks. By this point our guys were so gung ho that the taunting only made us work harder, and the extra training paid off. Against thirteen companies we won four different times and each week we won, we got the weekend off. The team's enthusiasm grew to the point where our final week of competition we came out on top in every single one of the ten events.

Coast Guard training in New Jersey was one of the best times of my life and I loved the opportunity to lead such a quality group of guys. The rest of my commitment was advanced training in Groton, Connecticut. We did well there, but it was a less competitive environment and couldn't match the fun we all had at Cape May.

In August, I was released from the Guard and was reaccepted to Brown for the fall semester. My father was fine with me going back to school but shortly after my return as a midterm sophomore, my original fears started coming true. He began to make negative comments about Brown and said he wasn't sure he wanted me to stay there. Things reached a head about six months later when I declared Classics as my major.

My most inspiring professor at Brown taught in the Classics Department. His name was John Workman and my first class with him consisted of a discussion format—much different from a big lecture as we'd deal in great depth with a single subject and really kick around ideas. We read classic writers like Thucydides and Virgil and we went deep into ancient Greek history. Workman was the first professor who really challenged me to think and I absolutely loved it—I couldn't wait for his class to come around. And it was largely because of Workman that I declared Classics as my major. Problem was, my father wanted me to study practical subjects that would prepare me for a career in business. But Brown didn't offer business courses, and even the economics classes were mostly theoretical. Regardless, my dad was furious and described his feelings to me in a long, rambling letter.

I reproduce my dad's letter here to provide insight into the kind of person he was and how he thought about me, and life, at that time:

My dear son,
I am appalled, even horrified, that you have adopted Classics as a major. As a

matter of fact, I almost puked on the way home today. I suppose that I am old-fashioned enough to believe that the purpose of an education is to enable one to develop a community of interest with his fellow men, to learn to know them, and to learn how to get along with them. In order to do this, of course, he must learn what motivates them, and how to impel them to be pleased with his objectives and desires.

I am a practical man, and for the life of me I cannot possibly understand why you should wish to speak Greek. With whom will you communicate in Greek? I have read, in recent years, the deliberations of Plato and Aristotle, and was interested to learn that the old bastards had minds which worked very similarly to the way our minds work today. I was amazed that they had so much time for deliberating and thinking, and was interested in the kind of civilization that would permit such useless deliberation. Then I got to thinking that it wasn't so amazing—after all they thought like we did because my Hereford cows today are very similar to those ten or twenty generations ago. I am amazed that you would adopt Plato and Aristotle as a vocation for several months when it might make pleasant and enjoyable reading to you in your leisure time as relaxation at a later date. For the life of me I cannot understand why you should be vitally interested in informing yourself about the influence of the Classics on English literature. It is not necessary for you to know how to make a gun in order to know how to use it. It would seem to me that it would be enough to learn English literature without going into what influence this or that ancient mythology might have upon it. As for Greek literature, the history of Roman and Greek churches, and the art of those eras, it would seem to me that you would be much better off by learning something of contemporary literature and writings and things that might have some meaning to you with people with whom you are to associate.

These subjects might give you a community of interest with an isolated few impractical dreamers, and a select group of college professors. God forbid!

It would seem to me that what you wish to do is to establish a community of interest with as many people as you possibly can. With people who are moving, who are doing things, and who have an interesting, not a decadent, outlook.

I suppose everybody has to be a snob of some sort, and I suppose you will feel you are distinguishing yourself from the herd by becoming a Classical snob. I can see you drifting into a bar, belting down a few, turning around to the guy on the stool next to you—a contemporary billboard baron from Podunk, Iowa—and saying, "Well what do you think about old Leonidas?" Your friend, the billboard baron, will turn to you and say, "Leonidas who?" You will turn to him and say, "Why, Leonidas, the prominent Greek of the twelfth century." He will, in turn, say to you, "Well, who in the hell was he?" You will say, "Oh, you don't know about Leonidas?" and dismiss him, and not discuss anything else with him the rest of the evening. He will feel that you are a stupid snob and a flop; you will feel that he is a clodhopper from Podunk, Iowa. I suppose this will make you both happy, and as a result of it, you will wind up buying his billboard plant.

There is no question but this type of useless information will distinguish you, set you apart from the doers of the world. If I leave you enough money, you can retire to an ivory tower, and contemplate for the rest of your days the influence that the hieroglyphics of prehistoric man had upon the writings of William Faulkner. Incidentally, he was a contemporary of mine in Mississippi. We speak the same language—whores, sluts, strong words and strong deeds.

It isn't really important what I think. It's important what you wish to do with your life. I just wish I could feel that the influence of those oddball professors and the ivory towers were developing you into the kind of a man we can both be proud of. I am quite sure that we both will be pleased and delighted when I introduce you to some friend of mine and say, "This is my son. He speaks Greek."

I had dinner during the Christmas holidays with an efficiency expert, an economic adviser to the nation of India, on the Board of Directors of Regents at Harvard University, who owns some 80,000 acres of valuable timber land down here, among his other assets. His son and his family were visiting him. He introduced me to his son, and then apologetically said, "He is a theoretical mathematician. I don't even know what he is talking about. He lives in a different world."

After a little while I got talking to his son, and the only thing he would talk to me about was his work. I didn't know what he was talking about either so I left early.

If you are going to stay on at Brown, and be a professor of Classics, the courses you have adopted will suit you for a lifetime association with Gale Noyes. Perhaps he will teach you to make jelly. In my opinion, it won't do much to help you learn to get along with people in this world. I think you are rapidly becoming a jackass, and the sooner you get out of that filthy atmosphere, the better it will suit me.

Oh, I know that everybody says that a college education is a must. Well, I console myself by saying that everybody said the world was square, except Columbus. You go ahead and go with the world, and I'll go it alone.

I hope I am right. You are in the hands of the Philistines, and dammit, I sent you there. I am sorry.

Devotedly,
Dad

We were really feuding now and this correspondence set me off. I decided that the best retaliation was to send the letter to the college paper, which reprinted it in full. The letter soon became the talk of the school. In subsequent days, to get a rise out of his students, Professor Noyes— whom my father knew to be an epicurean chef—ended class by telling students he was off "to make jelly." The room erupted in laughter.

My father described my move as "dirty pool" and his anger over the letter's publicity drove a further wedge between us.

I was in a bad place at this point. I sensed that my college days were numbered and I was really upset with my father. I could have gotten a commission to the Naval Academy but he didn't want me to go. When we settled on Brown he promised to support me for four years. His business was successful and he had more than enough money to pay my way. I don't know if any of his negative feelings about college had anything to do with the fact that he never finished a full four years himself but regardless, it didn't seem fair. Whenever I tried to talk to him about it, he'd only say that it was his right to do "whatever I damn well please," and the case was closed.

I worked for my dad's company again that summer, saving as much as I could to pay for another year at Brown. I was living with my father and new stepmother at their plantation home in South Carolina but since most of my friends were back in Savannah, that's where I'd go on weekends and evenings to enjoy some nightlife. Despite the strains on our relationship, my father let me borrow his car for these trips, only because he felt it was important for me to maintain a place in those social circles.

That summer he had a new Plymouth Fury. This was the fastest production car built in the United States at that time, able to reach speeds as high as 150 miles per hour. One night I was driving back roads through rural South Carolina, in a hurry to get to Savannah for a debutante party. I was going about 120 mph when I approached an unmarked railroad crossing. I'd gone this way a bunch of times and had never seen a train pass, so I assumed it was just a side track. This was back in the days when many crossings didn't have blinking lights or gates or other markings.

Slowing to about 90 to cross I noticed an elderly black man standing on my side of the road and when he saw me he started going crazy—waving his arms and jumping up and down. I didn't understand what he was doing until he was in my rearview mirror. Looking into that mirror as I skipped over the track, I saw a train flying through the intersection! I was going close to 100 mph and it had to be doing 70. We missed each other by a flash of a second. Once I was on the other side and realized what had just happened, my heart was beating out of my chest. I made it to the debutante party on time but when I got there my hands were still shaking. I came really close to dying that night—and I've driven more carefully ever since!

I don't remember us talking much about it but by the time I headed back to school that fall—for what would be the second half of my junior year—it was clear that my father would not be supporting me financially. My life savings at that point were about $5,000 and even back then that wouldn't get you far in a private college like Brown. I made some spending money working in the school cafeteria but I could never earn enough during school to make my room and board payments. I met with people at the admissions department to see if some kind of financial aid or academic scholarship might be possible. They were polite but made it clear that Brown University did not make a practice of extending these sorts of opportunities to the children of wealthy parents. I doubt they had ever seen a situation quite like mine and found it hard either to understand or sympathize with my predicament.

I managed to pay my bills those first few months and threw myself into my schoolwork, sailing, and partying.

I was proud to have been named captain of varsity sailing as a junior. I led the team to a successful fall season, but that campaign ended with a Thanksgiving regatta in Chicago. The trip there would turn out to be a low point in my life.

The school didn't provide transportation to these sorts of events. There were four of us heading out but the one car among us was a little Volkswagen. After cramming in all of our luggage and gear, we realized that only three of us could fit in for the ride. Rather than debating the solutions, as captain of the team I decided to let my luggage go with them and volunteered to hitchhike to Chicago.

Relieved by my gesture, the other three wished me luck and sped off. Without the money to do it any other way, I headed down the hill from campus prepared to hitchhike halfway across the country on Thanksgiving weekend. I was wearing an oxford shirt and tweed jacket and I had one of those tacky old raincoats that's "weather resistant" but not really waterproof. It started raining almost immediately and by the time I was picked up outside Providence I was already soaked. My first ride got me all the way to New York City and after standing in some more rain there I was able to catch a series of lifts that took me across New Jersey and onto the Pennsylvania Turnpike. The next ride dropped me off at about 2:00 in the morning in the middle of the Pennsylvania Mountains—miles from anywhere. Still soaked, I stood there with my thumb out as the temperature dropped. The rain turned to snow—it was freezing.

I remember saying to myself, "I'm going to die out here." It was as simple as that.

Adjacent to the exit where I'd been dropped was a sign that said "Next Rest Area 10 Miles." After standing there for more than an hour I grew desperate and decided to start walking those ten miles. About five miles into the walk a truck pulled over.

"Where's your car?" the driver asked.

"I don't have one," I told him. He said he couldn't pick up hitchhikers and I said, "Well, I'm going to die out here. Would you please take me as far as the rest area?"

He was kind enough to do that and when he dropped me off at the rest area I was the only person there. It was kind of like a Howard Johnson—it was comfortable inside and I just sat at the counter, trying to dry off and warm up. Eventually, another guy came in and sat down and I told him that if he were heading west I'd really appreciate a ride. He took me as far as Ohio and I made it to Chicago later that next day. I really thought I might freeze to death that night and was about as down as I've ever been. After we competed in the races that weekend, I volunteered to head back

alone—but only after we had pooled together enough money for me to take a bus.

Those final weeks and months at Brown
I was like a tragic character. I knew the
end was near but I couldn't figure a way
out. I burned the candle at both ends. I
was drinking, chasing women, staying up
late, and hardly going to class at all. It was
all coming to an end but there are two
commonly told stories about my final days
at Brown that I'd like to clear up. One is
that I burned down the Homecoming display and the other is that I was kicked out
for having a woman in my room. Both of
these tales are only partially true.

As for Homecoming, we did burn something down. Each fraternity built stationary
structures outside their house for a school-
wide competition. On Sunday night, after
Saturday's judging was over and everybody was taking their exhibits down, some
guys and I did get a little carried away and
instead of dismantling ours in an orderly
fashion, we set it on fire. Regarding having
a woman in my room, it is true that I was
caught and suspended (it was against the
rules back then but they allow it today—I
was ahead of my time on this one!). What's

not accurate is to say that this was the reason I left the school. I'd already run through nearly all of my savings—I knew this would be one of my final nights on campus so I figured I might as well make it a fun one. I got caught and suspended, but I was already preparing to leave.

Despite my father's assurances, the truth is he didn't support me through all four years at school. My college career was over.

4

Billboards

With my college career over I'm sure my father assumed I'd rush home to work for him once and for all. But I was in a state of rebellion and couldn't bring myself to do it. Peter Dames, my best friend and fellow mischief maker at Brown, had decided to take a leave of absence and we planned our next move together. It was just after Christmastime and turning cold in Rhode Island so we got the idea to head south, all the way to Florida. I bought a beat-up old car for about $100 and we packed it full of our belongings and hit the road. We stopped by my dad's place in South Carolina for a good night's sleep and a couple of meals and he was cordial, wishing us luck in our travels. He probably figured I'd be back before long. I might have been angry and rebellious, but I was also broke.

─────── A TED STORY ───────

"It All Sounded Good to Me"
—Peter Dames

Our idea was that we would pass through South Carolina to pick up Ted's Flying Dutchman sailboat. We'd sponge a few free meals off his old man, I would get to see his father's place, then we'd continue down to Florida where we would both get jobs and earn enough money to make his boat seaworthy so we could sail it around the world, get laid everywhere we went, and be the toast of every continent. I was brought up in New York and didn't know anything about boats other than the Staten Island Ferry but Ted was a good salesman, I was very gullible and it all sounded good to me. We stopped at my parents' house in Queens on the drive down and they weren't very happy with me. They were immigrants and the thought of me being educated was the most important thing in their lives; now here I was blowing it.

When we arrived at the plantation Ted's father was very gracious. We pulled up in that old jalopy and he met us in his smoking jacket. We had drinks and dinner with his father and his new wife. Ted was never much of a drinker and he wanted to get up early the next morning to go frog gigging or something so he went to bed early. Mr. Turner's new wife excused herself after dinner but the old man felt like talking so he and I stayed up and drank and talked into the wee hours. He gave me a lot of great insights.

By the time we left a couple of days later, our plans had changed. Right before we got to South Carolina a hurricane had come through the area. It was almost like the hand of God came down and the better part of an oak tree fell across Ted's sailboat and destroyed it into splinters. So that killed the original sailing-around-the-world idea. Now we had to get to Miami, get a job, and make that much more money so we could buy an even better sailboat.

For the first several weeks in Florida we lived out of our car like bums, completely down and out. Eventually we managed to find a cheap room in the Cuban section of town. Castro was still in the hills at that time but there was already a sizable Cuban population in South Florida. To save money, we ate peanut butter and jelly sandwiches off reused paper plates and ripped pages from public pay phone books to use as toilet paper. Work was hard to come by and the highest paying job I ever got was selling *Miami Beach Sun* subscriptions on commission. For one thirteen-week subscription I got $1.50 and on my best day I sold four. A $6 per day income just wasn't going to cut it.

We were low on cash and short on options. Dames decided to give up and go back north to New York for a steady job as a bank clerk. I then got the idea that now would be a good time to fulfill the two months of reserve time I owed the Coast Guard after leaving them that past summer. I could either attend evening meetings once a week for two years or go full-time and meet the requirement in just two months. Given my situation, the latter was the clear choice. Not only would they pay me $100 a month, they'd put a roof over my head and feed me three meals a day.

I was stationed in Fort Lauderdale on a search-and-rescue vessel called the *Travis*. The work was interesting but conditions on the ship were rough. We had to limit our possessions to what we could fit in our sea bag—a duffel that hung from a pipe. Sleeping quarters consisted of metal-rimmed canvas bunks stacked four-high. As a reservist and the newest guy there, I was given a bottom bunk beneath the fattest guy on board. His weight stretched his canvas down so low that I had to lie flat on my back all night—I didn't even have room to roll over.

I was comfortable being back in a military setting and I worked hard on every assignment they threw at me, but this time around I spent a lot more time contemplating my future. I realized it was time for me to stop delaying the inevitable. My father and I had a complex relationship but I loved him. I had a great opportunity in front of me and I really did enjoy the billboard business. If I could play by his rules, I felt that things would work out just fine. In the spring of 1959, when my two months were up in Fort Lauderdale, I went back to Savannah to begin my full-time career with the Turner Advertising Company.

By this time I'd spent eight full summers there and, given my range of responsibilities, I really understood the business well. From the age of twelve I'd been a water boy, gofer, and pole digger for the construction crews. I'd posted bills with the bill posters and painted signs with the sign painters, but my strongest skills became evident when I started working in the leasing department at age sixteen. I could handle the physical jobs, but once I had the chance to use my mind, my heart, and my salesmanship, I really started to shine. The job of a billboard lease man is to search the territory for the best sites for new signs—

the ones with the most traffic going by, best sightlines, and so forth. You then have to convince the property owner to let you install the billboard in exchange for about $25 a year. Some of these sales were tough, and none more so than when I tried to lease a location from a lady whose house was in the middle of the Sears Roebuck parking lot.

I was on summer vacation from McCallie. For years, the two billboard companies in Savannah had been pursuing this elderly woman who had wound up owning a home right in the middle of the Sears Roebuck parking lot. Years before, when she refused a sizable cash offer to move out of her house, the developer simply built around her. She was a strong, stubborn woman, and after refusing a lot of money to move, a little money from a billboard leasing agent couldn't convince her to allow for a sign that would cover up all the windows on one side of her house.

But I made it my mission to be the one to finally make this deal. I decided to start by getting to know her. She was a widow and that summer I spent a lot of time with her, almost like I was her adopted son.

When I explained that we figured out a way to build the board so that it would cover only the windows on the upper floor of her two-story house, she was still un-moved. I had to come up with an angle that no one else had thought of. Spending all that time at her home I discovered that it had poor air circulation, and being sur-rounded by an asphalt parking lot in the middle of a Savannah summer, the place got really hot. I talked it over with my father and he agreed that in addition to the usual cash offer, I could tell her we'd pay for and install an air conditioner for her. Pleased by my thoughtfulness and partly as a per-sonal favor to me, she finally said yes.

I learned a great deal during those sum-mers. My dad had some unusual ideas but he was a very clever businessman. He was also as ethical and honest as the day is long. (Before he got into billboards he owned a little car business and he called it "Honest Ed's Used Cars.") There were many days when he'd drive me to and from work and the entire ride he'd only talk to me about business. We'd cover every-thing from detailed accounting principles like depreciation to broader concepts like motivation techniques and the importance of hiring and motivating good people. As a boy I saw firsthand the value of hard work and customer relations. It was almost as though he gave me the business degree I didn't get in college. Oftentimes he'd punctuate his lessons with funny stories or memorable expressions. Once, to drive home a point about the difficulties of attracting good, loyal employees, he told me, "Heck, Jesus only had to pick twelve disciples and even one of those didn't turn out well." One of his favorite mottos was one I've used myself ever since: "Early to bed, early to rise, work like hell and advertise!"

He also impressed upon me the importance of good community relations. Local advertisers were the lifeblood of the billboard business and he worked hard to be on a first-name basis with every business owner in town. The industry was also frequently under attack, challenged by everyone from local municipalities changing zoning ordinances to environmental and beautification groups blocking us from developing new sites.

For all these reasons, my father made a point to be involved in the community and he passed that practice down to me. But as hard as he worked to make friends, his drinking helped him earn an occasional enemy. Unfortunately, when my dad drank he could become a different person, turning angry and insulting. I didn't frequent the bars myself so I never witnessed the arguments he got into, but on occasion I'd run into people in town who refused to do business with him because of insults exchanged in a bar. I remember pursuing a billboard sale one time with a Savannah business owner and before I could get the conversation going the man asked, "Are you Ed Turner's son?" When I told him I was he said he would never do business with him. When I asked him why, he said, "Go ask your father," so I did. My dad was honest but embarrassed to tell me of an argument he'd had with him after several drinks. It was difficult for me to see my father struggle with this but it taught me a great lesson about not only the importance of making friends but the negative impact of making enemies and what damage drinking could do.

"We're Going to Show the Flag"
—Peter Dames

Ted and his father persuaded me to
leave my banking job in New York and
come work with them at Turner Advertising. I was a salesman in Turner's
Charleston operation when Ted's father came in for a visit. He went to the
Carolina Yacht Club his first night in
town and got drunk. This was a very
exclusive club back then and somehow he got into a conversation with
one of the members about his heri-
tage and how his name, Robert Edward, comes from Robert E. Lee and
how he had a plantation in South Carolina with a family tree on the wall
showing where Robert E. Lee was
and where Edward Turner was.

Eventually, he and this other guy
got into a fistfight and he punched
the guy out. Well, in Charleston you
just didn't do that sort of thing. So the
word was all over town by the time
he showed up at the office the next
morning and he was chagrined and

hungover. He asked the manager to go to lunch with him and he said, "Oh, I have an appointment," and when he asked the sales manager it was the same deal. They were suddenly very busy. Finally he looked at me and said, "You, come on, we're going to have lunch. We're going to show the flag." So we went to the Colony House, which was kind of *the* place at that time so that he could show that he wasn't embarrassed. Why else would he want to be seen with me? I figured he just wanted to be seen with somebody having lunch in polite company.

When I made my decision to join my father I decided I would approach my work with him just as I had after my turnaround at McCallie. I was going to try my best to do everything right—I'd work the hardest, follow every rule, and seek excellence in everything I did. My father had made it clear that he wanted me to run the business one day and I was determined to show him that I was capable. As the boss's son, I made a point to impress the other employees by being the first one to arrive every morning and the last to leave at night. I was based in our Savannah office, working primarily with the sales and leasing departments. While we worked to grow revenues in our existing businesses, my father was on the lookout for new billboard companies to acquire and he purchased several small operators throughout the Southeast. With his major operations in Savannah and Charleston, my dad worked mostly out of his plantation home in South Carolina, halfway between these two cities.

Despite how busy his work kept him, and perhaps due to his excitement to finally have me officially under his wing full-time, my father became involved in my private affairs. Not only did he expect a full accounting of my activities on the job, he also wanted to know about and have input into every aspect of my personal life. He wanted to know who I was dating, what family they were from, where we went, what we did— *everything*. I was accustomed to my father taking an interest in me but this was getting to be too much so I worked up the nerve to talk to him about it. My desk in our

Savannah building was in an open area directly outside my father's office. Late one afternoon, I knocked on his door and said, "Dad, do you mind if we talk for a bit?"

"Sure son, come on in."

Taking a deep breath, I said, "Dad, all these years you've said you're going to leave the business to me and that's great. You didn't want me to go to the Naval Academy because you wanted me here right after college. I couldn't finish Brown so I came here even sooner than we had planned. I've been working on and off in this business since I was twelve. It's not always easy being the boss's son, but you know I love you to death. I'm glad to be your son and I'm proud and I'm doing everything I can to make you proud of me."

Having his full attention, I said something next that he didn't expect.

"You always say you're going to leave your business to me—but have you ever considered the possibility that what you really want to do is leave me to your business?"

He sat up straight in his chair. To his credit, he listened carefully to what I had to say and rather than respond immediately he said he wanted to think about it overnight. First thing the next morning he called me into his office and told me I was right and that he'd do his best to step back. I thanked him, and feeling a new confidence I said, "Dad, it just gets tough when you're involved in every aspect of my life. You tell me where I should live, who I should date. I'd just like you to consider letting me be myself a little bit. In my business life I'll do anything you say, but please try not to bug me so much about my personal life. When I want advice I'll ask for it, but if not, please let me try to work it out myself." He said that he understood, and things between us really did get better after that.

As I worked to become my own person, sailing also helped. The billboard company was my father's and as long as I worked there I'd be Ed Turner's son. But sailing was mine, and on a boat I could be Ted Turner and earn a reputation on my own merits. The sport also played an important role in Savannah society and being good at it helped me establish myself there.

While I was still shy of my twenty-first

birthday I decided that now that I was out in the real world, it was time I found a wife and settled down. At this point I'd not had any long-term relationships with women. Attending an all-boys military academy didn't help matters and during my wilder years at Brown I tended to have dates with several women as opposed to going steady with one. Living in the small town of Savannah I felt that I knew just about everyone there and I concluded that I'd have to look elsewhere to find a mate.

Given the increasingly important role that sailing was playing in my life, I figured that marrying someone who shared that passion would make a lot of sense. My thoughts turned to a woman I had met at a college sailing regatta. Her name was Judy Nye and she was a champion sailor on Northwestern University's team. Judy was very bright and fun-loving and so was her father. He was also a champion racer and after inheriting his father's tool-and-die business, he went on to start his own sail-making company. I remember the first time I met him was after a Chicago Bears game and he came in wearing a fur coat, a drink in hand, and laughing it up. Recalling these memories I gave Judy a call. We got together once or twice and got along pretty well. Looking back I don't think we were ever really in love but we were young and impulsive. After dating long distance for a while I called her up and proposed to her over the phone. She said yes, and began planning for a Chicago wedding in June.

That December, between our engagement and wedding, my sister, Mary Jean, died. She was just seventeen years old and it was a sad ending to a long ordeal for everyone involved. My mother had done all she could to keep Mary Jean stabilized and healthy but for many years it had been a question of when, not if, she would succumb to her illnesses. Since moving back to Cincinnati with my mom, Mary Jean was in many ways already out of my life, but that didn't make her passing any easier to take. And of course, the death of their only daughter was absolutely crushing for my mom and dad. Even now, it's painful to think about, and I've blocked all memories surrounding her death—how I learned of it, the funeral, the wake, my parents' behavior—I don't remember a single detail.

After that dark winter, our summer wedding was a welcome respite. Judy's family reserved a private club for our reception and it was spectacular. My father was my best man and very proud of his son that day. With our brief courtship, my sister's passing, and our June wedding, those months were a whirlwind. Judy and I settled into our first home together—a rented one-room apartment in Savannah—but we were only there for a few months before my father bought a billboard company in Macon and we had to relocate there. We found a nice little apartment but I'm sure that going from Chicago to Savannah to Macon was a tough transition for Judy. Frankly, deep down, I think we both had concerns that rushing into our marriage had been a mistake.

Even worse, once we got to Macon, I really threw myself into my work. My father had purchased Jones Poster Service earlier that year and their previous owner—Johnny Jones—stayed around for a while to help me out with the transition. He was beloved by everyone in town but he wasn't the greatest businessman. An elder in the Presbyterian Church, he was a fine, principled man, the kind of guy who would give you the shirt off his back. Unfortunately, his spirit of generosity often caused his business to suffer. When he sold us the company he was beginning a battle with cancer and wanted to get his affairs in order. He had no children to whom he might pass along the business, and was happy to sell to my father, who by now had earned a solid reputation across the industry.

At the time of our acquisition, Jones was a small company, with about two hundred billboards and revenues of just $55,000 per year. They operated twenty-four-sheet posters—those smaller billboards you used to see with aluminum trim around them—and his people had not put much effort toward maintenance, leaving many signs tattered and some even in danger of falling down. I inherited a lean staff, just six and a half employees including me. We had two bill posters and a three-man construction crew. The "half" was a secretary who worked mornings only (an answering service covered calls in the afternoon). The office itself was run-down and tiny, out on the edge of town near the railroad tracks. My secretary and I shared a one-room office and we had a cramped little garage at the back where they kept the paste cooker for the billboards and stored all the rolls of paper.

Despite the company's poor condition and my relative youth—I was still just twenty-one years old when I took over—I felt like I was in my element and knew exactly what needed to be done. To grow we had to add locations and raise advertising rates across all of our signs. I handled all the leasing and advertising sales. I staked out locations for new signs and went out with the crews to show them exactly how and where I wanted them built. I'd personally go down to City Hall to learn about local zoning rules and to apply for the permits required for new billboard sites. Having trained so many summers with some of the best in the business—including my dad—it all came to me naturally.

I was active in the Macon community,

becoming the youngest member of the local Rotary Club, and joining the board of the Macon Red Cross chapter and the United Way's publicity committee. Every year we'd donate signs to advertise events like the annual flower show or other charities that could use the space to their advantage. Not only did I enjoy the community involvement, it helped smooth the way for the growth of our business.

My father came to visit and he was happy with everything he saw. He was an active Rotarian and it pleased him when I brought him to a Macon meeting and several of the older members of the club made a point to let him know how much they thought of me and what good things I was doing in the community. I drove him around and showed him all our new signs and he was impressed by the locations I'd managed to secure and excited to see the improvements that had been made in organizing and managing the small staff. He was really high on the whole operation and when I drove him back to the airport, he said, "Son, you're starting out where most men finish," meaning that here I was twenty-one years old and running a business. A few days after he left I got a letter from him telling me what a great job I was doing and how proud he was of me. My father was usually very sparing with his praise, and nothing he ever did before or after that day ever made me feel so good.

Within my first two years in Macon we increased our number of billboards by 50 percent and doubled our revenue to $110,000 per year. Not only did I feel like I was becoming a strong leader of this small business, I developed a sense that my dad and I were becoming a great team.

I had no way of knowing at that time just how special and precious our days together would later prove to be.

5

Tragedy

Turner Advertising Company was already one of the larger billboard companies in the South by the summer of 1962, when my father put together a deal that would make it the biggest.

Over his years in the business, my father had developed a close relationship with a successful billboard operator in Minnesota named Bob Naegele and together they hatched a deal proposal. They would go in together, purchase General Outdoor, and then split it into two pieces. Based in Atlanta, General Outdoor, Inc. had been one of our greatest competitors. They owned properties not only in the Southeast but across the Midwest and Northeast as well. Naegele's company would take the properties in the North while my father would own the markets in the South. Together, they made an aggressive offer and General Outdoor accepted.

While our company had grown large, the cities where we operated—Charleston, South Carolina, Macon, Savannah, and Columbus, Georgia—were relatively small. Not only would this merger quadruple our revenues overnight, it would put us in major, higher-profile markets like Atlanta and Richmond. The sales price was about $4 million, a value roughly equal to what our entire company was worth at the time. To afford the deal, my father had to finance nearly all the purchase price, but successful billboard companies generated a lot of cash, so taking on this debt really didn't present a problem. When the dust settled on the General Outdoor acquisition, my father moved into our new headquarters in Atlanta as CEO of the biggest outdoor advertising company in the South.

My father asked me to move as well. He was pleased with my work in Macon and while he didn't feel I was quite ready to run the much bigger operation in Atlanta, he did think I could do a good job there heading up the leasing department. My father was convinced that General Outdoor had been missing out on growth opportunities and believed that an aggressive leasing effort was in order. Adding new signs had been part of my job in Macon but now it would take up 100 percent of my energy and I was excited about the prospects of tackling a major market like Atlanta.

But while my professional life was humming along, my marriage was not working. Almost from the very beginning, Judy and I realized that not only had we rushed into things and married too young, we barely even knew each other. My work and sailing schedule made it hard to become better acquainted, and unfortunately, when we did spend time together, our personalities were not compatible. I did plenty of things to make Judy mad and it wasn't long before we were fighting a lot. I had real difficulty putting my bachelor lifestyle behind me and it didn't help that from an early age my father taught me by word and example that men are by their nature polygamous—"like roosters in a hen yard," that "real men run around." I however had felt the need to settle down and get married, but as soon as I made the commitment I realized I wasn't ready to fulfill it. Even more, Judy was tough—in addition to sailing at Northwestern she was captain of the varsity field hockey team—and during a few of our fights it was everything I could do to keep her from beating me.

While we both knew that our marriage was in trouble, we did have some good times together. One of the brightest of these was the birth of our daughter, Laura Lee, in July of 1961. I was racing on weekends back then and when Judy went into labor on a Saturday, I was off sailing and missed the birth. Laura was a beautiful child who brought us a lot of joy, but sleepless nights and the demands of parenthood put even more strain on an already shaky relationship and it was becoming clear to both of us that it wasn't going to work. We got a quick divorce but it wasn't long after our separation that Judy realized she was pregnant with our second child. We agreed to get back together and to give our marriage a second chance and almost as soon as we did, I was presented with my new job opportunity in Atlanta. Given all the transitions we had already experienced, Judy and I agreed that it would be best if she and Laura Lee stayed put in Macon while I rented an apartment in Atlanta and came home on weekends.

With the General Outdoor acquisition in place and being reunited with my father in Atlanta, the fall of 1962 was an exciting time. Dad was elated—the most energized I'd ever seen him. He looked around town for a classier headquarters and traded in his Buick for a Cadillac limousine that Jimmy Brown drove. Unbeknownst to all of us, this upbeat behavior came just as he was approaching the brink of a collapse. He was like an engine that runs at its fastest right before stripping its gears.

My dad had always had his mood swings, but almost overnight his behavior became significantly more erratic and un-predictable. One day he'd be high as a kite and the next he'd be in a state of ab-ject depression. He'd always been a fairly large man, but now he was putting on more weight and growing a big potbelly. After years of smoking two or three packs of cigarettes a day he had developed a bad case of emphysema that, combined with his drinking and weight gain, took a heavy toll on him physically. I'm sure that Mary Jean's death had a lasting impact on him as well. Her illness was lengthy and her passing was long anticipated, but it can't ever be easy to lose a child. I know how devastating it was for me to lose Mary Jean and I can only imagine the grief it created for Dad.

Despite my father's obvious ambition, it's clear to me now that reaching new heights in business and material wealth actually could have undermined his mental state. He told me a memorable story on the subject. He was preparing to enter Duke University just as the Depression hit. His parents lost nearly everything and they struggled to tell him they could no longer afford his tuition. At that young age he consoled his mother, saying, "Don't worry, Mom. When I grow up, I'm going to work really hard and I'm going to be a success. I'm going to be a millionaire and I'm going to own a plantation and a yacht." Given their circumstances at the time these were very lofty goals, but by the time he shared this story with me he had achieved all three. He said that having now checked off each of these goals, he was having a really tough time reevaluating things and coming up with a plan for the rest of his life.

He then told me something I've never forgotten. He said, "Son, you be sure to set your goals so high that you can't possibly accomplish them in one lifetime. That way you'll always have something ahead of you. I made the mistake of setting my goals too low and now I'm having a hard time coming up with new ones."

In addition to achieving all that he had ever hoped to, this new acquisition seemed to trigger other insecurities in Dad. Seeing his parents lose everything in the Depression created a deep-seated concern about going too far into debt. His post-acquisition interest payments were big and the company needed large capital investments to continue its growth. Still, we were doing well and generating plenty of cash. My father knew the billboard business cold and while most of his advisers assured him that he wouldn't have trouble meeting his obligations, an irrational fear of losing everything began to consume him.

He tried to get his addictions under control by checking into a place called Silver Hills in Connecticut. They managed to curb his drinking and smoking but right around that time he'd also been prescribed a variety of medications. He said they were for "his nerves," and I'm pretty sure they included Quaaludes and a variety of other uppers and downers. In effect, my dad basically swapped alcohol and tobacco for prescription drugs. Everyone around him was concerned. Jimmy Brown, the one person who probably knew him better than anyone, told me many times that he feared that the drugs were not good for him. I tried to convince my father to take a vacation but he wouldn't do it.

Dad was in bad shape and his unpredictable behavior was tough on the company and particularly hard on me. During the first six months or so after the General Outdoor acquisition my weight dropped from 180 pounds to 135. I developed a preulcerative condition and my doctor made me swear off coffee. I'd get so tired and agitated that one of my eyelids developed a twitch. I'd hold one finger over my eye to hold it still but when I did that one of my feet would start to twitch so I'd have to put one foot on top of the other foot just to make it stop. People walking by my desk must have thought I was crazy.

I was working like mad during the day, visiting Judy and Laura Lee on the weekends, and watching my father unravel right before my eyes. I didn't know how to help him. I talked to him a few times about getting off the pills but he wouldn't. After years of grooming me to succeed him, all of a sudden he seemed in a panic about the company's future, and by March of 1963 I was practically ready for a nervous breakdown myself. Then things got worse.

It was in the middle of the week and I was in Atlanta working. My phone rang, and it was my father calling from South Carolina. He'd gone there to spend the week with his wife, Jane. I had hoped he was relaxing there but I soon realized he wasn't. He said he was calling to tell me that he was selling a large chunk of the company—all the recent acquisitions and major market operations—to Bob Naegele.

I couldn't believe it. I was stunned and I tried to talk him out of it. I told him we were finally in the big time, that the company was doing well and there was no doubt in my mind that we could make our debt payments and then some. When it was clear I wasn't getting anywhere my shock gave way to anger and I said, "Dad, all my life you've taught me to work hard and not be a quitter and now you're the one who's quitting! What's happened to you? How could you do this?" Dad remained surprisingly calm and unmoved. I hung up the phone dazed and disappointed.

Just a few days later I got another call from South Carolina, but this time it was my stepmother, Jane. Dad was dead. After Jimmy Brown had served him and Jane a relaxed breakfast, my father walked up to his bathroom, climbed into the tub, and shot himself.

As worried as I'd been about him, I never thought it would come to this. I felt I had lost my best friend.

6

Picking Up the Pieces

Jimmy Brown was the first to reach my father, rushing up the stairs after hearing the gunshot. Dad was still clinging to life but passed away before an ambulance could get him to a hospital.

Looking back it's easy to see the warning signs. In addition to his erratic behavior at work, Dad had made some dire statements to friends and colleagues, suggesting that his life was a failure and that his most recent acquisition was going to sink him. Also, just days before taking his life my dad wrote a $50,000 check and gave it to Jane. It has always frustrated me that she didn't see this as a sign that something was going awry. My stepmother had been unable to help my father during his final struggles and it has never been clear to me how close she and my dad ever were as a couple. I never discussed this with my own mother, Florence, but I've heard stories from my Cincinnati relatives that my father asked her to take him back on numerous occasions, and that his final such call to my mom was not long before his suicide.

Regrets about missing signals and not connecting dots naturally follow tragedies like this and I've done my best to try to put them behind me. My memories of the hours and days after learning of his death are hazy. I was in tremendous shock. I remember his funeral as a simple one, held in Savannah at the Episcopal church. He had many friends and admirers in town and the turnout was big.

I'd already been a nervous wreck for the past several weeks but now my head was really spinning. As confused and startled as I was about my father's death, there was one thing I knew for sure—the man who agreed to break up his company was

not the real Ed Turner. He had been running himself ragged. He had replaced two
addictions, smoking and drinking, with prescription pills. His behavior was manic, and
in a way I had never seen before, he was
scared. I also knew he wouldn't have wanted
me to spend my time grieving. Turner Advertising represented my father's life's work.
He loved the company, and what he'd really want me to do was save it.

But first we had to sort out his estate.
Unbeknownst to me my father had named
me executor of his will, a document we
discovered to be fairly straightforward.
When he died, my father had a net worth
of about $2 million (more than $13 million
in today's dollars). Roughly $500,000 of
that went to pay estate taxes. To my stepmother he left $500,000 worth of company
notes that were to be paid out over ten
years. My mother would continue to collect
her note payments, while the rest of the
estate—worth a little less than $1 million—
was left to me.

Outside of his blood relatives, Jimmy
Brown was probably closer to my dad than
anyone, and after rushing to find him in
that bathroom he'd also been given the

grim task of cleaning that awful mess after my father was gone. Jimmy loved and respected my dad and on top of his grief he was now faced with an uncertain future. Sometime during those difficult days he came to me and said, "Mr. Ted" (he always insisted on addressing me in that formal fashion), "your father told me once that if anything ever happened to him, you'd be sure to take care of me." I told him he had nothing to worry about. After my father, Jimmy was my closest friend in the world and without hesitation I assured him he'd always have a place in the Turner family. (As testament to the admiration Jimmy had for my father, years later and after I had become well known, Jimmy was asked, "Why aren't there more people like Ted Turner?" and he responded, "Because there aren't more fathers like Ed Turner.")

With these personal issues ironed out, I turned my attention to the company. My father's accountant, Irwin Mazo, confirmed that my dad had in fact agreed to sell the General Outdoor assets he had acquired less than a year earlier. The deal document was informal—just a handwritten note—

and my father signed it the day before he killed himself. Bob Naegele would pay the original purchase price plus $50,000. It was a great deal for Naegele and most people probably saw it as a good deal for me. Naegele would take away the big markets of Atlanta and Richmond, but in the process he'd remove our heavy debt load and put an additional $50,000 of cash in our account. Yes, I would have to move back to Macon but I'd still have a business to run, albeit a significantly smaller one. I could have made this all work, but it just didn't seem right.

A day or so after the funeral I explained to Irwin Mazo that I intended to try to keep the company together. He was polite and appreciated my desire but explained that the deal was done and given my youth and lack of track record with banks or access to capital there was no way I could come up with enough money to change Naegele's mind. Truth be told, I doubt he thought I was up to running the business anyway. After all, it wasn't long before that my father had declined to give me even the top job in the Atlanta operation. It didn't matter. I was determined to see if I could save the company.

The first thing I figured I had to do was buy some time. I contacted my father's lawyer and doctor to see if they could help me make the case that my father was not of sound mind when he entered into this agreement, therefore making it null and void. Neither of them thought this argument would hold water. Despite this discouragement, I knew that Naegele was fond of my father, and I hoped that his friendship and closeness would make him more sympathetic to my plight and more aware of the fact that my father's behavior had been out of character. He agreed to meet with me.

His billboard success had made him a wealthy man, and as it was still March and cold in his hometown of Minneapolis, we met at his vacation home in Palm Springs, California. Naegele made it clear to me that while he admired my father and mourned his death, he had no intention of going back on the deal. My case about my father's mental state didn't move him a bit. Naegele was a huge player in the billboard business and I'm sure part of him was wondering, "Who does this twenty-four-year-old kid think he is?" He probably thought that if he held firm, I'd fly back home, realize I had a pretty good thing going with the old Turner Advertising, and leave him alone.

If he thought that, he was wrong. In fact, heading back to the airport, instead of giving up I kicked into a higher gear and came up with another way to complicate the sale. It was aggressive and hostile, but it was the only card I had left to play. Before boarding my plane, I called the head of our five-man leasing department back in Atlanta. This group had grown loyal to me and I knew they'd help me out if I asked them to. Fortunately, Naegele neglected to place non-compete clauses on any of our employees so there were no legal issues holding us back. In the billboard business, a company's leases are its most valuable assets, and if you really wanted to foul up a competitor, "jumping" the leases was a great way to do it. I explained my plan to the team in Atlanta and they agreed to help me execute it.

To understand lease jumping, let me explain how billboard leases work in the first place. Back then, about 95 percent of a typical company's signs were on leased ground: someone else's parking lot, the roof of a tire company, and similar such sites. You paid the owner of the property a certain amount of money each month to maintain the lease but the termination triggers on the property owners' side were generally pretty short, and most leases could be canceled within sixty or ninety days. This left billboard companies vulnerable to a very destructive competitive tactic known as lease jumping.

To jump a competitor's lease, you'd call the owner of one of his billboard sites and find out what he was being paid. If he tells you it's $50 per month you tell him that as soon as he's able to cancel—which often would be no more than ninety days and could be as soon as tomorrow—you'll pay him $75 to take over the location. No matter what the property owner does next, the current lessee gets hurt. If the property owner agrees to your price, he cancels the current deal. If he doesn't cancel, he goes back to the sign owner and tells him there's a new rate he has to match.

As a result, the company's cost structure gets thrown out of whack. Lease jumping was an effective tactic to disrupt a competitor but since it virtually guaranteed a deadly price war, it was rarely put into practice.

The first step of my plan was to take the leasing team off the Atlanta payroll and make them employees of our company in Macon (an operation that was not included in the pending sale). These same guys could now call their Atlanta contacts but now they'd be doing so on behalf of a different company. In the case of leases that were expiring within the next few days, they'd tell the property owners that they'd like to transfer the lease over to a different company—a simple act of changing some paperwork. For leases that had several weeks to run, they would offer a higher renewal price to move the lease over to our Macon company. My team and I worked the phones feverishly and within a matter of days we caused significant damage to the assets Naegele hoped to acquire. He could now tell that I didn't intend to go quietly into the night.

With that in mind, he met with his advisers and came up with a new offer, presented in the form of two $200,000 alternatives. If I agreed to return all the leases and simply go away, he would pay me $200,000 cash. This was 1963, I was twenty-four years old, and that was a ton of money (more than $1 million today). My other option, if I wanted to retain the General Outdoor assets, was to pay $200,000 to Naegele and for this price he would tear up the agreement he had reached with my father. I'm sure Naegele thought I'd jump at their offer to buy me out. But without considering how in the world I would come up with another $200,000, I agreed on the spot that I would take the second option. This was my chance to save the business and I wasn't going to blow it for $200,000.

They were so surprised by my response that they asked for a few days to think about how they wanted the deal for tax purposes. Now they were the ones who were stunned and I had them back on their heels. After further consideration they said they'd accept my $200,000 but I had to make the payment within ninety days. If I defaulted, the deal was off and they'd keep the company.

Suddenly, I was like the dog that finally catches the bus—I had a deal but what could I do next? My recent inheritance came in the form of company equity and personal property, not cash. Turner Advertising had very little disposable cash, as we'd been making capital investments and had just six months to come up with $600,000 to make our first debt payment to cover the General Outdoor acquisition. Working through these challenges, I learned a lesson that would stick with me throughout my career. When the chips are down and the pressure is on, it's amazing to see how creative people can be. And with a ninety-day clock ticking, we had to get really creative very fast.

I was very fortunate to have Irwin Mazo on my side. He was an accountant, and he realized that nearly all of the $200,000 cash payment to Naegele and his other partners would go straight to the government. Since their deal with my father was only a couple of weeks old, this payment would be treated as a short-term capital gain and would be taxed as ordinary income. Back then, guys like Naegele would have been in a 90 percent tax bracket so taking the cash would not have been much of a deal for him. Armed with that knowledge and short on cash, we went back and offered to pay them $200,000 in Turner Advertising stock. That way, they could hold their value in equity as long as they needed to shield themselves from the heavy tax on short-term gains. By the time I presented this proposal, they'd figured out these tax issues themselves and they probably assumed they'd have another shot at our company in six months after I failed to make our first big debt payment. Who knows—but at that point they may have simply had enough of me and wanted me to go away. Regardless of the reasons, they accepted my offer.

So far so good. I had kept the company out of Naegele's hands and it didn't cost me a single dollar of cash. Energized by this victory, I went a million miles an hour sorting out solutions to keep the company on track and to make sure we made that big first payment. We created an employee stock purchase program, convincing as many employees as we could to invest their money in the company's shares. I also convinced some big advertisers like Coca-Cola and Anheuser-Busch to pay cash in advance in return for discounted prices. Turner Advertising owned some small pieces of commercial real estate that we could live without, so I sold them off. Part of my inheritance included my father's 1,000-acre plantation in South Carolina. It was mostly cattle farm. After he died I'd gone there once to collect some of his personal items. Given what had happened there, I never wanted to go back again and it was put up for sale.

Eventually, somehow, we managed to keep it all together and we made that $600,000 payment in September. It was beyond my control to save Dad, but I'd done everything I could to save his company.

I knew he would have been pleased.

7

On My Own

Dad died on the fifth of March, 1963, and by the end of that month I'd managed to keep the company together and assumed the roles of chairman and president. During this intense stretch, Judy was in Macon taking care of Laura Lee and preparing to deliver our second child. A beautiful baby boy arrived on May 23 and less than three months after his grandfather's passing, I was proud to name my first son Robert Edward Turner IV. We called him Ed after my father (he would later become known as Teddy) and we both loved him dearly. Adding a second child to our family, though, would not change the dynamics between Judy and me. Our marriage was simply not going to work.

Ironically enough the very thing that brought us together—the sailing competition—would ultimately be the setting for our final straw. It was late in 1963 and we were racing against each other. I had developed a lead over Judy's boat and when she thought the time was right, she made a move to pass me to windward. Judy was a great sailor, but her pass was made so close to my boat that she violated the rules. Just like in a car race, when you overtake someone in a sailboat you have to keep a safe distance. We were really at each other's throats at this point so when I saw who was making this move I figured "all is fair in love and war" and I gave her a sharp luff and tapped her boat out.

When the contact drew the attention of the judges, they realized that Judy's pass was illegal and they disqualified her from the race. She hurled insults at me like you wouldn't believe. After the race she packed her sails as quickly as she could and we parted for good. Judy decided to move back to Chicago to be closer to her family and while divorce is never easy, it was particularly hard for me to be separated from my two young children. With everything I was trying to do at the company and with racing taking up so much of my time, I knew I wouldn't see them very much.

I wasn't looking to marry again anytime soon but with Judy and the kids gone I found myself needing companionship. Despite the fact that I was now a divorced father of two I was still just twenty-five years old and Atlanta was a great place to be young and single. By this time, my old college friend Peter Dames had transferred to our Atlanta sales office. Young, single, and knowing his way around town very well, Peter told me that if I really wanted to meet smart, good-looking women I needed to go to one of the Young Republicans cocktail parties. I wasn't involved in politics at all back then and my worldview was still very conservative, so I figured I'd get along well in a room full of Republicans, especially attractive female ones.

The first event I went to was a fundraiser for Barry Goldwater's 1964 presidential campaign. Peter was right—there were pretty women everywhere—and one in particular caught my eye. Her name was Jane Smith and the attraction was immediate. From across the room I could tell she was beautiful and from our initial conversation I knew she had a great personality. I asked her out to dinner on the spot and our courtship began.

Janie—as most people called her—was a graduate of the University of Alabama and when we met she was working as a flight attendant for Delta Air Lines. Her dad was a successful executive and former president of his local Rotary Club and he and Janie's mom seemed to have a great relationship. For me, after failing in a marriage with a northerner from Chicago it felt reassuring to be with a southerner.

Janie and I spent a lot of time together and had a lot of fun, and after dating for almost a year we first discussed the possibility of getting married. In retrospect, it was probably too fast, but I felt I had failed at one marriage, and when I fail my impulse is always to try again. So we flew to Las Vegas for a quick wedding, then settled together in a modest Atlanta apartment. Before long we welcomed our first child

together, a boy we named Rhett, after my
favorite fictional character, Rhett Butler. I
was happy to be a new father again, and
Rhett was the apple of Janie's eye.

The company continued to move at a
pace every bit as hectic as my personal
life. We were generating solid cash flow
and once we made our first big debt payment I was eager to expand. The first opportunity I found was a billboard company
in Chattanooga, Tennessee. The price
was steep—$1 million—and back then
most sellers expected to receive about 30
percent of the purchase price up front as a
down payment. We couldn't produce that
kind of cash and still continue to meet our
debt requirements, but with Irwin Mazo's
help, we figured out a way to make the acquisition with no money down. After convincing the sellers to finance 75 percent of
the purchase price over seven years at a
high interest rate, we found a bank in Chicago to fund the balance. The bank had
been looking to expand their investments
in the South and they lent us the rest of
the money in return for equity in the Chattanooga company. (My father had always
maintained many of the different billboard

businesses as separate legal entities, in part to provide this sort of flexibility; we could offer equity in the Chattanooga company without diluting our ownership of Turner Advertising. This arrangement also allowed for periodic reorganizations to offset potential capital gains liabilities.)

Our next purchase was also in Tennessee, this time in Knoxville. This was a much smaller deal than the Chattanooga one but the details were pretty colorful. I can't remember the original owner's name but after several years of mismanaging the business, he passed away. Like a lot of billboard markets, Knoxville was a two-company town and for years the guy's competitor, run by an Air Force reserve colonel named Tom Cummings, had been cleaning his clock. It was widely assumed that once the company came up for sale, Cummings would be the only interested buyer and could easily take it at a low price. But since Knoxville would be a logical addition to a company that now owned signs in Atlanta, Richmond, Roanoke, Savannah, Charleston, and Chattanooga, I felt like I should go there and check it out.

The company would be sold at auction

out of the deceased owner's estate. I figured that Cummings assumed he'd be the
only bidder, and not wanting to disabuse
him of this notion, I did everything I could
to make sure my Knoxville visit went unnoticed. I rented a car under an alias and
drove around the town to check out his
signs and locations but never went near
the offices for fear of being spotted. The
company clearly needed some work but it
looked to me like an opportunity worthy of
at least a lowball bid. Our Atlanta attorney
found a Knoxville lawyer to represent us at
the auction and I gave him explicit but unusual instructions.

"I want you to put on the crummiest suit
you have," I told him, "and right before the
deadline you walk in there looking like
the poorest guy in town. Drop the bid on
the lawyer's desk just a few minutes before the noon deadline on the final day."
When he asked me how much I wanted to
bid I had to think about it a little. I can still
remember staring up at the ceiling in my
office. This was a one-time, sealed bid
auction so I thought it might help us to bid
an uneven amount. I also figured that Cummings wouldn't go in for more than about

$50,000, so I picked the number $50,300 out of the air, wrote it down on a piece of paper, and handed it to the attorney.

Sticking to our script, our Knoxville lawyer walked into the auctioneer's office just before noon, dressed in a cheap, unpressed suit and scuffed-up shoes. Cummings was sitting there in the lobby with his lawyers, and thinking they would have no competition they had yet to submit an offer. When they realized that this scruffy-looking guy was walking past them to submit a competing bid, they panicked. After a flurry of activity between him and his team, Cummings scribbled down a number, stuffed the paper in an envelope, and handed it to the lawyer for the estate.

A few minutes later the bids were unsealed. Sure enough, Cummings had offered $50,000. He had lost by $300 to Turner Advertising of Atlanta and he was stunned. He called me later that afternoon screaming bloody murder. He told me he'd pay me $110,000 for the business—*doubling* my money in a matter of hours. I let him know that I was serious about the Knoxville market and wouldn't sell to him for anything less than $250,000. He said that was too rich for his blood and he passed. Once we took ownership I sent Peter Dames to Knoxville to run the company and he turned things around, expanding the business from three hundred signs to four hundred. We had a lot of fun competing with Cummings and quickly became a serious player in the Knoxville market.

Our business was hitting on all cylinders and I was really in my stride. Outdoor advertising wasn't the most glamorous business but we did manage to be creative. I remember one time when a marketing person at Coca-Cola declared that billboard advertising was old hat and that they were going to redirect their dollars into television. They were one of our biggest customers and probably had about a hundred signs in Atlanta alone.

By coincidence, around the time they made this announcement, rumors were circulating that Coke was considering moving its headquarters to New York. Their executives vehemently denied this but the stories wouldn't go away. That gave me an idea. I went to our creative department

and told them to draw up a simple billboard design that said, "Goodbye Coca-
Cola, We'll Miss You!" I figured this would
stir up some controversy and when it did,
it would prove to Coca-Cola that people
really did pay attention to billboards! Our
lawyer at the time, Tench Coxe, convinced
me that this was not a good idea. We argued about it and even though we'd already had several signs printed, those
boards never did go up. (The lawyer was
probably right. Coke never did leave town
and they remained great clients of Turner
for the next forty years.)

We continued to grow our billboard, but
I wanted to expand into new lines of business. By the mid-1960s, outdoor advertising was increasingly under attack. While
her husband was president, Lady Bird
Johnson actively promoted a variety of
environmental initiatives. One of the most
high-profile of these was the Highway
Beautification Act, which called for the
banning of billboards from all federal highways. The billboard business had taken
off during the 1950s when the federal
highway system was built and losing these
signs would be a devastating blow to

Turner Advertising and the entire billboard industry. As it turned out, the law as it eventually passed was watered down significantly. It continued to allow signs in commercial and industrial areas along the highways and offered compensation to companies whose signs were removed.

Still, this pressure at the federal level, combined with constant threats from local municipalities, made me think I didn't want all my eggs in the billboard basket. At the same time this legislative pressure was building, more and more advertisers—like Coca-Cola—began to see television as more glamorous than outdoor signs. I was trying hard to stay focused on the road ahead and to me it seemed pretty clear that the medium with the brightest future had to be television.

Looking around the industry I found two companies that I could try to model myself after. The first was Metromedia, run by John Kluge, and the other was Combined Communications, headed by another entrepreneur named Karl Eller. Both of these companies had diversified beyond just one medium. In Metromedia's case, Kluge started with TV and radio and later added billboards, while Eller's company went the other way, beginning with billboards before moving into television and radio station ownership. Their strategies made sense to me, but I would need greater access to capital, or have to wait and accumulate cash from operations if I were to diversify Turner Advertising beyond its current base of business.

Up until this time, our company had remained private. My father had always owned a majority of his shares and I inherited these holdings when he passed away. In addition to using our stock to help finance acquisitions, we also allowed employees to purchase some as well. That worked fine but whenever we let our people buy stock or when an employee left the company or wanted to sell shares, we had to negotiate with them over the valuation. I always felt like I was selling our stock too cheaply and buying it back too high. It seemed to me that by going public, we could raise the capital we'd need to diversify while allowing the market to decide what we were worth. But I was advised that now would not be the right time for a public offering, so given our limited resources and the high price of television stations, we decided to start our diversification efforts by going after radio properties. Our hope was to take advantage of efficiencies in sales and promotion by buying or merging with radio stations in markets where we already had billboards.

Around this time a guy named Peterson had recently beaten me to the purchase of an AM station in Chattanooga. Since he also owned billboard properties I decided to meet with him to discuss the possibility of some creative combinations of our various holdings. He had a struggling outdoor operation in Norfolk, Virginia, and said he would agree to sell me the Chattanooga radio station if I would also purchase his Norfolk company. Wanting to get into radio and confident that we would be able to turn things around in Norfolk, I made the deal. Shortly thereafter, a South Carolinian named Chuck Smith agreed to merge into our company three of the radio stations he owned: two in Charleston, South Carolina, and one in Jacksonville, Florida. Both Peterson and Smith sold to us for stock and a small amount of cash.

While it was fun moving into a new business, I never developed a passion for radio the way I later would for television. It had been hard enough selling billboard ads against one competitor in a market, but in radio you competed with a dozen or more stations. We also had a lot of personnel issues at the stations we bought. At this point of the 1960s drugs seemed to be used heavily by a lot of the disc jockeys. A low point came when one of our on-air guys in Chattanooga got caught taking an underage girl across state lines and wound up going to prison. This all gave me a pretty bad feeling for the new business and I determined that radio would not be the final stop for Turner Advertising.

With my professional and sailing careers continuing at a breakneck pace and with a young child at home, things were hectic for Janie on the home front but she worked hard at it. After helping raise me, Jimmy Brown had transitioned into helping out Janie and me around the house, and he served as a caretaker for Rhett. We were also fortunate to have Jimmy Brown in our lives, especially as things were about to get significantly more complicated.

In the spring of 1967, when Laura and Teddy, now five and three years old, came to Atlanta for a customary Christmas holiday visit, something was clearly wrong. Laura was obviously unhappy and young Teddy was covered with bruises. I took them to the doctor and it didn't take us long to conclude that the children had been physically abused. Teddy had been taking the worst of it and there was evidence that he'd had some broken bones, including one in his arm that hadn't been properly set. It was terribly sad for me to see my two young children in this condition and there was no way they could go back to Chicago. Judy had remarried by this time and when I called her she explained that her husband was the abuser. Apparently, he had battled with drugs and mental problems and for whatever reason took out his frustrations on his stepchildren. (He was a very troubled person who eventually spent time in jail and committed suicide.)

Judy knew this was a serious problem and as heart-wrenching as this was for her, she offered no protest when I told her the children had to remain in Atlanta. She would later say that when she put Laura and Teddy on that flight to Atlanta, part of her knew that they were not coming back. After a few months, being away from her children became so difficult for Judy that she impulsively flew to Atlanta to try to take them back. That was a very difficult scene at our home. I never would have let the kids go back with her anyway but when seven-year-old Laura outright refused, it was clear even to Judy that this couldn't happen. She knew her visit had been a mistake and after seeing Teddy and Laura in their new environment, Judy decided that the best, least confusing thing she could do for her children was to let this become their home once and for all. Judy returned to Chicago and had very little contact with her children from that day forward.

But knowing that taking care of Laura and Teddy was the right thing to do didn't make the job any easier for Janie. Already tending to young Rhett, who was by this time just a year old, she now had to look after two older children from another marriage. Less than a year later, in January of 1968, Janie gave birth to a second boy, Reed Beauregard Turner, whom we called Beau. Thirteen months after that—February 17, 1969—marked the arrival of our daughter Sara Jean (or Jennie, as we called her), and at this point we had five children under the age of eight living under our roof. It was all very difficult for Janie, and frankly it was also tough on my two older children, whom she would always have difficulty treating as her own. Jimmy Brown and I did our best to try to balance the equation, but varying forms of unequal treatment would be an issue for our kids for years to come.

———— A TED STORY ————

"Janie Really Was Not Happy"
—Laura Turner Seydel

Janie really was not happy. First of all, my father was off sailing and he'd come home with his dirty laundry and as soon as things were clean he was off again. She was pregnant and now his kids from a former marriage were being shoved on her. Janie was trying but this was more than she bargained for and she couldn't stand the situation. After all these years Janie and I have now become best of friends but back then she really couldn't stand us. Teddy and I spent a lot of time down in the basement with Jimmy Brown and with my dad being away so much, he almost became like a surrogate father for us.

_____ A TED STORY _____

"The Benevolent Dictator"
—Teddy Turner

Having Jimmy Brown around was almost like having a grandfather living with you. He was kind of strict and kept after you but he also had that tender side so where your parents might not have given you ice cream after dinner, Jimmy would. My dad was a dictator, but Jimmy was the benevolent dictator when my dad wasn't around. And he had a big job because there were five kids and a household to take care of. In some ways he had zero authority but all the responsibility, which is a very, very difficult job but he was great at it. And Dad was gone a good bit between sailing and work but I really don't think anybody holds it against him because ultimately he was very successful in both. It's not like he wasn't around because he didn't want to be there—as a kid that would really upset you—that wasn't what he grew up with and he was away doing big things. We were proud of him doing it and were very happy when he was around. Things were very different when he was around; there was always life and activity and buzz and schedule and stuff. Dad makes the most of every moment while Jimmy was a little more laid-back. We did a lot but it wasn't at the frantic pace of my father. With Dad, when it was a weekend or a vacation the term was "maximum fun." His view was that if you didn't get it all in you've wasted time and haven't had your maximum fun.

I read a lot of books on parenting and tried to do my best as a father. Jimmy helped out with just about everything and as a team, he, Janie, and I did our best to raise children with good manners and the proper respect for their elders and each other. We taught them the importance of honesty, integrity, and hard work. I was so busy with work and sailing that I wasn't around as much as I would have liked, but my children always knew I loved them.

8

Sailing Gets Serious

By the mid-1960s my passion for sailing grew to be nearly as intense as my drive to succeed in business. This was a time in my life when I was doing everything at an increasingly fast pace. My father had enjoyed fast cars and now that I was on my own and could afford one, I thought it would be cool to own a Ferrari. I bought a used one that was still in good condition and while it was great for getting me around town, it posed a challenge when it came to getting my boat in and out of the water at the Atlanta Yacht Club and the other places I sailed in the area. I owned a Flying

Dutchman, which was just a two-man boat but it was heavy for a Ferrari. I couldn't see the practicality of buying a four-wheel-drive truck just to tow my boat so I took the Ferrari to a mechanic and had them install a trailer hitch to the back of it. I may have been the first person ever to trail a boat off the back of a Ferrari and this made for quite a scene whenever I drove down the highway or pulled into a boatyard but I never minded all the stares and laughter.

The more races I entered the better my sailing became and, as always, I had a strong desire to move up to the next level. For years I had read about bigger boats in *Yachting* magazine and now, with the company doing as well as it was, I realized that I might be able to afford one. A friend of mine named James Schoonmaker, from Miami, suggested I charter a boat and enter the Southern Ocean Racing Conference, or SORC. We checked with a yacht broker and were able to find someone to lease us his Block Island 40 out of Pimlico Sound, North Carolina. At forty feet in length, she was much bigger than anything I had ever sailed and I doubt its owner would have leased his boat to me had I not had a partner with Schoonmaker's experience. After we worked out terms and signed all the papers, Schoonmaker decided to take off for a race in Brazil. I was left on my own on the biggest boat I'd ever sailed.

With Jimmy Brown's help, I pulled a local crew together and Irwin Mazo came up from Atlanta to be our navigator. (He had learned navigation on a destroyer in the final days of World War II.) By the time of our scheduled departure for Charleston, the weather had turned cold and the manager of the marina recommended we spend another night there. But it didn't seem so bad to me and I was eager to get going so we went out anyway, motoring into the darkness singing sea chanteys. We made it between the first few sets of buoys but then somehow took a wrong turn. Thinking we were heading into a channel we were actually going full steam into a shallow bay. The next thing we knew—CRUNCH—we had run aground. We were stuck in Pimlico Sound and the wind started blowing harder.

Waves started to lift up our boat and then would drop us down hard on the sandbar with a loud crash. Normally waves like these can help you dislodge but that night the wind was blowing us back into the shallow bay and we couldn't get off the sand. As the waves kept pounding, Mazo grabbed the radio and started calling "Mayday! Mayday! Coast Guard!" only to discover that the radio didn't work. We started to worry that the boat might crack up, and knowing that there was no rescue on the way, we got the life raft out and put on our life jackets. We were prepared to abandon ship but as a little more time passed we realized that the boat was not breaking up and we never manned that raft. That was a good thing because if we had set out in a lifeboat in those conditions we probably would have all drowned or died of hypothermia.

After a rough night, the storm passed in the morning and we dislodged from the sandbar. The boat was okay but our psyches were damaged. Everyone was exhausted because it had been impossible to sleep that night. If you went belowdecks, there was a constant BAM, BAM, BAM that was so loud there was no way you could relax, let alone sleep. At first light we could see where we had made our wrong turn. It was back just a quarter mile and so we were able to make a quick correction. Regardless, the crew's confidence was shaken. I think Mazo and Jimmy Brown may have been the only guys on board with any real experience at sea. It was like I had pressed a bunch of old men into military service, gave them shovels, pointed them to the front lines, and asked them to take Berlin from the Germans!

Mazo wanted to make an unscheduled stop in Morehead City to get the radio fixed. This made obvious sense but given my crew's low morale I suspected that if I pulled up to the dock they would desert. I held on to the tiller and said, "We are *not* stopping at Morehead City." They asked if we couldn't just go there to get the radio fixed and check the condition of the hull and I said, "No!" Morehead was a big fishing port and when we passed the inlet on our way out to sea, it looked like the entire fishing fleet was coming in. Without a working radio, I should have taken this as a sign that the weather at sea might be getting rough. I think that

Mazo was even considering jumping overboard and swimming ashore.

I was determined to keep moving and sure enough, less than a hundred miles from Morehead City we ran into the worst storm I had ever experienced. Winds were over 50 mph and it was a struggle just to keep the boat from going around in circles. The trip to Charleston was only two hundred miles but it took us two brutal days to get there. Mazo spent almost the entire trip under a blanket belowdecks and when we put in at Charleston, he came on deck looking like someone just released from a concentration camp. The entire crew of three left me except for Jimmy Brown (and if he didn't work for me I'm not sure that even *he* would have stayed).

The next week's race was scheduled to start in St. Petersburg, on Florida's west coast, and to sail there from Charleston we had to go all the way around the Florida Keys. I managed to assemble an entirely new crew (in addition to Jimmy) in time to start this trip and while the weather was pleasant as we headed out, we ran into another storm in the Gulf of Mexico. As soon as conditions turned rough, the crew folded up their tents and left all the work to Jimmy and me. I remember one guy who got so sick that he wouldn't leave his bunk. He just lay there on his back and when he started throwing up it shot up into the air and back down on top of him.

I couldn't get anyone but Jimmy to work up on deck, so I decided to take advantage of the Gulf's shallow waters by pulling down our sails, dropping anchor, and riding out the storm. I was so exhausted from all that work that I managed to sleep that night but it proved to be a mixed blessing. I awoke the next morning to find that the anchor line had parted and we were adrift. We had no way of knowing how long the line had been broken. We were out of sight of land and I was so inexperienced that I didn't yet know how to operate the radio direction finder. The only thing I was sure of was that the wind had been blowing in a southerly direction and since we dropped anchor in the Gulf of Mexico I figured that if we sailed due east we'd have to bump into Florida. We did that, and as the weather started to moderate we came into sight of land. We ran alongside a fishing boat and the skipper let us know we were off the coast of Naples. We then managed to sail north to St. Petersburg and got there just in time for the race.

I learned a great deal about ocean racing in that first year. I sailed over a thousand miles and I felt like I was becoming experienced. In addition to my own first-hand knowledge I also learned a lot from Jimmy Brown. He had been around a lot of boats in his years, and he helped us learn about racing by getting information from our competitors. Jimmy would sit down at a bar next to a veteran racer and before you knew it, the guy would tell him some secrets. Jimmy was a great conversationalist, and given the makeup of the sport, which was very elite and very white, I'm sure these other sailors couldn't see how this black man they were drinking with could ever be a threat. It was amazing how many valuable insights they passed along to him. For example, Jimmy came back one night to say that one successful skipper explained to him that most people focus on what happens during daylight hours and fail to understand that races can be won and lost at night. I used this information to my advantage the rest of my sailing career.

We did poorly in our first couple of races but we managed to win a few trophies before the series was over: a second place finish in one race and a third in another. In the process, I fell in love with ocean racing. I liked everything about it—being out on the open ocean, the teamwork, the preparation, the challenges—everything. It really was a lot like running a business. You had to recruit a good crew and you had to be able to motivate them. From my early misadventures I realized that when conditions were good, you couldn't tell how strong your crew was. Heading out and singing chanteys everyone looked great, but once the going got tough, the weaker guys would fold.

Early on, I figured out that in both business and sailing, it's important to assemble a strong team with talents that are complementary. In many ways, a good sailing crew is like a good football team. In football you need some guys with brawn, some who are agile and quick, and you have to have a good quarterback calling the shots. In sailing, the quarterback is the skipper or helmsman. He has to be able to look out ahead and make the right calls and strategic decisions. You need the stronger, quicker crewmembers to grind winches and pull in the sails. You also need an experienced navigator. Today, technology has made navigation much easier but back then you had to rely on a sextant and dead reckoning and the job required a lot of skill.

Sailing around the clock, crews are split into two watches. While one watch sleeps, the other takes over and keeps the boat on course at top speed. Watches are normally four hours long and two teams shift out six times a day. I tried to be flexible with my own schedule to make sure I could be on deck when the sailing was the most difficult and the decisions most critical. For example, sailing into the wind requires the greatest skill so I would try to stay on deck when we were going upwind. I'd try to rest when things were at their easiest but given the fickle nature of weather at sea, I often had to get by on very little sleep.

While I had been successful on smaller boats I found that my skills were better suited for ocean racing. Not only did this sport reward leadership, recruiting, and motivating a team, it also required a lot of hard work—often around the clock—and numerous split-second decisions. The more I raced, the more I got the feeling that this was a sport in which I might compete successfully at the very highest level.

I decided it was time to buy my own ocean racer. Sizing up other vessels during my first SORC season I decided to order a new Cal 40, a thirty-nine-foot sloop made of fiberglass. We took delivery in the fall of 1966 and named her *Vamp X* (after the "Vamp from Savannah"). With a new boat and a season's worth of experience I was able to attract a stronger crew. Everything came together that year and we took the overall SORC championship. It was the biggest series I'd ever won and I let the success go to my head a little. (Privately, I used to tell people I wanted to become the world's greatest sailor, businessman, and lover all at the same time.) In public, for the first time in my life I had reporters interviewing me. The sailing culture was very conservative in those days and when I was quoted saying things like, "Man, we blew those other boats away," I rubbed some people the wrong way. My crew and I were green, brash, and from the South; and that combination didn't always go over well in places like the New York Yacht Club. But we loved to win and challenging the establishment was all part of the fun.

I also had a great time with our crew. In those earlier years, I'd sometimes cover for my lack of experience with an oversized sense of bravado, but the guys I sailed with knew how to put up with it, and occasionally they were able to put me in my place. One of my favorite stories along those lines was a time when we were out on *Vamp X,* not racing but bringing her back home from one of the SORC events. We ran into some bad weather, and after breaking our mast we had to ride out the storm using the motor. As we made this change, Jimmy Brown began hooking up a radio antenna and I said, "What are you doing?"

He said, "I'm putting up the antenna in case we need to use the radio."

I barked, "Well knock it off. Columbus made it through waters worse than this, and if Columbus didn't need a radio, I don't need one, either!"

"Okay, then," replied Jimmy, and he went right on rigging the antenna. An hour later, the engine ran out of gas. Jimmy looked at me and said, "Okay, Columbus, time for you to take over!" Thank God the radio worked. We called the Coast Guard and they came and towed us to port.

I learned a lot of lessons the hard way, but no matter how skilled a sailor anyone becomes, if you spend enough time at sea, you're going to run into trouble. One of my worst experiences came in January of 1968. By December of 1967 it became clear that the next boat I was having built would not be ready for the 1968 SORC and I needed an alternative. I had a good boat broker and while it was late in the year to be looking for a replacement, he was able to find an older boat called *Bolero* in Oyster Bay, Long Island, that was available for charter. By this time, most new ocean racers were constructed out of fiberglass but she was built in the 1940s out of wood. She was also big, running seventy-three feet long and weighing about fifty tons, far bigger than anything I had ever sailed. My broker said she had already been decommissioned and placed in winter storage but the owner was willing to make her available. Given her age and condition, and since I already had a new boat in the works, I had no desire to buy her. I told my broker to let the owner know that while I wasn't interested in purchasing the boat, having a champion crew race it would enhance its market value. The pitch worked and the owner agreed to let us take her south, but if we were to make it on time we'd have to move quickly.

Bolero was in the water and ready to go by the end of December and I got to New York just after New Year's. Our first race would be at the end of January so we only had a couple of weeks to get her down to Florida. Complicating matters was a record cold snap that had gripped the Northeast for weeks. Oyster Bay was covered with nearly six inches of ice. The night before we were supposed to leave, two of our crew slept on board with electric heaters and one of the guys forgot to pump out the water after using the head. Stepping out of their bunks the next morning, their feet slipped on the ice. A pipe had frozen and burst, and while they slept water filled the bottom of the boat and froze. While this went on, the boat began to sink. Fortunately, this all took place at a shallow dock and with just three feet of water beneath *Bolero*'s keel she only sank that far. Water from the pipe covered the engine and the battery as well, so once they pumped out the boat and fixed the piping they also had to change the battery and tear down the engine to get all the saltwater out. This cost us another couple of days and as we waited, the cold spell persisted. By the time we were ready to head out, the ice was frozen for about a mile and we had to hire an ocean tug to break the ice and lead us out. We made it down Long Island Sound and into the East River, but around the Battery in lower Manhattan, the pack ice was so thick we became stuck and had to wait for an incoming freighter to help us break free.

It was a struggle getting *Bolero* out to the open ocean, but once we did, it was a thrill. It was cold but sunny and the wind was blowing out of the north at about 15 to

20 knots. To race a boat of this size would require a crew of about eighteen but to get her down to Florida I only had six on board in addition to myself. *Bolero* was a yawl, meaning she had two masts. To race at full speed we'd want to put up full sail but with a tailwind and a small crew, I started out with just the mainsail up. As we cleared Sandy Hook, New Jersey, and headed due south we were going about 10 knots. We were making real progress. The air temperature was still cold but when you sail downwind like that, the boat sits upright and doesn't throw waves.

In addition to staying dry, when you sail with the wind at your back, you don't feel its full force. For example, if you're running at 11 knots in a 25-knot tailwind, you only feel 14 knots of wind, but if you're going into the wind at 11 knots with a 25-knot wind, you feel 36 knots of wind and you have waves and spray on top of it. It's not to say conditions on board were good, but they could have been worse. For those first two days we had about a quarter-inch layer of ice all over the deck so it was really hard to walk around. When I leased

Bolero I assumed that a boat of that size would have steam heat on board but in fact she didn't have any. Our water tanks froze, so for drinking water we were forced to warm ice on the stove. (Jimmy Brown later would say that on that trip the warmest place on the boat was in the refrigerator.)

On trips like this one, Cape Hatteras is the turning point. Conditions are generally much better on the southern side, but getting around can be rough. South of Cape Hatteras the Gulf Stream warms the water significantly and this differential often contributes to very windy conditions. When we passed the Cape the wind was swirling in a clockwise direction and once we were to its south, we faced very strong headwinds. This is when things got really bad. I had been fighting the flu and another one of our stronger guys had hurt his hand. A third crewmember turned out to be a real loser and was no help at all. We were reduced to just three able men and we had a difficult time trying to get our sails down as conditions worsened. When waves started crashing over the boat we discovered that during the two months when *Bolero* was decommissioned, her wooden deck and sides had dried up and opened up slightly and now she was taking on water.

The bilge started to fill and as it did we found out that the electric pump was broken. Our next option was a set of hand pumps but the rubber diaphragms inside them were rotten and they proved worthless. The water wasn't rising so quickly that we were in danger of sinking but we knew that if it got much higher it would flood our batteries and we'd lose electric power, and once that happened we wouldn't be able to start the engine or operate our radio. Our only remaining option was to start a bucket brigade. As the winds continued to build (we'd later learn they blew upwards of 70 mph), the three able guys on the off watch used buckets to bail the boat. That process worked but it was never-ending—if we took a break, the bilge would start to fill up again.

Despite the heavy seas and wind we did manage to get all our sails down but sediment buildup in our engine caused it to stall and we couldn't restart it. At this point, darkness was setting in and we had all been working flat-out for about twenty-four hours straight. Between fatigue and the cold (it was still below freezing on the boat) we finally decided it was time to give a Mayday call to the Coast Guard. We radioed their station at Cape Hatteras where they had one of their most durable all-weather boats. They were only about forty miles away to our north and made an attempt to come get us, but they turned back after deciding the seas were too rough. The Coast Guard called and told me that a two-hundred-foot oceangoing tugboat had been dispatched from Morehead City, but since that was more than a hundred miles to our south, it would take them all night to get to us. As we considered hunkering down for the night, the wind continued to roar in from the southeast and we were afraid it was pushing us right back into Cape Hatteras, which was now only about twenty miles away. One of the most dangerous features of Cape Hatteras, in addition to its frequently bad weather, is a shallow sand bank called Diamond Shoals. Jutting out about ten miles, this area has been called the "Graveyard of the Atlantic," since so many ships have wrecked there in conditions just like the ones we were facing.

As the rest of the crew tried to sleep, I could see the light from the Cape Hatteras lighthouse and I figured we only had about three hours before we had to start worrying about the shoals. I decided that I should let everybody sleep and gather some strength, then when we got a little closer I would wake them up and try to raise at least one small sail to steer her out of the way. Fortunately, we didn't get that close. As the night went on the wind shifted around to the south, so instead of blowing us toward the shoals it moved us slightly farther away. Through the night a freighter had been keeping an eye on us from about a quarter mile away. They had heard our distress call and decided to stay close until the tug got there. I'm not sure we'd have ever been able to transfer ourselves onto that ship in that weather but regardless, they were great to keep a lookout for us, just in case.

First thing the following morning, with a bit of sleep and the storm finally letting up, we decided to give the motor another try.

The engine started but it turned out that the ropes that had been tying our sails was dragging overboard and had wrapped around and choked our propeller, so that was the end of that. Fortunately, the tug made it to us about an hour later. They shot us a line that we tied to our mast for a five-hour tow to Morehead City. It was a relief when we were finally safe on dry land. With the weather now calm, we had a scuba diver remove the rope from our propeller and we left the next afternoon to motor our way down to Charleston. We made it there safely and the following week, with an entirely different crew, Jimmy Brown and I reached St. Petersburg in time for the first race.

I will never forget that night near Cape Hatteras. I really thought there was a decent chance that I wouldn't see the sunrise the next morning. I remember taking a picture of my wife and kids out of my wallet and just sitting there in my bunk looking at it. I kissed it several times and hoped that I'd have a chance to see them again. It was the most harrowing time I had ever had at sea, but it couldn't diminish my enthusiasm.

I was determined to learn from the experience and to continue racing. I had found my sport and nothing was going to stop me now.

9

WTCG: "Watch This Channel Grow!"

By the late 1960s we owned five radio stations but I was frustrated to be based in Atlanta and not have one there. I looked around but it was clear that there weren't going to be any twenty-four-hour stations for sale anytime soon. I might have been able to get my hands on a daytime AM station but those seemed to be losing propositions. The situation was frustrating. I had energy to burn and knew I'd be restless if the company didn't keep growing and diversifying.

At about that same time I noticed an ad on one of our billboards for a UHF TV station called WJRJ, Channel 17. I wasn't following the television business back then—to be honest, I didn't even watch much TV. I remember having to ask someone what UHF stood for. ("Ultra High Frequency," was the answer, which I soon learned was a fancy way to describe a station most people couldn't see because their antennas couldn't receive it.) Still, this business intrigued me. The VHF—Very High Frequency—stations in Atlanta were all strong network affiliates that were probably worth more than my entire company. But since the VHF stations were so strong and because they basically split the market three ways, I figured I might be able to get my hands on a UHF competitor at a price I could afford. As I asked around town, it appeared that WJRJ was not doing well and might be on the block. The idea of getting into the TV business was exciting and if my options came down to buying a lousy radio station or a lousy TV station, I wanted to bet on the medium that looked like it would grow.

Channel 17 was owned by Rice Broadcasting, which was run by Jack Rice, Jr. (not only was his name on the parent company, his initials provided the call letters for WJRJ). I went to see him and my visit confirmed that the business was indeed in bad shape. They had just gone public (the market for new issues was really hot at that time), but the station was bleeding cash. This wouldn't be the worst thing, though, since our radio and billboard businesses were quite profitable and we could use these losses to lower our tax obligations while we turned the station around. I also came up with another way our company could squeeze value out of this deal. In an average month about 15 percent of our billboard inventory went unsold. With signs all over Atlanta, I could put the unsold ones to use promoting our station, just as we had done to promote our radio stations. The more I studied this deal, the more I wanted to do it.

My board, on the other hand, thought I was crazy. The directors were mostly friends of my father's and they were having trouble getting used to my more aggressive style. They also read reports from analysts who did not believe that UHF stations would ever be successful. (I remember one who referred to UHF as "the lunatic fringe of broadcasting.") But after considering it carefully I wanted to go ahead. Television would be a new challenge and it looked like it might be a lot of fun.

Rice was represented by Atlanta investment bank Robinson-Humphrey, and everyone involved was prepared to make a deal. Disappointed with the station's performance, they thought that now might be a good time to merge with a partner or make an outright sale. They valued the company (which consisted entirely of the TV station, WJRJ) at $2.5 million. At the time the rest of our company was probably worth about $7.5 million, so this would be a big deal for us. There was no way we could pay cash, so we negotiated a stock swap that would leave me as the largest single shareholder in the combined company but would drop my percentage ownership to about 47 percent. My board of directors continued to raise objections but they knew I had voting control of the stock and in the end my enthusiasm wore them down.

Despite getting my board's blessing, closing the deal would take a while. The

Federal Communications Commission must approve any change of control at a station using the public airwaves. It's a slow, bureaucratic process and between their scrutiny and all the other details we needed to resolve, it took nearly six months to go from a letter of intent to closing. A few months into this process a second UHF station signed on in Atlanta. They were part of a bigger group called U.S. Communications and they came into town with their guns blazing. They had catchy call letters for the Atlanta market—WATL—and they kicked off with a huge promotional campaign. We were pretty sure that their monthly programming budget was four times that of Channel 17's—$100,000 to our $25,000—and after just two months on the air, their ratings were higher than WJRJ's, which had been in business for two years.

The already small UHF market in Atlanta had thus been split in two and while our decision to buy Channel 17 was looking worse by the day, television was still where I wanted to be and I was determined to give it a try. Radio and billboards were okay but this was a chance to get into an exciting new game with some real upside. I was sure that some portion of TV's growth in advertising had to come at the expense of radio and outdoor so this move made sense from a diversification standpoint. I knew how to sell advertising and assumed that the rest of the TV business couldn't be that hard to learn. I had confidence in my abilities and figured things at the station couldn't be so bad that we couldn't turn it around.

Our deal finally closed in January of 1970. Upon taking control of WJRJ we changed its call letters to WTCG, for Turner Communications Group, the new name of our newly diversified media company.

I had a lot to learn about the TV business so I dove in headfirst. My radio and billboard experience gave me a good sense for the advertising side of things but television programming was a whole new world. When I was a kid we didn't have a television set at home and the military prep schools and Brown didn't have them either. Once I was out of school I was too busy to watch much TV—maybe a football game or a movie here or there. I bought a couple of books about the industry and subscribed to the TV trade journals. I also talked to a lot of people, including general managers of other stations and anyone else I could think of who had some knowledge to share. Even my local competitors were pretty forthcoming. I was kind of like Jimmy Brown getting information from those skippers; they didn't see me as much of a threat and they didn't mind telling me what they knew.

Unfortunately, the more I learned about TV stations, the more I realized that ours was a disaster. Most of the thirty-five employees we inherited were either lazy, on drugs, or both. The terrible work ethic started at the top. When I'd walk into the GM's office he'd be sitting there with his feet propped up on the desk reading *The Wall Street Journal*. I'd say, "What are you doing reading the newspaper? This place is going broke! You need to get out and hustle!" It was the most poorly run business I had ever seen. We hired new people, bought some new equipment, anything we could afford to help turn things around. Of the thirty-five people who were on the payroll when we took over, only two were still there a year later—the custodian and the receptionist.

Our shows were weak, so I decided to make programming my top priority. As an independent station without prime-time commitments to a Big Three broadcast network (which back then were ABC, NBC, and CBS), we had flexibility and opportunities to be creative. During late night, after prime time, the three Atlanta broadcast affiliates ran programs like Johnny Carson and Dick Cavett. I loved movies and figured there had to other people out there who would prefer to watch them instead of talk shows. Sure enough, when we put films on in late night, our ratings improved. Sunday mornings were a similar story. The other stations all ran religious programming and I knew there had to be viewers who would appreciate another option. This was in the days before VCRs, and broadcast TV was the only way people could see movies at home. We began airing our best films in *Academy Award Theater* and I actually served as the show's host. After being introduced as "R. E. Turner" I'd walk to my easy chair, sit down, and introduce the movie. It was a lot of fun and I think viewers liked seeing a live local person taking part in the programming. *Academy Award Theater* was our first big hit.

I've made a lot of programming decisions this same way ever since. I look around to see what the competition is running, figure out whose tastes aren't being met, and provide them with an alternative. From watching the competition I believed that most of what the networks were airing was garbage, full of gratuitous violence, sex, and stupidity. Knowing how quickly TV viewership was growing, it troubled me to see how much junk people were watching. With limited choices and so much poor programming, I felt that a station like ours could compete if we offered something that was more wholesome. I concluded that the great old TV shows could compete against new, crummy ones and for years that became a guiding principle for how we programmed the station.

About six months into our ownership of WTCG, a bankrupt UHF station in Charlotte went on the market. But Channel 17 looked like it might lose as much as $900,000 for our first full year and there was no way I could convince the board, let alone our bankers, that this was a good time to add another struggling station to the company's portfolio. Still, I made an exploratory trip to Charlotte and the station seemed to have a solid infrastructure and lots of new equipment. I was convinced that TV was where I wanted to be, so I decided to buy the station on my own. And because it was in bankruptcy, I was able to buy it for less than $1 million.

Even though I executed this transaction separate from the company, my board was not happy, concerned about me trying to manage two money-losing stations in big, competitive markets. Most displeased of all was Irwin Mazo, my chief accountant (and onetime ocean navigator). He had been a close friend of my dad's and after doing everything he could to keep me from buying the Atlanta station, the Charlotte deal was the last straw; he resigned from the board. (Later I found out that before Mazo left, he tried to have me replaced as the company's president, but he realized that I owned too much stock for anyone to push me out.) Not long after Irwin left, Jim Roddey, who was running the company day to day, decided he'd also had enough, and he resigned as well. These were big blows given all we had in front of us, but I've always considered myself to be a good open-field runner and I was more determined than ever to make it work.

I renamed the Charlotte station WRET (which happen to be my initials), and quickly discovered that despite the better-looking physical plant and equipment, the operation was in poor financial shape. Complicating matters, I had committed myself to a serious schedule of sailing races and I was away a lot. Fortunately, I hired a smart guy from Price Waterhouse named Will Sanders. Will was great with the numbers and tough on spending, but even after his effective work keeping things on track while I was gone, WRET was clearly undercapitalized. It got to the point where we couldn't pay some of our key suppliers, without whose forbearance we'd have to go off the air.

When we were beginning to get desperate, Sid Pike, who was running station operations in Atlanta, came to me with an idea. He suggested we go on the air with a telethon but instead of raising money for a charity we'd ask for viewers' pledges to save our station. I thought it was worth trying and since we didn't have any better ideas we gave it a shot. All weekend we ran movies but instead of putting ads on during the breaks, I'd come on and tell people that if they wanted us to stay on the air, we needed their help in the form of a direct cash loan. I'd say things like, "By the rules of business, we're failing, but before we go off the air we're asking for your support. We air about three thousand movies a year, so it's probably worth a few of your own dollars to help keep us afloat." Well, the money started rolling in. Little kids brought in their piggy banks and we had policemen and firemen come on the air and tell us why they felt the need to give. It was a lot of fun and when all was said and done, we raised about $25,000 and generated tremendous goodwill in the community. (By the way, we kept receipts for every donor for whom we had a record and when we turned the corner three years later we paid every single one back with interest—$4 for every $3 we borrowed— about a 10 percent annual return.)

As scary as things could get on occasion, this was a great time for the company. Every day was a battle but we refused to quit. The telethon (which later became known as the "beg-a-thon") helped keep us afloat and from that point on we started taking more creative, fun chances with the programming. As in Atlanta, we ran a lot of old movies but tried to do it with a little twist. One of our more memorable showcases was a horror feature hosted by a guy we called "Dead Ernest." At the start of the show he'd be lying down in a coffin and then he'd slowly sit up like a vampire and introduce the picture. Sandy Wheeler was our GM then and he had a lot of great creative ideas like this. We also made some important decisions when it came to series reruns. One was a programming swap with another station in town owned by Cox. We had rights to *Ironside* and *Marcus Welby,* two shows that were highly regarded on their networks but which turned out to be duds in syndication. We swapped them for *The Andy Griffith Show,* which turned out to be a huge hit—one that really helped turn the station around (and made us a lot of money for years to come).

We were also aggressive and creative when it came to ad sales and I personally went on a lot of calls. When potential advertisers criticized us for running old black and white shows when color TV was all the rage, we'd tell them that our black and white programming would help their color commercials pop out of the clutter. Others would say that since our shows were older and old-fashioned that our viewers were probably that way, too—not as smart or wealthy as the people watching our competition. I'd tell them they had it backward—our viewers were actually much smarter than our competitors' because you had to be a genius to figure out how to pull down a UHF signal!

———— A TED STORY ————

"Just Plain Fun"
—Terry McGuirk

(TERRY MCGUIRK BEGAN WORKING AT TURNER COMMUNICATIONS BETWEEN HIS JUNIOR AND SENIOR YEARS AT MIDDLEBURY COLLEGE IN VERMONT. HE WENT ON TO WORK AT TURNER FOR MORE THAN THIRTY YEARS, ULTIMATELY BECOMING

THE COMPANY'S CHIEF EXECUTIVE OFFICER. HE IS NOW THE CEO OF THE ATLANTA BRAVES.)

I was looking for a job for my final college summer and my father recommended I interview at Channel 17. My dad was general manager at the CBS affiliate in Atlanta but they had a serious nepotism policy so a position there was out of the question. Fortunately for me, my father was one of the few people in town who had respect for Ted and what he was trying to do and he thought a summer at Turner would be a good experience for me. I wound up having so much fun that summer that I worked there again the following Christmas vacation and Spring Break and after my graduation I went to work there full-time.

Having just earned my bachelor's degree in history I went to Atlanta thinking this job would be a placeholder before I went on to teach or pursue some other very different kind of career. The only problem was, the job was just plain fun. There were only about thirty full-time employees at the station and almost all of us were in our early or mid-twenties. Toward the end of that first summer I was still thinking about what I really wanted to do for a career when Ted came walking into our little sales office. At this point I was the tenth man on a ten-man advertising sales team and Ted told us he had just bought a station in Charlotte. "I'm losing $50,000 a month," he said. "It's a total disaster and I need a couple of guys to pick up and go there to help straighten things out." Everybody ran into the bathroom or hid under their desk. Sitting in the back of the room I raised my hand and said, "I'll go."

I was the only guy from Channel 17 who went and I arrived in Charlotte shortly after WRET's famous "beg-a-thon." That stunt had helped the situation somewhat but things were still in rough shape. The new salespeople Ted hired were following a group that had earned a very bad reputation in town. I can still remember making a call to a local furniture store only to have the owner chase me out of his store with a gun. Our general manager was a guy named Sandy Wheeler. I don't know where Ted found him but he was quite a character and every single day at 10:00 A.M. there was an all-staff prayer meeting in the confer- ence room. Everything at the entire station just stopped. For many of us in the sales department, this was not our cup of tea and we made sure to be out of the office on calls every day at that time.

Almost everything we aired was taped syndicated programming. About the only show that aired live from our studios was a religious program hosted by a young couple named Jim and Tammy Faye Bakker. Well before they went on to national fame, they got their start with this local show in Charlotte and before long they were bringing in more money in a week than the entire station made in a month.

It really was a wild place to work. That station had a culture and beat of

its own like nothing I've ever seen before or since.

The first year under our ownership
WRET and WTCG each lost almost $1
million, but we were making significant
progress. More people started buying UHF
antennas, which helped enlarge our audience, and as a result more advertisers
started spending money with us. Still, even
as our revenue grew, Will Sanders was
smart enough to realize that the company
needed more capital and he pushed me to
shed some assets. With TV becoming my
focus, we sold our radio station in Jacksonville, Florida, and the billboard company we owned in Roanoke, Virginia.

I've been lucky many times in my career
but what happened next was one of my
greatest breaks ever. Out of the blue, WATL
went off the air. Their parent company was
losing money on each of its six UHF stations and they decided to pull the plug on
WATL rather than continue to fight it out
with us. Just like that we went from being
one of two independents in the market to
being the only one, and I knew that instant

that this was a huge moment for us. Our direct competitor had capitulated and I was so excited I decided to throw an on-air celebration. It was literally a televised cocktail party. I'm sure people wondered what we were doing and it didn't make for great TV but I couldn't contain how happy I was and didn't mind sharing our success with our audience.

With WATL out of the way, we were now the only independent station bidding on syndicated programming rights for Atlanta. The three network affiliates bought a limited number of newer movies and some syndicated series from the Hollywood studios and aired them selectively in local time periods, while the network supplied the bulk of their high-profile programming—prime time, soap operas, national news, and such. The film studios sold their products on a market-by-market basis and with WATL gone, no one else in Atlanta was buying old movies. This left literally thousands of titles with no one else competing to air them in our market. These old films were long since fully amortized by the studios, and in the old days the actors and actresses were paid a flat fee up front and didn't participate in any "back end" revenues from syndication (after all, TV didn't even exist when most of these movies were made). This meant that any revenue they generated from the Atlanta market would be found money that would drop straight to their bottom line.

As a result, we were able to get good pricing, and we bought just about every movie we could get our hands on, striking long-term deals whenever possible. I did business with nearly all the major studios, including Paramount, Warner Brothers, and MCA. (There was one studio that refused to sell to me. MGM decided they would forgo revenue from Atlanta rather than sell to me at the bargain-basement prices I was paying everyone else. It would take me many more years to gain access to the MGM library but I would get there eventually.) Working on these deals I became acquainted with the executives at the movie companies, from salesmen in the field all the way to the top executives like Barry Diller and Lew Wasserman. I'd always loved movies and now I was having fun with these guys while I learned the business and grew our library.

In addition to counterprogramming with movies and old series I figured out another chink in the armor of our competitors. The Big Three networks made their money by selling national ads that ran across their affiliated stations. They wanted this programming to air on as many affiliates as possible to deliver nationwide coverage and a large audience. Because of conflicting programming commitments, especially with locally produced shows like pro sports, affiliated stations would sometimes preempt national programming, costing the network coverage in that market. Once I learned this, I got an idea. I decided to call the network people in New York and offer to air their shows on Channel 17 whenever they were preempted by their Atlanta affiliate. It took me a while to track down the right people but when I did they said yes. They preferred to have their affiliate clear their shows, but we were better than nothing. When we reached the point of having four preempted NBC shows running in our daytime lineup I had our people put up some billboards saying "THE NBC NETWORK MOVES TO CHANNEL 17" in really big letters (smaller letters mentioned what these four shows were). The owners of the NBC station—Cox Broadcasting—threatened a lawsuit and our attorney, Tench Coxe, advised me to have them taken down. Meanwhile, the controversy was mentioned in Cox's own *Atlanta Journal-Constitution* newspaper and we got some free publicity out of it.

The Atlanta ABC station carried the Hawks basketball games, so during the NBA season they had a bunch of preemptions in prime time. This gave me the same opportunity I had with NBC, and ABC's executives were more than happy to have us clear Atlanta for them. We even got to air the 1971 premiere of *Brian's Song.* Starring James Caan and Billy Dee Williams, it was one of the biggest made-for-TV movies of its time. We got a 17.0 rating—our biggest audience ever. That same night the Hawks game on the ABC affiliate did something like a 4.0 or a 5.0.

The next time period I focused on was the morning. The ABC station's big hit was a local kids program called *Tubby and Lester.* It cost them a lot to produce but the other stations ran news in that time slot so the show got big ratings with kids. We decided to put on licensed cartoons and pull some of the kid audience away. The plan worked—we split the non-news audience and they eventually canceled their children's programming. We did so well shaking things up and growing our ratings that I started telling people that WTCG now stood for "Watch This Channel Grow!"

I knew we needed sports to really jump to the next level. I'd already taken professional wrestling from the ABC station (and we produced the events in our own little studio—it was cramped in there but somehow we made it work), and while these shows did well, getting big league rights would really put us on the map. The Atlanta Braves were relatively new in town, having moved from Milwaukee in 1966, but they were already popular. If we could somehow get the Braves on WTCG it would be a huge coup. Not only would our ratings go up, but also we figured that many Atlantans who didn't have UHF antennas (about 50 percent of the market) would buy one just so they could see the

Braves games. With more of these antennas in place, the potential audience for all of our shows would grow automatically.

It was widely known that the Braves had lost money since moving to Atlanta—some said as much as $1 million a year—and as a result I was confident that an offer of more money for their TV rights would at least get their attention. WSB was paying the Braves $200,000 per year for the right to show twenty away games. Back then many teams hesitated to put too many games on TV—particularly home games— fearing that this exposure would hurt ticket sales. WTCG was turning the corner to profitability and I was willing to pay for an asset as valuable as rights to a major sport. I called Bill Bartholomay, who led the group that purchased the Milwaukee Braves and moved them to Atlanta. He lived in Chicago and was also a sailor so we knew some of the same people and had a lot in common. From our mutual friends I also learned that he was a trustworthy, stand-up guy.

I met with Bill and said we would offer the Braves $600,000 per year—three times WSB's fee—but in return we wanted sixty games instead of twenty. While WSB would have the wherewithal to increase their payments to the Braves, I figured they would not be willing to commit to airing that many more games—especially since they knew Channel 17 would be happy to air the NBC programming they'd have to preempt.

My hunch was right. The Braves needed the money and after some negotiating Bill agreed to take my offer. Given the team's broad relationship with WSB's parent, Cox Communications (they owned the Braves' flagship radio station in addition to the *Atlanta Journal-Constitution,* the paper the Braves counted on for extensive and hopefully positive coverage of the team), Bill felt the right thing to do was to give them a courtesy call before they heard about this deal secondhand. I was worried but I had no choice but to agree.

The Cox people were furious. They told him I was a nut and that WTCG was a "Mickey Mouse UHF station." Since all Bartholomay had with me was a handshake, they said he should walk away from our deal and that if he did, they would match my terms. They even went so far as to suggest to Bill that if his deal with WTCG went through, the team should expect to see their newspaper coverage buried in the *Journal-Constitution*'s classifieds, not on the cover of the sports section. That subtle threat was a bad idea because then, as now, the government had a lot of concerns about media concentration in local markets and how that power might get abused. If Cox stole our deal with the Braves, this comment would give me leverage in a complaint to the government.

After his unpleasant meeting with the Cox people, Bill met with me again and asked if I'd reconsider releasing him from our deal. I said, "Bill, I've been told that a handshake from you is as good as a signed contract and that's why I agreed to let you talk to Cox before our announcement." He just slumped over his desk and said, "You're right, but it would really be best if we just forgot about our deal. WSB is willing to give me the same deal you are."

I said, "Look, a deal's a deal," and that was that.

As hard as it was for him, Bill was a man of his word. He stuck by his guns and we got the Braves.

With this big new jewel in our crown, we set our sights on other teams' TV rights. Tired of us stealing their network shows during their prime-time basketball telecasts, the ABC affiliate passed on renewing their Hawks deal and we picked it up. We also carried Atlanta Flames hockey (before that NHL franchise moved to Canada) as well as professional soccer from the now defunct NASL. Those other sports couldn't touch the Braves in terms of ratings or interest but every little piece added to our popularity and helped us get noticed.

WTCG was on the map and our financial performance started to improve dramatically. We cut our losses from $900,000 in 1970 to about $600,000 in 1971. We doubled our revenues and broke even in 1972, and for the full year of 1973, Channel 17 generated more than $1 million in profits. We were on a roll.

Putting so much of my energy into work and sailing didn't leave as much time for a family life and things were chaotic on the home front. Janie did her best to manage a household with five young kids but it was a struggle. She never embraced the idea of caring for Teddy and Laura and their unequal treatment continued. As the step-children, they would often spend meal-times down in the basement with Jimmy Brown, eating different food than their half siblings enjoyed upstairs. Thank goodness for Jimmy. He worked very hard and took great care of the children. He drove them to school, cooked many of their meals, and did lots of fun outdoor activities with the kids like catching butterflies and sled-ding in the winter. He was also great about teaching them manners and respect.

But Jimmy had his challenges, too, and in addition to battling with his weight he also struggled with alcoholism. There were times when Jimmy and Janie would argue, and these arguments would sometimes trigger Jimmy to go on a drinking binge. For weeks at a time, he would remain com-pletely sober, but then he would go on a bender and behave like a completely dif-ferent person. He'd become paranoid and stay in the basement for days at a time be-fore he'd eventually come out of it.

———— A TED STORY ————

"Those Weren't the Best of Circumstances"
—Rhett Turner

When Jimmy was up and running he'd take us to school, and everywhere we needed to go. We walked to the store to return bottles and to buy marbles. He always had deep pockets full of change that we would use to buy candy. He was the best guy in the world for that. The few times when it snowed in Atlanta he'd take us to the golf course to go sledding all day. He could go three months being a great person doing everything he needed to do but then for a week and a half or two weeks he'd stay down in the basement, drunk, until he ran out of alcohol and food. You wouldn't want to walk into the room because it smelled terrible. And with my dad not around, my mom would have two weeks of crises waiting for Jimmy to wake up and Dad's not there. Somehow we all got done what we needed to get done but those weren't the best of circumstances.

This wasn't the healthiest environment for our children and I tried to step in when needed most, but in truth my presence at home was not consistent. The obvious question is why and it's not an easy one for me to answer. I'm a product of my environment and I grew up with an intense desire to achieve and to be successful. My father was a driven man who instilled in me an intense work ethic and the schools I attended also stressed discipline and achievement. From an early age I always had a lot of energy and when I became an adult, my drive and that energy were channeled toward trying to be the best in sailing and business.

Growing up, my own family life was far from the traditional ideal. My father wasn't around much for the few years I was home as a child, so while he was a strong role model and taught me a lot about business, he didn't set an example in terms of being home for dinner every night. Life at home wasn't always the happiest for me, either.

My dad was unpredictable and tough and when my sister got sick, being around the house could be difficult. This, combined with the fact that I spent so many of my formative years at boarding schools, created in me an orientation that was not centered on a family life at home. But regardless of the reasons, I simply wasn't around as much as I probably should have been. When I was able to be there, I tried to be a good disciplinarian, with a big emphasis on manners and respect. I always thought my father's treatment of me was harsher than it needed to be, so while I did spank my children on the rare occasions when they were particularly out of line, I was never as harsh on them as Dad was with me.

—————— A TED STORY ——————

"A Drill Sergeant"
—Jennie Turner Garlington

Whenever my dad was home there was tons of excitement around the house. He always made everything fun. It would be pitch black dark outside and every morning before school

Dad would rattle off all our names like a drill sergeant. He'd yell, "Beau!" and he'd answer, "Yes sir!" "Rhett!" "Yes sir! "Teddy!" and so on. We knew we'd better get our butts out of bed fast and once we did, Dad would start singing "Hi-ho, Hi-ho, it's off to school we go." We'd eat breakfast and then everyone crammed in the tiniest Toyota you've ever laid eyes on. Then he would get out of the car in the middle of our neighborhood, he would flag down our neighbors in their Cadillac and make them roll down their car window and say "Hey, why don't we all carpool to school?"

When Dad wasn't around, Jimmy was our Rock of Gibraltar; a pillar of strength in the kindest and gentlest of ways. Even with five wild banshee children running amuck he never once raised his voice or his hand to us. He always kept us busy selling lemonade at the corner of the street, doing homework projects in the very unfinished basement. That basement was our haven, with Jimmy sitting in his chair, answering every single one of our millions of questions.

By the time Laura was approaching the sixth grade we reached the decision that it would be best for her to go to Cincinnati to live with my mother. There she would be surrounded by relatives on my mother's side of my family. This wound up being a good solution for everyone. Laura needed a break from what was an increasingly turbulent household and her moving away took some of the pressure off Janie. It also turned out to be a great thing for my mother. After all that she had gone through with my little sister, having a healthy granddaughter around was a blessing. She told Laura that God must have sent her there as a replacement for my sister and she even mistakenly referred to her as "Mary Jean" on occasion. It was a happy time for the two of them and they developed a very special relationship.

A few years later, Teddy also left home to attend McCallie. My alma mater was no longer a military school but it still accepted boarders and maintained much of their philosophies about discipline and citizenship. As in the case of Laura's departure, getting away was a good thing for Teddy and home life in Atlanta settled down for Janie and the other three children.

10

The Braves

The Braves were a huge shot in the arm for us. Ratings for the games were strong and our ad sales team had solid success selling them. We also estimated that moving these telecasts over to our station prompted about 100,000 people in Atlanta to buy UHF receivers, so not only were our ratings high for the Braves games, but viewership increased across our entire schedule since more people could see the station. Being associated with the team was also a lot of fun. I hadn't been a baseball fan but now that we were carrying games I went to the ballpark often and watched a lot of the other games on TV.

As helpful as the Braves were, we'd have been much better off if the team had won more games. Advertisers like being associated with a major league franchise, but they prefer that team to be a winner. The Braves of the early 1970s were pretty bad, but after posting consecutive losing records our first two seasons carrying games—1972 and 1973—they started turning things around in 1974. In April, Hank Aaron broke Babe Ruth's all-time home run record and the team went on to win eighty-eight games for the season. Atlanta was really excited about baseball—nearly a million fans went to the ballpark and our ratings improved. But the team did a total 180 degree reversal in 1975. They traded Hank Aaron to Milwaukee the very season he broke Babe Ruth's record, lost ninety-four games, and saw their attendance drop almost in half (530,000 fans for eighty one games—fewer than seven thousand people a game). I went to Fulton County Stadium for one of the last games of that difficult season and there were barely six hundred people in the stands. The Braves were losing and it was obvious that the fans weren't the only ones who had packed it in; the players had, too. The whole experience was depressing. I got restless. I walked up to the club level to see Dan Donahue, the team's president, and I said, "Dan, I consider us to be partners, and we need to add some more excitement next year. What are we going to do to get the team on track?"

Donahue looked at me and said, "Well I don't know what you're going to do next year but I know what we're going to do. We're selling the team."

"What!" I was shocked. The Braves meant a lot to my business and there were constant rumors that someday they might move out of Atlanta.

"Who're you going to sell it to?" I asked.

"To you," Donahue answered.

"*Me?*" I was stunned.

My dad taught me early on that long-term relationships with your customers and partners are important because you never know; the guy who you're friendly with today might be able to help you out tomorrow. He was right. For the past few years I'd demonstrated to Braves management that the team was important to me and now they were offering me a first-look chance to buy the franchise.

I caught my breath and I said, "Okay, but if I'm going to consider this, I need to know a little more about your business. How much money will you lose this year?"

"About a million dollars," he replied.

"Okay, how much do you want for the team?"

"Ten million."

Ten million dollars! For a business that was losing a million dollars a year? We'd paid $2.5 million for Channel 17 and $1 million for Charlotte. Our company's biggest acquisition ever—my father's purchase of General Outdoor—was $4 million. And that company was profitable and in our own industry. My first reaction was that this was completely out of the question, but before I said no I asked him for a couple of days to think about it.

After the initial shock wore off I spent the next couple of days taking long walks in the woods. I've often used long walks to clear my head and in this case it cleared quickly. The Braves were a key asset and I *had* to go for it. Major League Baseball

was high-quality programming for Channel 17 and by owning the team I would
control its long-term TV rights. Plus, buying this franchise would really put our company on the map. There was just this one
little problem—I couldn't afford it. Our
other businesses were performing pretty
well but we still had a lot of debt and even
if I could scrape together $10 million it
would be hard to justify paying that for a
business that was losing a million a year.

I might have had room to negotiate on
price, but I decided to focus on terms. I
told Dan, "Look, I'll buy the team, but I
can't afford to pay cash. How about I give
you a million dollars down and you give
me nine years to pay the rest, with interest?" He said he'd need to talk to his partners and would get back to me. I knew
that since I'd been given the first look I
needed to put in a strong bid. My offer was
unconventional, but it would allow them to
tell the world that they got their $10 million
asking price. (Incidentally, throughout my
career I've been criticized for being a poor
negotiator and overpaying for things. But
by not hesitating to make quick, aggressive bids, I usually got the deal and even

my higher-priced acquisitions have turned out to be good investments.)

Dan got back to me quickly and told me my offer had been approved. I was elated, but we were only halfway home. The next hurdle was approval from the Major League Baseball owners. In addition to my not fitting their mold, I think I was the first person to try to buy a team with less than 100 percent cash. Some were also concerned about my ultimate intentions on the TV side of things. I would be just the second owner who controlled both a team and its broadcast station (Gene Autry of the California Angels was the first), and I had made a few comments about distributing WTCG on cable outside Atlanta. Some owners worried about what this might mean in terms of TV competition in their home markets. But the Braves were a bad team in a relatively small southern city and I don't think many of them saw me as a threat.

Still, I couldn't take any chances so I went into full sales mode and did everything I could to get into baseball's good graces. In a lucky break, the guy running national sales for Channel 17 just happened to be Stan Musial's son-in-law, and when it came time for me to meet with commissioner Bowie Kuhn and the rest of the owners, none other than "Stan the Man" provided my flattering introduction. I was also careful to make sure that Bill Bartholomay agreed to stay on as Braves chairman after our deal closed. Through our previous rights negotiations I learned that he was a man of integrity and I knew that the other owners liked and respected him. Major League Baseball was a new world to me and Bill's presence would be very helpful.

We successfully resolved our financing and league approval issues through the fall of '75, and in January '76 Turner Communications Group took over as owner of the Atlanta Braves. It was a thrill for all of us at the company. The team might have been losers, but they were in the big leagues, and now so were we. I'd become successful in billboards, broadcasting, and sailing through dedication, motivation, smarts, and plain old hard work. I assumed that baseball would be no different. I figured I'd simply go in there, fire up the team with enthusiasm, and we'd be tearing up the league in no time.

Boy, did I have a lot to learn!

The first thing I figured out was that to be good in baseball you needed to be able to hit, run, field, and throw. If you couldn't do those things well, no amount of motivation or enthusiasm could make the difference. Unfortunately, this was precisely the situation we inherited with the '76 Braves. I did make the effort, though. I remember inviting all the players up to our station offices on West Peachtree. I packed the team into a small conference room and introduced myself and told them a little about our company. I told them about my sailing and business experience and my belief that a lot of the keys to success in those fields applied equally to baseball: play as a team, be disciplined, work hard— these all were essential whether you were racing boats, selling ads, or playing baseball. The players relaxed, laughing, and excited about being part of a new ownership team.

Enthusiasm was high across the league the first part of that off-season. The 1975 World Series between the Cincinnati Reds and the Boston Red Sox was one of the greatest ever played and drew some of the highest TV ratings in history. Then a labor dispute almost blew the whole thing. By February of '76, discussions around free agency and the reserve clause grew so difficult that the owners locked the players out of spring training. There I was, all geared up for my first season, and we were going to shut down. It was very frustrating for everyone.

Because of the lockout, we would now lose spring training games that we had sold to sponsors and were counting on airing. The players weren't allowed to have official practices but they got together informally to stay in shape and be ready as soon as the season began. Meanwhile, I became friends with Bill Veeck of the Chicago White Sox. Bill was known for being a lot less traditional than his peers and he and I hit it off. Together we decided to get our nonroster players together to play what we called a "nongame" that we could televise back in Chicago and Atlanta. As a show of support for our advertising partners, we gave them free airtime in the telecast and it turned out to be a big win all the way around. The players got some practice, the fans saw a game, our sponsors got free airtime, and we generated a lot of good publicity. The lockout ended a couple of days later, but if it hadn't, I'm sure we would have tried to do more games.

─────────── A TED STORY ───────────

"A Real Breath of Fresh Air"
—Terry McGuirk

Shortly after buying the team, Ted moved some of our offices down to Fulton County Stadium. In addition to freeing up space at West Peachtree, it gave our sales team a little cachet to be housed at the ballpark. By being around the front office I had gotten to know a lot of the guys pretty well and one day Ted walked into my office with Eddie Robinson, the team's general manager. They explained that they wanted me to go with them to Florida the next morning for the opening of spring training, and literally out of the blue, Eddie said, "You're going to put on a uniform and pretend you're a nonroster invitee. You're going to play with the team during the day and at night you and Ted can get together and he can ask you questions."

Ted wanted to learn more about baseball and this was his solution! I couldn't believe it but it sounded like it could be fun. Dave Bristol, the team's manager, and one of the coaches were in cahoots, but my identity was a secret to all the other players and coaches. So the very next day, there I was suited up and training with the Atlanta Braves. I did this for about three weeks and debriefed Ted every night. He is such a quick learner and his memory is so strong that his understanding of the game of baseball went from zero to 100 percent during that short period.

It all finally ended one day when we were playing the Mets in one of our first spring training games. We were in one of those stadiums where the bullpens are open and just off the foul lines and Dave Bristol had sent me out to guard the pitchers and catchers from foul balls. The game was a long one and came to the point where we had played practically everyone on the roster. If he were ever going to put me in a game, now would be the time. But Dave was a serious baseball man and couldn't bring himself to do it. At that moment it became apparent to Ted and me that the jig was up. The next day, I came clean with the other players and coaches and let them know I was heading back to my real job in Atlanta. My last night there I took a bunch of guys out for dinner and we all had some good laughs over the whole thing (and I did well enough that they offered me an AA contract!).

As strange as the whole thing was, I think it confirmed to everyone that Ted was going to do things his way and for most people in the Braves organization he was a real breath of fresh air. For me, it was just another example of how my career with Turner would never be dull.

During the lockout I decided to stir things up and jump into the middle of one of that year's highest-profile player negotiations. As I learned about the game, everyone told me that strong pitching would be the key to turning the team around, and the big free agent going into 1976 was a pitcher many considered to be among the league's best. His name was Andy Messersmith. As you might imagine, I wasn't the only one interested in him and I soon found myself in the middle of a bidding contest with, among others, George Steinbrenner of the New York Yankees. Steinbrenner was every bit as competitive as I was and he was in the country's number one TV market and had deep pockets. He saw free agency as a huge opportunity and he wanted to make Messersmith one of his first blockbuster signings. As hard as it was going up against the Yankees, Messersmith's agent did nothing to help matters. I was pretty sure he was simply using my offer to increase the bidding by Steinbrenner and the other interested owners. By the end of March, the Yankees were declared the winners of the Messersmith sweepstakes.

Shortly after the public announcement from New York, Messersmith claimed that his agent had negotiated the contract without his authority and he didn't want to be a Yankee. Apparently, their money was good but New York put in a bunch of other clauses Andy didn't like. For example, in addition to taking a big share of his endorsement income, the Yankees included their standard clause that required their players to have short haircuts and no facial hair. That wouldn't be a problem for me—heck, I was the owner and I had a mustache. Suddenly, we were back in the running and I moved quickly. With Steinbrenner out of the way I was in front of Messersmith with a big smile and a big offer, and about a week later, he signed with the Atlanta Braves for more than $1 million over three years. That doesn't sound like much today but it was big money back then. This was a high-profile signing and the fact that we'd landed him ahead of the New York Yankees really pleased our fans. We hadn't played a game yet, but we'd created a ton of excitement going into opening day.

We opened that season on the road,

winning two out of three in San Diego against the Padres. Heading back to Atlanta after that encouraging start, I wanted to make sure our home opener was a big, fun event. Helping matters was the fact that we were playing the Cincinnati Reds, the team that had just won the dramatic 1975 World Series. That night, after the Reds and Braves lineups were introduced, I ran out to a microphone on the field and gave the entire stadium a pep talk. Then, with a full marching band behind me, I led the fans in singing "Take Me Out to the Ballgame." I'm sure some of the players didn't know what to make of the whole scene but our fans ate it up.

These ceremonies caused the game to start a little late but before the first pitch I took my seat down next to the field. Many owners sit upstairs in glass-enclosed suites but I thought watching a game in a suite was like kissing a girl through a window. I wanted my seat in the front row, right next to the home dugout. So there I was sitting field-side and in the bottom of the second inning with no score, Ken Henderson, our outfielder, came up to bat. We had acquired him in the off-season and there was a buzz in the stadium when he stepped to the plate. In his first at bat with the Braves he hit the team's first home run of the season. The crowd—me included—went absolutely wild. I was so caught up in the excitement that without even thinking I jumped over the wall in front of my seat and ran onto the field. By the time Henderson rounded third I was standing at home plate with the other players ready to shake his hand! Not being a big fan I didn't think that what I had done was all that unusual but by the time I made it back to my seat I could sense that I'd created a stir. Henderson's homer wound up being the Braves' only highlight that game and we lost 6–1. Still, the opener that night gave our fans a feeling that this season might be different.

Braves fans might have enjoyed my on-field activities on opening night but when we played those same Reds on the road, I realized that some of the other owners weren't quite as enthusiastic. Cincinnati gave me field-level seats that I'd requested but when I got there I found a security guard with his back to the field, facing me. The Reds front office placed him there specifically to keep me off the field and they notified our promotions department that if I went on the field in Cincinnati, I'd be arrested. Welcome to Major League Baseball!

I went on many road trips in those early days and made a point to meet with as many of the other teams' owners and executives as I could, in part to get to know them but also to learn the business and figure out how to do a better job of running our franchise. On one trip I realized other teams put out onions and relish for hot dogs and hamburgers, but in Atlanta, we only had mustard and ketchup. I ordered that we add onions and relish. In every business I've ever been in it's been clear that doing even the smallest things to take care of your customers is essential and running a ball club was no different.

I found that hanging out with the players was just like spending time with my sailing crew or the guys at our TV and radio stations. I was still in my thirties and a few times in spring training I even went out on the field with the guys and did calisthenics and wind sprints. Since most games were at night, when I traveled with the team we all had a lot of time to kill during the day. Some of the players liked to play poker, and on occasion I'd join them. These were low-stakes, nickel-and-dime games—if you were lucky you'd win $10 or $20—but everyone had a great time. When word of this got around the league, Chub Feeney, who was National League president, told me to knock it off.

"Owners aren't supposed to play poker with the players," he told me.

"Why not?" I asked. I wasn't trying to challenge him, but I truly didn't understand.

"It just isn't done," was his reply.

This all seemed wrong to me. There was clearly a huge gulf between players and the team owners. It was like they were on different teams and the owners didn't treat their players as equals. When I first came in the clubhouse the guys were saying "yes, sir," and "no, sir" and I said, "You call me Ted just like everyone else." At the owners meetings everyone complained about how the players were taking them to the cleaners and the union was too powerful. I'd ask them why didn't they get to know their guys any better? Go out and have a beer with them or invite them over to your house for a party? Who knows— maybe if they had tried that in the past, there never would have been a union in the first place.

I wouldn't let the baseball establishment get me down. I had worked my way into the broadcasting and sailing communities and I was determined to do the same in baseball. Fortunately, I had great people around me. In addition to keeping Bill Bartholomay, I was able to retain Bob Hope, the team's marketing director. He wasn't related to the famous comedian but Bob did have a great sense of humor. He was constantly generating ideas and I was just the guy to let him run with them. I didn't even mind participating myself when I could. One time, we held ostrich races on the field. We dressed up in horseracing silks and silly hats and I rode out first to kick things off. Sometimes we even involved opposing players. On one occasion I agreed to an offbeat race with colorful Tug McGraw of the Philadelphia Phillies. We had to push baseballs from first and third base to home but we couldn't use our hands or feet, just our noses. We got down on all fours and as I pushed my ball as fast as I could, I nudged it off the edge of the grass and on to the rougher base path. I refused to quit and as I kept going I skinned my face raw in the dirt. I beat Tug by about six feet and when I stood up and raised my arms in victory there was blood all over my face. Our fans loved this kind of stuff but I also did it in hopes of making an impact on our players. I wanted them to know I was a competitor—that I would do anything for the team, even if it meant getting down on all fours and bloodying my face.

Having their dad as the team owner was also a lot of fun for the kids. They got to be batboys and girls on occasion and we'd have players over to our house for birthday parties. I did everything I could to keep the relationship between the players and myself, and between the team and our fans, as informal as possible. In our TV ads we called the Braves "The Big League team with the Little League spirit!" and Bob Hope thought it would be fun for our home uniforms to have the players' nicknames on them instead of their usual names. So instead of "Jones" it might say "Jonesy," or for the famous knuckleballer Phil Niekro, his jersey said "Knucksie." Andy Messersmith, our high-profile pitcher, also had a flair for the dramatic and came to me and said, "Hey, Ted—how about giving me number seventeen and making my nickname 'Channel'?"

What a great idea! Next thing you know, one of the most famous pitchers in the game is taking the mound with "Channel 17" on his back—I loved it! Unfortunately, commissioner Bowie Kuhn didn't. He told me this was considered advertising and there were league rules against putting commercial messages on jerseys. Oh, well. It was fun while it lasted and we drummed up publicity in the meantime.

Off the field, when it came to the Braves front office I could tell right away that our costs were too high. People were flying first class, staying at fancy hotels—all luxuries that were customary across the league but the kind of expenditures we simply couldn't afford. I had to make some changes and one of my more controversial ones was the time I fired a guy named Donald Davidson. He had held various jobs with the team but when I came along he was the traveling secretary, and it just so happened that he was only about four feet tall. I had nothing against him personally but I could tell right away that he didn't particularly like me.

Like a lot of other career baseball people he thought I was just some rich guy who didn't know what he was doing. When it came to the game on the field, I did have a lot to learn, but off the field I could tell when money was being wasted. For example, when the Braves traveled, Davidson stayed in the huge VIP suites. Seeing the guy who booked the rooms staying in a luxury suite made me angry. Digging into the situation I realized that the traveling secretary basically booked flights, hotel rooms, and bus trips to the stadiums. It didn't seem like all that much work and at the same time our three TV and radio announcers, who were also on the team's payroll, hung out all day without much to do. I decided to cut Davidson and assign the travel secretary duties to the announcers.

You would think that dismissing the travel secretary wouldn't make a lot of news but Davidson had previously worked in PR and it turned out that he had friends at the paper, in the Atlanta community, and all over baseball. People were questioning how I could fire this likable little guy. I told them that I liked him, too (and by the way, he went on to work in baseball for twenty-four more years, eventually passing away in 1990 while working for the Houston Astros), but I believed we needed to make some changes. One reporter asked me how I could justify signing a pitcher to a million-dollar deal, and then turning around and saying I wouldn't find money to pay for nice hotel rooms. My answer was simple. The million dollars spent on Messersmith could help us win games, put fans in the seats, and pull in viewers. If anyone could show me that bigger rooms for front office staff would help us accomplish any of those things, I'd have paid for those as well.

Basically I couldn't cut everything. The ball club was a complex organization. We had about 125 players on six different teams (the Braves owned all of our minor league franchises) and we had twenty-five scouts looking at players not only in U.S. high schools and colleges but also down in Latin America and the Caribbean. This was complicated because it wasn't like in pro football where, with a TV and a VCR, you could see just about every player you wanted to, playing for his college team. Here, you had thousands of high schools and a lot of colleges that didn't get TV coverage. And with the potential for trades you had to keep an eye on players on the other teams across the minors and the majors. Those totaled about 125 teams with twenty-five players per—more than three thousand players. Once I understood how complicated this was I concluded that the general manager I inherited was not up to the job. He was a pleasant guy and had been around the game a long time but I didn't think he was good enough. I remember him walking me around a minor league complex and when we'd pass a player I'd ask, "Who's that?" Half the time he didn't know. The way I saw it, the players were our investment, and as the person running the business, he should be familiar with them. For some major league owners, the teams were just a hobby. After being successful in other fields, owning a team satisfied their egos and gave them publicity. I felt like some of that trickled down through the management ranks and a lot of these guys didn't work as hard as I felt they should.

I decided to make a change and hired an executive from the Boston Red Sox named John Alevizos to be our new general manager. He really knew the game, but not long after joining us his aggressive style got him in trouble with Bowie Kuhn and our team was fined $10,000. The charge was for something called "tampering." Alevizos had asked Gary Matthews, a star on the San Francisco Giants, whether he'd like to join the Braves when he became a free agent after the 1976 season. From my business experience, this didn't seem like a big deal but I learned from the commissioner's response that you just don't do that.

Shortly after being slapped with this fine I made matters worse. I've never been particularly good at holding my liquor (my friends used to call me "Two Beer Turner") and at a World Series cocktail party I'd had a few before getting into a conversation with Bob Lurie, the owner of the Giants. I told him that no matter how much he was willing to pay Matthews, I would offer him more. I was speaking too loudly and was overheard by others in the room, including some baseball writers. Lurie filed a complaint with the commissioner and it looked like I might be in trouble. I pressed on, and we ultimately managed to get Matthews and sign him to a contract. Then Commissioner Kuhn called me into his office and told me that because of these repeat offenses he was going to suspend me from the game for a year and take away our first round draft choice.

I replied, "Suspend me, but please don't take away our number one draft pick!"

He refused, and we had no other choice but to litigate. It took several weeks for the judge to make his decision, and I was getting anxious (although by that time I was planning to race for the 1977 America's Cup and could have used an excuse to be away from the team for the summer). Meanwhile the team was on a terrible streak. After losing our sixteenth game straight I decided to shake things up. I thought about firing our manager, Dave Bristol, but instead I decided to just give him some time off. After telling the press that Bristol was away on a "scouting trip," I put on a Braves uniform and served as the team's field manager.

In the dugout I really didn't do a whole lot other than crack some jokes and yell encouragement. I didn't know the signs, so I had to sit next to one of the other coaches and when I thought we should steal or bunt, I'd have to tell him so he could relay the signal. Phil Niekro pitched a complete game that night so I never even got the chance to walk out to the mound. Despite his strong performance, we lost 2–1 but we broke a lot of tension on the club and we ended our losing streak with a win the very next game.

Unfortunately, I wasn't in the dugout that night. The baseball establishment didn't like the idea of me managing the team and I received a telegram from National League president Chub Feeney the morning after my debut, telling me that my first game would also be my last. I retired with a life-time record of zero wins and one loss.

Not too long after, the judge passed down a split ruling on the tampering case. He upheld my suspension but let us keep Gary Matthews and our first round draft choice (which we subsequently used to select future All-Star Bob Horner). As a result, I was free to head to Newport without people wondering why I wasn't at the Braves games.

In our first years as Braves owners, we set an embarrassing record, becoming the first team since divisional play began to finish in last place four seasons in a row—'76, '77, '78, and '79. I went to nearly every home game, watched the away games on TV, and did my best to stay positive, but all that losing was not the toughest thing that happened during those lean years. Far worse was the passing of Bill Lucas, who replaced Alevizos as general manager in 1977. When we bought the team, Bill was director of player personnel—the farm director. It was a big job but Bill had a tremendous work ethic and a knowledge about his players that really impressed me. When I promoted him, I didn't realize he would be baseball's first-ever black general manager—I was simply putting the best guy I knew in the position. He did a great job, and in the process, we became close friends.

Then, early in the 1979 season Bill suffered a massive aneurism and passed away. He was only a couple years older than I and the news floored me. Seeing such a young, vibrant guy taken away also made me stop and think about what a short time we all have on this planet and I became more determined than ever to keep moving—to grow the company and make a difference in the world. (Incidentally, Bill's wife, Rubye, worked with me for many more years as head of our company's community affairs efforts and ultimately served on our board of directors. Their daughter, Wonya, later became head of marketing for CNN and is now chief marketing officer at Discovery Channel Communications. Bill's memory is honored next to Turner Field, where one of the streets bordering the stadium bears his name.)

Those initial years in baseball were lean, and I made a lot of bad deals. We did manage to win our division in 1982 before being eliminated in the playoffs by St. Louis in three straight games. (By the way, I'm pretty sure I set another record in that series. I personally caught two foul balls in three games—one in Atlanta and another in St. Louis—I'd be willing to bet that an owner has never done this before or since.)

At the press conference in 1976 when we bought the team I promised that we'd win a World Series within five years. After our four straight last place finishes, the Braves beat reporter from the *Atlanta Journal-Constitution* called me and said, "Well, Turner, this is year five coming up. Are you going to win this year?" This was back during the Cold War when the Soviet Union was rolling out all those five-year plans that never panned out so I said, "No, I'm going to be like the Russians and start a new five-year plan!"

Winning the World Series would take much longer than we had expected, but it would be worth the wait.

11

The SuperStation

With WTCG and WRET both making money I was more confident than ever that television was where I wanted to be, but even as we moved out of the red I was concerned that our options for meaningful growth were limited. WTCG's share of the Atlanta market had grown from next to nothing to about 15 percent, but against the tremendous resources of the three network affiliates it was hard to see us pushing that number much higher. Prices and sell-out levels of our ad inventory were growing, as were the number of homes with UHF receivers, but these variables could only increase so much. It was time for another quantum leap. I concluded that what we needed was a bigger footprint—a broader territory and larger number of viewers. Broadcast networks accomplished this by assembling a string of owned and/or affiliated stations across the country but from where we were, duplicating that model was almost impossible. I had to figure out a different way. I used to compare myself to the bear that went over the mountain to see what he could see, and now it was time to take another look.

In the mid-1970s, Channel 17 was the only independent station in a major southeastern market outside of Florida, and the Braves were the only Major League Baseball franchise in the region. I knew that our programming would be of interest to viewers outside Atlanta. I also saw that in places like Albany and Macon, Georgia, people were signing up for a new service to get local stations they were unable to tune in with their antenna and/or a better picture for stations they were already receiving. This technology was often referred to as CATV, for "community antenna television," or more simply, cable TV. I concluded that our next big opportunity would be to push WTCG's distribution beyond Atlanta—to become an independent station that served the entire Southeast—and we would use cable to get us there.

To learn more I decided to go to my first National Cable Television Association, or NCTA, meeting. There I learned about experiments undertaken by broadcasters and cable operators to use microwave technology to relay signals from broadcast towers to the cable plant. From there, the signal was sent down a cable into the subscriber's home. This made sense to me and I could see an immediate, clear path toward expanding WTCG's reach. I learned a lot at this meeting and I met some great industry people, including an NCTA researcher named Don Andersson. Don was a smart guy, and not only did he understand how these new technologies worked, he also grasped the promise they held for aggressive independent broadcasters. Realizing I needed someone with Don's expertise I hired him and put him in charge of figuring out how we could use microwave technology to expand our territory and market our service to the young cable industry.

Microwave distribution technology was straightforward, but there were limitations. Signals were relayed from one transfer tower to another, but the stations required a direct line of sight between them and could be no more than twenty-five miles apart. With one of these relays costing about $35,000 to set up, it took about $150,000 to go just one hundred miles in one direction; a lot of money for fledgling cable companies. Making this investment even riskier, consumers were accustomed to getting their TV signal for free. Convincing them to pay was no small challenge but the cable TV companies understood that independent programming from distant markets was a logical way to entice subscribers and WTCG was a good candidate to play this role. Before long, Channel 17 was delivered to places like Birmingham, Tuscaloosa, and Anniston, Alabama; Albany and Savannah, Georgia; and Tallahassee, Florida. These early systems only had capacity to carry a maximum of twelve channels, but once ours was in these lineups we were just as easy to tune in and our signal was just as clear as the others. Not only did we reach new markets, once we got there, we competed on a level field.

With Don Andersson's introduction I became friendly with cable TV operators. Always believing in keeping one's customer happy, I was eager to get to know these new affiliates and I wanted them to like me. I remember a guy who was running a cable system in Atlanta inviting me to Myrtle Beach for a meeting with the Southern Cable Television Association. He wanted me to speak to them about my ideas for microwave transmission and told me how I'd be the first friendly broadcaster they'd ever met. Back then, broadcasters saw cable operators as the enemy. For many years, local TV stations had a monopoly and they viewed cable operators with fear and suspicion. It was one thing when cable helped them improve their signals and get full penetration of their home markets, but quite another when they started importing distant stations. One time, the manager of a Florida station got angry when Channel 17 starting coming into his area. He asked me to stay out of his territory and I replied, "What do you mean, 'your territory'? If we can get our signal there, it's our territory, too!" As far as I was concerned, our territory was the United States, and later the world!

This all sounded great but the truth was, adding new viewers via microwave and cable did not help us generate much incremental advertising revenue. When we spoke to media buyers outside Atlanta, all they wanted was ABC, NBC, and CBS. They were used to making two different buys—local and national—and a regional outlet like ours didn't fit in their plans. We quickly concluded that the only way to generate revenue from our expanded audience was through direct response ads—the ones that sell the latest record compilation or steak knives and end with a phone number to call to purchase the products. To make the most of this opportunity I hired a merchandising man from Atlanta's Rich's department store and sent him to all the trade shows where people showed off their latest inventions.

The best products to sell via direct response are unique little gadgets and gizmos whose producers have trouble getting retail distribution. This allows you to call them "Exclusive TV Offers!" and say things like "Not Available in Stores!" We managed to find all kinds: super-glue, steak knives, and vinyl repair kits, among others. Since most of these companies couldn't afford it, we often produced the TV commercials ourselves, and in some cases both the products and the ads were pretty amateurish. One of the worst that I can remember was a piece of cheap jewelry called the Party Ring. It was magnetic and came with about eight different-colored stones that you could change to match your outfit. The commercial was so bad it was almost funny. It featured an attractive African-American couple out on a dance floor, and in the middle of their dancing the guy says, "Hey, what's that ring you've got there?" She holds it up to the camera and says, "That's my super-bad Party Ring." The ads and the products may have been silly but we did manage to sell a lot of merchandise. Direct response revenue would prove to be vital for us while we worked to convince traditional advertisers that we were worth considering.

These challenges on the advertising front, combined with the complications of assembling a series of microwave hops, suggested that being a regional player would provide less upside than I had hoped. It was in early 1975 that I saw an article about communications satellites in *Broadcasting* magazine. Reading it through I realized that instead of using an antenna in Atlanta and hopping across microwave points throughout the Southeast, I could use one satellite "antenna" that's 22,000 miles up in space and cover all of North America. Our microwave experience proved that cable operators were interested in carrying us and I thought that if we put enough quality programming on the channel, they might even consider expanding their business into major metropolitan areas (at the time, their business was centered primarily in smaller markets where signal quality and availability were the issues). Satellite delivery looked like a great opportunity that might even be our ticket to compete head-to-head and on a national level with ABC, NBC, and CBS.

The *Broadcasting* article mentioned that Home Box Office (HBO), a relatively new for-pay movie channel, was planning to start distributing their signal via satellite and that Western Union would be their distributor. I called Western Union's marketing director—a man named Ed Taylor—and set up a meeting at his office in New Jersey. They sent a car to pick me up at Newark Airport and it was clear that they wanted my business. Shortly into the meeting with Ed, I understood why. Not only was HBO their only other television client, their deal was short-term and as soon as RCA launched their satellite, HBO planned to switch over to them. I learned a lot from Ed during that visit and unfortunately for Western Union, I was convinced that we had to be on the same satellite as HBO. At the time, satellite-receiving antennas cost cable operators about $100,000 apiece, but if I teamed up with HBO, they'd get two channels for the price of one.

I decided to try to coordinate efforts with the head of HBO, a guy named Jerry Levin. I'd met Jerry once before, shortly after he'd gone to work for Time Inc., HBO's owner. In the past few years since then he had become a passionate advocate for satellite distribution.

—————— A TED STORY ——————

"This Is an Amazing Guy"
—Jerry Levin

I think Ted and I first met around 1973 when HBO was very small and just a tiny part of Time Inc. We must have had fewer than ten thousand subscribers and were kind of going nowhere, but we had the interest of a guy named Jim Shepley, who was our corporate president at the time. Jim happened to be a sailor and he said there's somebody I'd like you to meet. His name is Ted Turner and he's interested in the cable business. Why don't you give him a call? That was all I knew about Ted when I set up our meeting. He came into my office in New York and started talking nonstop about everything he was doing in Atlanta and at one point I think he even got up on the top of my desk. This was in the Time-Life Building where we were already a little bit left to center but it was still a pretty staid environment and I thought, "Oh, my God." After the meeting I reported back to Shepley and said, "This is an amazing guy—a hell of a personality— I just don't know what we can do together right now."

That was our first meeting and we saw each other again on a few occasions at cable conventions but the serious conversation began when we announced that we were going on the satellite. When Ted and I got together then, he said, "You know, if you can get HBO up on the satellite then I can turn my Atlanta station into a national thing. You're pay TV and we're advertising support so together we can really lift the cable industry." That was the beginning of what I thought was a beautiful friendship.

Jerry and I had a great meeting and he liked the idea of teaming up with me since he knew that the more programming we could offer via the same satellite the better HBO's chances were for getting distribution. With Jerry supportive of my plan, I went to RCA to negotiate a deal. They were more than happy to work with me but there was one major problem. Before you could distribute a channel via satellite you had to get your signal up to the satellite in the first place, and to do this required the use of a send station, or uplink, at the signal's origination point. In 1976, uplinks existed only in New York (where HBO's was located), Chicago, and Los Angeles. They told me that by being based in Atlanta I was out of luck since no one planned to build a send station there for at least the next several years.

I thought that over and said, "Well, what would prevent us from building one?"

They had never considered this option but could see no obstacle other than the expense: about $750,000. I asked them if there was anyone in Georgia who could build one for me and they suggested I contact a company named Scientific Atlanta. By now, I was determined to make this work and I quickly set up a meeting with Sydney Topol, Scientific Atlanta's CEO. He said that while they expected satellite technology to be a big part of their business they had yet to build an uplink. I asked him how much he thought this would cost and he said he would have

to do some research and get back to me.
I liked Topol and trusted him so I told him
that if he offered me a reasonable price,
I'd do the deal with him. I can't exactly remember what price he came back with
but it seemed okay and we reached an
agreement. We bought a small piece of
property in a remote area on Atlanta's
northwest perimeter that would serve as
our site and the Scientific Atlanta people
got to work.

Sometime around the completion of the
uplink, another problem emerged. My lawyers explained to me that the FCC had
rules against broadcasters sending their
own signal outside their broadcast tower's
footprint. Microwave distribution passed
muster because the cable operators owned
the relays, but in the case of satellite distribution our company wasn't allowed to own
the uplink or the lease for the satellite transponder. A third party, or "common carrier," would be required. We looked at
different scenarios like putting the uplink
company in my wife's or my children's
names, but the lawyers made it clear that
the distributor had to be completely independent from the broadcaster.

I had to find someone to run an independent satellite uplink company so I called the first person I'd met in the satellite business, Western Union's Ed Taylor. I explained to Ed that I needed to set up an independent company to carry the TBS signal and asked him if he would leave Western Union to own and run our common carrier. He told me he was making about $60,000, and with RCA poised to take the HBO business, he didn't see a bright future for Western Union's satellite operation. I assured him that by this time, Don Andersson, Terry McGuirk, and our sales team had spoken to enough cable operators to know that a great many would pay for Channel 17 and the fee we had discussed was 10 cents per subscriber per month.

We expected our subscriber base to start at close to a million households and grow quickly into several million, so the revenue for this business could get very big very fast. The math was easy and Ed knew this could be a great opportunity. When he asked me how much it would cost him to take all this over I asked him to hand me a dollar bill. After he pulled one out of his wallet and handed it to me, I shook his hand

and said, "Congratulations, Ed. You're now our common carrier!"

Ed started a new company called Southern Satellite Systems but he needed more capital to get it off the ground. The primary expense was the lease on the RCA satellite, which was about $100,000 per month. I knew he didn't have this kind of capital but by this time our company had a lot of experience borrowing money, so Will Sanders, our CFO, agreed to help him raise the cash he needed. It wasn't long before Southern Satellite Systems became an extremely profitable business and I think it's safe to say that Ed Taylor made one of the greatest $1 investments in American business history.

———— A TED STORY ————

"A One-Man Circus"
—John Malone

(JOHN MALONE JOINED TELE-COMMUNICATIONS, INC., OR TCI, IN 1972 AND BY 1981 HAD HELPED BUILD IT INTO THE LARGEST CABLE OPERATOR IN THE COUNTRY. TODAY HE IS CHAIRMAN OF LIBERTY MEDIA CORPORATION.)

I remember the first time Ted came out to the old TCI headquarters in Denver. We had all of our management team gathered in a conference room and Ted was there to pitch us on carrying WTCG as a distant independent station and perhaps even getting together to help put up the money to get him on satellite. I think I had met him before at some industry functions but this was the first real meeting I'd ever had with him. Not knowing him too well, we all thought he'd had too much coffee or something. He put on a real dog-and-pony show—a one-man circus like only Ted can. I remember at one point he got down on the floor and crawled around on all fours and said, "Whose shoes do I have to kiss?"

I thought he was hilarious and had a great sense of humor but I do recall trying to explain to him that there were legal restrictions on the importation of distant broadcast signals and the local cable company had to pick the two that were closest to them. We also told him that satellite receivers at that time had to be ten meters and had to be fully licensed—that this would be quite an economic impediment to keep him from distributing his station in a very large-scale way. The reality was we were desperate for more content and there was no question that if he could get it up there, by God we were going to carry it. The real question was how realistic he was being about all the obstacles in his way.

But he didn't care about any of that, and that was classic Ted. Ted asks himself the question, "If a rule doesn't let me do something that's so logical, it must be a bad rule. And if it's a bad rule I ought to be able to change it or it should just go away." He's always had that kind of basic, almost childish, logic about him that refuses to accept artificial impediments. I think one of his big secrets of success over the years is that the things that most of us would sit there and ponder—all these regulatory and legal reasons why it might not be something you could do—Ted would just say, "Oh, hell, you can overcome those kinds of things," and he'd just go do it.

The first satellite transmission of WTCG occurred on December 17, 1976. Months before, someone in our promotions department had come up with the idea of calling the local station "Super-17." I liked that a lot but once we were beaming the signal off the satellite I thought we needed something more. I was playing around with the word "super," when it just came to me— "SuperStation!" The name had a great ring to it and would convey to people exactly what it was. I also decided to change the station's call letters. Since we had moved into broadcast media we changed our corporate name to Turner Broadcasting System, Inc., and I decided to convert WTCG to WTBS. Now that we were competing on a national level, I also liked that "TBS" sounded like "CBS" and we were soon referring to the channel as "SuperStation TBS."

Once it became clear that I was serious about getting national distribution for a local station, we ran into problems with our program suppliers. Our syndication deals with Hollywood gave us rights in the Atlanta market only. Pushing farther into the Southeast via microwave didn't seem to bother them, but going national on the satellite certainly got their attention. As for the Braves, Major League Baseball knew when I bought the team that I had been considering broader distribution but I don't think they thought it would ever really happen. It was one thing for Braves games to be beamed to places like Montana or New Mexico where a competing franchise didn't exist but it was quite another to go into major markets like Detroit or St. Louis and compete for viewers against their home market team. We were also carrying Atlanta Hawks games at this point and the NBA raised similar concerns. Local broadcasters also lined up in opposition to us, claming that the SuperStation violated established rules about the redistribution of local TV signals. (Leapfrogging a signal via microwave had been bad enough, but satellite, in their view, was far worse.) They claimed that since the

SuperStation beamed into their territory with shows that they had licensed for that market, we were violating their rights to exclusivity.

In a short period of time we'd managed to alienate Hollywood, the sports leagues, the broadcast networks, and local stations all over the country. Each one of these groups had big-time lobbying presence in Washington and with the FCC and Congress ultimately presiding, Washington became a primary battlefront and I started spending a lot of time there. I participated in numerous hearings and tried to be on a first-name basis with as many influential politicians as possible (including a young congressman from Tennessee named Al Gore). My early training as a debater served me well at congressional hearings. My opponents had skilled lobbyists and a strong case against me. Logic was not always on my side so I had to be passionate and appeal to people's emotions. When those testifying against me said that I was "stealing" their programming or encroaching on their territory, rather than defend my own position I would go on the attack.

"If there are any real thieves here it's ABC, NBC, and CBS!" I argued. *"They're* the ones who convinced the government to hand over incredibly valuable VHF licenses all over the country completely free of charge! They've used the public airwaves to make a fortune and never once paid a dime for that right!" I'd go on to argue that no one would ever dream of letting a paper company cut timber on federal land or an oil company drill offshore without putting those rights up for bid. So why should TV companies get these rights for nothing? A free license might have made sense in the beginning when the business was just getting started but what about now, when these broadcasters were making millions? "When these licenses come up for renewal every three years, why not put them up for bid?" I asked. "These companies would probably fork over enough money to pay off the national debt!"

When it came to the sports leagues I painted a picture that the owners basically sat around a table a long time ago and said, "Okay, I'll take New York, you get St. Louis, and the guy over here gets Chicago."

They colluded to create local monopolies, I said, "And I thought that one of the roles of government was to regulate monopolies!" I asked legislators to imagine a world where the heads of Ford, GM, and Chrysler sat down and the Ford guy says, "I get everything east of the Mississippi. General Motors, you get west of the Mississippi, and Chrysler, you can have the state of Michigan. If we agree to this, we eliminate competition and we can charge $10,000 for a car instead of $2,000 and we'll make a lot more money."

Baseball's commissioner, Bowie Kuhn, tried to counter by saying that the importation of games into other markets would disrupt things to the point where the league's viability might even be threatened. "How is that possible?" I asked. "The owners are all millionaires, we're paying millions to our players, and guess who gets left holding the bag—our fans!" And whenever I debated league rules in Washington I always tried to conclude my point by saying, "The law of the land takes precedence over the law of the league!"

My overall theme in Washington was consistent. I was the underdog—an entre-

preneur trying to compete in a world dominated by oligopolists. Television needed
an independent voice offering more choice
and more variety. While the broadcasters
were filling the public airwaves with a lot of
garbage—sensationalized news, violent
dramas, and such—the SuperStation, with
its wholesome movies, sitcoms, and sports,
would provide a welcome alternative.

These issues were uncharted territory.
All of us—the regulators, broadcasters, program suppliers, and leagues—were sorting things out on the fly. My hope was that
if I could just keep moving and stay on the
offensive, we might have a chance to pull
it off. I was working as hard as I could. I'd
go all out during the day, working on sales,
distribution, regulatory issues, whatever
the battle happened to be, and I'd work
right up until it was time to fall asleep. I
had a pull-down Murphy bed in my office
and I would literally work until the point of
total exhaustion. Then I'd put my head on
the pillow at night worried about problems,
then wake up and spend the entire next
day trying to solve them.

All the hard work paid off. The FCC ruled
that as long as our signal was distributed

by a common carrier, the SuperStation could continue to exist as is. The programmers may not have liked what we were doing but over time we worked out terms (in many cases, increased license fees) that everyone could live with. The sports leagues were frustrated but eventually learned to live with the idea that Atlanta games would be seen all over the country (and it wasn't long before we started calling the Braves "America's Team"). Meanwhile, cable operators were thrilled to add a wholesome, high-quality channel to their lineup and, as I'd predicted in Washington, consumers wound up being winners, too.

At first, being delivered nationally via satellite didn't make the job of selling advertising much easier. Nielsen, the company that measures viewership of television stations, refused to document our audience outside Atlanta. They claimed that it was prohibitively expensive for them to measure a channel whose distribution was so spotty across the country, but I was suspicious that their real motivation was to avoid upsetting their customer base—the broadcast networks and local stations that were our competition.

Regardless of their motivation, Nielsen's refusal to work with us forced us to devise our own ways of proving to national advertisers that people were actually watching. I had hired a creative research specialist from Cox Communications named Bob Sieber, and he realized that, once again, direct response advertising could be a solution to our problems. Since many of our orders for direct response products came in the form of personal checks mailed directly to our Atlanta offices, we could tell where they were coming from based on the postmarks. Every day, Bob would bring in a mail sack and dump it out on the conference room table. He and a couple of others would then sort the mail—one stack for letters postmarked in Atlanta, and another with letters from places outside Atlanta.

As the SuperStation gained distribution, not only did the overall volume of letters increase, postmarks from places in Alabama, Mississippi, and Florida were soon joined by others from as far away as New Mexico, Illinois, Hawaii, and Alaska. With Nielsen reporting our viewership levels in Atlanta, Bob and his team would count the number of letters mailed in locally, then tally the number of letters we received from elsewhere and back into a rough estimate of what the size of our non-Atlanta audience was. This was hardly a bulletproof scientific process but it was the best we had. Part of the fun was watching how quickly the "non-Atlanta" stack grew, going from just a handful of letters at first to a pile that ultimately dwarfed the size of the local one. The mailbags started to get so full they looked like Santa Claus's in *Miracle on 34th Street*.

While sorting this mountain of mail I also came up with a way to save the company a little money. Occasionally, I'd find letters whose stamps had not been processed by the post office and before tossing these on to the pile, we'd carefully remove the stamps and use them again on our company's outgoing mail. I don't remember what regular stamps cost at the time, but there were days when we'd collect almost $20 worth. Every little bit helped at that point. We were really strapped for cash and I had to do everything I could think of to keep us above water.

—— A TED STORY ——

"Captain Teddy's Kiddy Hour"
—Tom Cousins

(TOM COUSINS IS A PROMINENT REAL ESTATE DEVELOPER AND CIVIC LEADER IN ATLANTA. SOME OF HIS CLOSER FRIENDS CALL HIM CUZ.)

I remember going over to his little office on West Peachtree Street. His shirt had this frazzled collar and he sat behind a crummy, low wooden desk. I mean it looked like absolute poverty in a business office. He was asking me for a loan. He told me the banks wouldn't lend him another dime and he was worried that he might not be able to make the next payroll coming up in ten days or something. I wasn't much better off than he was back then, but I said, "Yeah, absolutely Ted. I'll loan you the money." He brightened up then and he said, "Cuz, I'll tell you what. I'm going to be the fourth network," and I'm thinking, "Oh this poor guy, he's out of his mind."

And he says, "I'm doing an earth station out in Cobb County and I'm getting on a satellite." I barely knew about satellites at that point and I certainly didn't know what an "earth station" was. Then he said, "I'm going to beam my signal up on this satellite and I'm going to be able to put Channel 17 all across America and I'm going to get national ad rates. And you know what I'm going to do next after I have the fourth network?"

I said, "No, Ted, what's that?"

"I'm going to run for president and be elected."

Now I thought to myself, "This guy is absolutely nuts—and I've just agreed to lend him all this money!" I said to Ted, "Oh, Ted, don't tell anybody else about that, okay?" And he said, "Cuz, your trouble is you don't understand the power of television. Let me show you." He pulled a little book of matches out of his desk drawer and he said, "Okay, it's Saturday morning at 7:30 and it's *Captain Teddy's Kiddy Hour,* and I come on television and I say, 'Hey kids, today we're going to play a

game and it's going to be so much
fun. Now, don't tell Mommy and Daddy,
this is our secret between Captain
Teddy and you. Now, everybody go
get some matches. See Captain Teddy's matches? Go get some just like
this.'" Then he goes over to his window he says, "All right kids, everybody
got your match? Go to the window and
strike your match and light the curtain
or the drape," at which point he struck
his match right near the old cheese-
cloth thing he had hanging in front of
his window and then he flung the window open and he said to me, "At that
point, I'd look out over Atlanta and
watch it burn." It was an incredible performance.

In the first place, he made his point.
Television is so powerful that could
happen. But number two it absolutely
confirmed my conviction that he might
be nuts.

Armed with the research data Bob Sieber cobbled together, we did our best to
convince advertisers that the SuperStation

was a smart place to put their money, but at first it was a hard sell. Early on, we were available in about 2 million households while the networks were seen in roughly 75 million. Our advertising sales team really had it rough. They were like that first wave of troops landing on the beaches of Normandy—they never really had a chance. Not only did people turn us down, more than a few literally laughed in our faces. I remember telling one buyer about how we planned to use TBS to compete as a "fourth network," and he threw his head back and laughed so hard that his chair tipped over backward and he cracked his head on his office radiator. He almost died laughing at our sales pitch! It was nearly two full years before we got any meaningful national buys. Our first major customer was Jack Irving, at the advertising firm of Dancer Fitzgerald, which at the time represented some major advertisers, including General Mills and Toyota. Once we were able to work out some creative pricing plans, he became the first national advertiser to pay for TBS coverage outside Atlanta. What we were doing was so new

and so unique that everyone was slow to
adapt, but once a few of the bigger players validated our concept, the rest began
to follow.

Our lack of Nielsen ratings continued to
hold us back, so I kept after them to add
us to their service. It became increasingly
clear that the only reason they were freezing us out was because of pressure from
ABC, NBC, and CBS and I decided that
my only option was to threaten a lawsuit.
My argument was that Neilsen's refusal to
measure our networks amounted to anti-
competitive behavior by them and the networks. Estimating that they were costing
us $10 million a year in lost revenues, I
said I would seek treble damages in the
amount of $30 million. This got their atten-
tion and it wasn't long before they came
back and said they would work on a rating
plan for us.

Once we were being measured we tried
everything we could think of to grow our
ratings and as I was looking at the listings
in *TV Guide,* it occurred to me that every
other channel started and ended all their
programming at the top and the bottom of

the hour. Why don't we try to break out of the crowd, I thought, and instead of ending a show just before 7:00 and starting the next one on the hour, what prevents us from extending a program through the end of the hour and starting the following one at 7:05? I envisioned that people watching our competition would start flipping around at the end of their show and while the other channels would all be running commercials, we'd be showing programming! (Besides, with a lot of shows the last five minutes are the best part.) Once a viewer came to us they'd be five minutes into the other networks' shows so they might as well stick around and see what we had on at 7:05. Another benefit of this strategy was that we got our own little slot in every program guide. A group of channels would be listed together at the top and bottom of the hour, but we were all by ourselves on the :05 and :35. We tried it and immediately our Nielsen ratings improved. Before long, people referred to this practice as "Turner Time," and it provided another way for us to stand out from the crowd.

Looking back, one of the lessons I

learned from all of this is that when you start out on a new entrepreneurial venture, you might think you know what the roadblocks will be but you don't really have any idea until after you get started. As an entrepreneur, you're like a running back in a football game. He knows what hole he's trying to run through, but once he's through he's in the open field and now he has to improvise. At first, the SuperStation's big hurdle was getting the signal to the satellite but as soon as we did that, I was fighting in Washington with our program suppliers. Once that was sorted out, Nielsen and the advertisers became our problem. The list went on but the key for us was that we kept fighting. We never knew what wall we'd come up against next but whatever it was, we figured out a way to knock it down.

It was really an exciting time. Cable and satellite delivery were about to revolutionize the way people consumed television and viewers' range of choice would increase in a way that few could have imagined. As a programmer in the middle of all this change, I spent a lot of time trying to invent other channels. A twenty-four-hour sports service made perfect sense and it wasn't long before ESPN's plans were developed (they ultimately launched in 1979). An all-movie format was also logical but HBO had a big first-mover advantage there. The other concept that struck me all the way back in 1975, when we first considered satellite delivery for Channel 17, was an all-news channel. To me, it was obvious, but it was also clear that the companies best positioned to do it were the Big Three broadcasters, or one of the news wire services. It would be an expensive venture and they were the only ones with the necessary infrastructure—from studios to bureaus to on-air talent—to pull this off. I assumed it was just a matter of time before one or more of these joined the cable fray with a new channel and for the next few years I read the TV trades to see which one would announce their news channel first.

Honestly, I was surprised that this window remained open long enough to give us the opportunity. The SuperStation was becoming a success, and it was only the beginning.

12

The America's Cup

In every field that I've entered I've tried to do my very best. When I got into the television business I owned just two small UHF stations but I wanted to compete with the broadcast networks, and after buying the last-place Braves, winning the World Series was my goal. But in no part of my life was my competitive drive stronger than in my sailing career, and around the time of the SuperStation's launch, my focus was on winning the sport's ultimate trophy—the America's Cup.

I first thought seriously about the America's Cup in the late 1960s when my ability improved to the point that I was holding my own against the world's best. By 1970 I was near the pinnacle of the sport, winning the SORC and the 5.5 Meter Gold Cup and performing well in several other high-profile competitions (including a first place finish in the World Ocean Racing Championship and a fourth place finish in the Fastnet Race). The sailing establishment took notice of my achievements and at the end of the season I was named 1970's Yachtsman of the Year. When the America's Cup was held that September I didn't compete, but the Australians asked me to skipper their "trial horse" boat during their training. Helping these guys practice couldn't match the excitement of the real competition but I did get a sense for how special the America's Cup competition was and my appetite was whetted for my own run in 1974.

For me, the first step in pursuing the Cup was to be selected by a syndicate—a group of partners who finance the operation, build or acquire the boat, assemble the crew, and so forth. When George Hinman put his team together for a 1974 syndicate, he asked me to join. This was a great recognition for me, as Hinman was well respected in sailing circles and was in a position to pursue the best people in the sport. A great skipper in his own right, Hinman was also a former commodore of the New York Yacht Club. (The club's custom was for their former chiefs to continue to be referred to as "Commodore," and this was the case with George.)

While some Cup teams competed with existing boats, Hinman's syndicate was building a new one specifically for the 1974 Cup races. To design his boat he hired Brit Chance, and the job of building the boat went to Bob Derecktor, who ran a yacht yard in Mamaroneck, New York, and was also considered to be at the top of his field. With this first-rate team assembled, Commodore Hinman's next task was to raise the funds necessary to build the boat and run the operation. The total cost back then was about $1 million (more than $4 million in today's dollars), and since this was before corporate sponsorships entered the sport, the money was generally raised from a group of individuals, with a half dozen or so putting up $100,000 or more. With no real financial return to be expected, these contributors were generally wealthy people who loved the sport and liked being associated with this prestigious event. (For example, included in Hinman's group of investors that year were Reynolds du Pont and Texas oilman Perry Bass.)

Our boat would be named *Mariner,* and the plan was for her to be designed and built through the winter and spring of 1973–74 and launched in time for the preliminary trials, which were scheduled to begin in June. We'd spent the better part of the summer competing against other American boats for the right to represent the United States in a best 4 of 7 series against the winner of the foreign trials. By the early 1970s, a team from the United States had held the America's Cup trophy for more than one hundred years, so the trials were usually the toughest competition. That summer four American yachts would compete. In addition to *Mariner* were the 1970 Cup winner *Intrepid,* another older yacht financed by Hinman's syndicate called *Valiant,* and a new boat called *Courageous*.

I went into this campaign with high

hopes but the summer of 1974 would prove to be one of the most difficult times in my life. Looking back, it is clear we were doomed from the start. For one thing, Brit Chance and I did not get along. Commodore Hinman had put us together, but if Chance had his choice of skippers or I my choice of designers, this pairing would not have been the result. We were two headstrong individuals and there was tension between us from day one. Fortunately Commodore Hinman allowed me to select my crew and I assembled a good one, consisting mostly of crewmen who had sailed with me over the years. One of the people with whom I didn't have much experience was Dennis Conner, but I knew he was one of the best and I wanted him on my team.

Mariner would be just the second twelve-meter yacht ever built from aluminum (*Courageous* being the first) and it featured a radical design. Below the stern was a unique step feature that had never been tried before in a sailing boat. Chance was known for pushing boundaries and we were all concerned that *Mariner*'s design was a big gamble. When we sailed her, our concerns were confirmed. She was slow. In early June we sailed informally against *Courageous* and were beaten badly.

The crew and I were convinced that we had a bad boat, but Chance told everyone that my team and I weren't sailing her properly. *Mariner* had been built quickly and before we could conclude that the design was a problem, we wanted to be sure we did everything else we could to get her in good sailing condition. Later in June, with minor adjustments made, we sailed in the first of three sets of trials held by the New York Yacht Club, the entity responsible for deciding which boat would represent the United States. We had our backs against the wall and everyone grew increasingly tense. Chance continued to criticize my sailing but Hinman and others were concerned enough about *Mariner*'s design that we made the decision to rebuild the back third of the boat. Had she been built of wood, we wouldn't have had this opportunity, but since *Mariner*'s hull was aluminum, it was possible to make rapid construction changes. Still, our boat would not be ready for the next round of trials in July, and instead, my crew and I watched the races from the sidelines. We were able to size up the other boats and observe their tactics but it was frustrating not being out competing. I tried my best to keep morale up but it wasn't easy.

The New York Yacht Club's objective was to choose the fastest boat for the final races against the challenger. To this end there is often some mixing and matching of crews and boats during the trials. Commodore Hinman asked me to skipper *Valiant* in a handful of these July races. I didn't do very well in these, and while *Courageous* and *Intrepid* emerged as the favorites, my poor showings with *Valiant* led to more whispers from Chance and others that I might not be the best guy to lead *Mariner* once her redesign was complete.

This was the insecure situation I found myself in as we prepared for the August trials—the final races to determine who would sail for the Cup in September. Managing both *Valiant* and *Mariner,* Commodore Hinman decided to pull Dennis Conner from my crew and let him skipper *Valiant.* Everyone assumed the new *Mariner* to be faster than *Valiant,* so when Conner beat me a couple of times, things really got difficult. Hinman called for a full crew switch, putting the *Mariner* crew and me on *Valiant* and shifting Dennis and the *Valiant* crew to *Mariner*. I was disappointed but I kept my chin up and, as *Valiant*'s skipper, I managed to defeat *Mariner* in a couple of races.

Time was running out and Commodore Hinman had to make a difficult decision. He believed that *Mariner* was slightly faster than *Valiant*, but he needed to decide which skipper was going to sail which boat. The next morning the Commodore called Conner and me into his office and delivered the news. I was being reassigned to *Valiant*. Dennis would not only skipper *Mariner* but he could also have his pick of crew. I knew that people had been questioning me but when this finally happened it was really tough. In effect, I had been fired. The final trials were only a few days away and my family and friends were coming— including my mother. I briefly considered packing up and going home but decided to stick it out and do my best with *Valiant*, fully realizing the only yachts with a realistic chance were *Courageous* and *Intrepid*.

Dennis Conner couldn't make *Mariner*

go any faster than I had and when it came time to remove boats from competition, the selection committee eliminated *Mariner* and *Valiant* on the same day. It was the end of a long, tough summer and with my crew out of the racing, we all went out for one last party before departing Newport. *Courageous* wound up representing the United States and easily defeated the Australian challenger in the finals. Dennis Conner had been added to the *Courageous* crew as tactician and so managed to win his first Cup. For the crew and me it was a relief just to have it over and be able to move on. The lessons learned by such a crushing defeat would stand me in good stead for the rest of my life. When I suffer a setback, I don't think of myself as losing, I'm simply learning how to win.

My work made it easy for me to put the summer of '74 behind me and it wasn't long before I began to consider the Cup's next running, to be held in 1977. My fate was largely out of my control since I would have to be chosen by one of the syndicates, and coming off the results of 1974 I knew I would not be at the top of their list. In 1976, a man named Lee Loomis was organizing a syndicate to race two boats in the trials. One would be *Courageous,* the boat that took the prize in 1974, and the other was a newly built boat to be called *Independence.* The latter would be the syndicate's "varsity" boat and Ted Hood had already been selected as its skipper. As she would be racing against boats designed specifically to beat her, *Courageous* wasn't considered to be a major contender, but after my experience with *Mariner* I felt more comfortable going with a proven winner than one that was still untested.

When I heard that Loomis was still looking for someone to skipper *Courageous* I contacted him. He told me they appreciated my interest but that I needed to understand that they still had to raise more money. I decided to make him an offer. I would take care of the cost of the *Courageous* campaign, but only if they let me sail her all the way through. Win, lose, or draw, I would get to stay with her no matter how much faster (or slower) the other boats might be. I was willing to put my heart and soul—not to mention some cash— into this venture but not if there was any chance of a repeat of my awful experience in 1974.

Loomis agreed to my proposal. Since *Courageous* wasn't a new boat and we didn't have to incur such costs as design, construction, and tank tests, our campaign was budgeted at about $400,000, far less than the $1 million–plus that the rest of the field would pay for theirs. With my own money and some help from friends, we raised the needed funds, and I was good enough at running a lean operation that I knew we could be competitive on a smaller budget.

Courageous was the clear underdog going into the summer trials. Not only was she the number two boat in her own syndicate, the third challenger, *Enterprise,* was another new yacht designed by world-renowned Olin Stephens and skippered by an Olympic champion named Lowell North. These were formidable competitors and their boat was one of the first to use computer technology not only to design the sails and the hull but also to calculate recommendations during the races themselves. Realizing the deck was stacked against me, I had to make sure my competitors would share their sails with me before putting up money for *Courageous*. For years, the ethic in these races was for teams to share their sails to help insure that the trials selected the very best boat and crew and didn't reward one group who might have won only due to superior sails. As a fellow syndicate member, Ted Hood would share with me, but since both he and North were professional sailmakers, I assumed that pride would keep them from working with each other. When North told me he would share with me, I moved ahead with my plans.

Over the years I had managed to develop great loyalty among my crew, and of the eleven men on my team in 1974, seven agreed to sail again three years later. The syndicate provided them with room and board in Newport but they didn't get any cash compensation and even had to pay their travel expenses to get to and from Rhode Island. In those days, nobody sailed for the money. They did it for the challenge, the competition, a love for the sport, and the camaraderie of the crew. Ocean racing was a sport that demanded attention to detail and I tried to make sure we were well organized and prepared before and during the races.

I worked hard and even if we were up against experienced teams in newer boats, my crew always knew I was doing everything in my power to make sure we had a chance to win. I was tough when I needed to be but I also tried to keep things light whenever possible. As a team, we went through a lot of difficult times together, but we also had a lot of fun.

One of the four new members of our 1977 crew was a young sailor named Gary Jobson. Gary had gotten my attention after developing an outstanding reputation in college racing and later in events in which he and I competed. As in business, in sailing I always tried to get the best people on my team and decided to pursue Gary to be my tactician. He agreed, and we developed a great relationship. He was excited to be on an America's Cup crew and I was pleased to have someone with his knowledge and ability at my side. Heading into the summer, with a strong crew and a battle-tested boat, I felt like we had a chance.

"Larger than Life"
—Gary Jobson

The first time I really got to know Ted was 1972 at a regatta in Barrington, Rhode Island. Ted was still in his thirties but he was already larger than life. This particular race was an interesting test—each of the three days you had to sail a completely different kind of boat. Ted was one of the skippers invited and so was I. I don't know where Ted ended up—seventh maybe—but I finished second and was leading much of the way. At the prize ceremony Ted came up, put his arm around me, and said, "You know, we're going to do some sailing together someday."

Fast-forward four years and it's October of 1976 and he's seen me around the waterfront, my name's popping up in the magazines—nothing more than that. I'm going to the Chicago Yacht Club to pitch the U.S. Yacht Racing Union on why they should hire me to put together training clinics with them. I walk in the door and Don Cohan, who won a bronze medal in the 1972 Olympics, walks up to me and says, "Hey, we need somebody like you to be on the Olympic Committee and help us out. You know about all this new training, we don't know anything about it and we need help, why don't you do that?"

"Oh, that sounds good, thanks!"

I walk ten feet into the cloakroom to put my coat up and there's Ted Turner. "Hey, I need a tactician next summer. Why don't you come sail with us in the America's Cup?" So here I am, I walk into the Chicago Yacht Club ready to pitch doing these clinics and next thing you know I'm on the Olympic Committee and sailing in the America's Cup just like that!

By sheer coincidence, that same night Ted and I are both flying back to Washington—I was coaching a team in Annapolis and he was going there to sail in the fall series—and we manage to get seats together on the plane. We get airborne and he pulls out a copy of the Delta Air Lines magazine.

He turns to the map of the United States and starts explaining to me how he's going to become a billion-aire. "Make sure you buy my stock. I'm going to be a billionaire and here's why. I got the Atlanta Braves here. There's not another baseball team around and we're going to dominate this market and I'm going to put this station up on a satellite and I'm going to get a news thing going—sports, movies and news."

I'm twenty-six years old, sitting there having my beer thinking, "This is pretty cool," and then he says, "You know, you're going to help me sail, and we're going to win some races. You're going to help me out and I'm going to help you with your business. How much do you make a year?"

"Uhh, fourteen thousand?"

"Oh, jeez you need help, I'm going to help you out!"

And that's exactly what we did. I helped him win races, and by teaching me and letting me sit in on meetings, he taught me a ton about business.

I have a lot of memories from that

1977 campaign but one of my favorites happened in early April. We were up in Boston with the crews of our syndicate's two boats and Ted took me out on a deck overlooking *Courageous* and *Independence,* which were moored down below. They looked so impressive and so beautiful that my mouth was hanging open.

Ted said, "When you were fifteen years old, did you ever think you'd be sailing on a twelve-meter?"

"No," I responded.

"Neither did I," he said with that huge smile. "Isn't this the greatest thing that ever happened to you?"

His enthusiasm was so genuine and so infectious that I'll never forget it.

Sometime during our spring practices, Lowell North called to let me know that he was going back on his word; he would not let me use any of his sails. He said he didn't have his syndicate's authorization when he made his promise and now they were telling him he couldn't do it. I was furious. I told him I thought he was a man of his word and never would have agreed to fund *Courageous* had it not been for his commitment. He was in his forties and certainly had the financial wherewithal to stand up to his syndicate and tell them he couldn't go back on his pledge. It was a bad turn of events but other than getting angry, there was really nothing I could do. I contacted some friends who had helped me with our financing and when I explained the situation they said they'd commit more resources for sails if that would be helpful. This wouldn't allow me to access sails from North, but at least I knew I'd be able to buy new ones if I needed them while the trials were underway.

After an encouraging series of spring practice races with *Independence,* the *Courageous* crew was in fine form heading into the first trials in June. There, we sailed against *Enterprise* and *Independence* four times each and won seven out of eight races. Our only loss was to *Enterprise* by just eight seconds. We didn't use any tricks or pull any surprise moves; we simply played it right up the middle and raced hard. Lowell North and the *Enter-*

prise team were disappointed. They had spent big money and did extensive testing on their boat in San Diego before bringing her out to Newport. Loomis was also caught off guard. He spent at least three times more money on *Independence* than we had on *Courageous*. Both *Enterprise* and *Independence* had been designed specifically to beat *Courageous,* making our victories in June that much more satisfying.

Our crew performed beautifully during these races and Gary Jobson and I were working together very well. We developed a very specific routine at the trials. Our crew all stayed at the same house in Newport and after breakfast Gary and I would walk the mile or so distance between the house and our boat. During the walk we'd discuss what we planned to do that day. Then, after a long day on the boat, while the crew put everything away, we'd take the same walk back home. Our afternoon stroll was like a post-game meeting; we'd talk about how we thought the crew did, how the boat performed, things we could have done differently, how well the two of us were communicating, among other such matters. Our routine was simple but effective and I think the fact that Gary and I worked so well together rubbed off on the rest of our team.

Of course, this was still a busy time back at the company. I had a satellite dish installed at our Newport house so I could watch the Braves games at night and every afternoon I got a package of mail from my office. Some of our executives would fly up to Rhode Island on occasion to watch the races and give me updates on important matters. I even had the Braves come in as a team one day when their schedule allowed. They had done so much losing that I thought it might be a good idea for them to be exposed to a team that was really working together well.

Our kids were on vacation and they stayed in Newport for much of that summer. As usual, it was hard for me to spend large amounts of time with them but it was great to see them and I think they enjoyed the carnival atmosphere in Newport and the chance to see their dad at the center of this competition. Janie stayed with the crew and me while Jimmy Brown took care of our kids.

━━━━━ **A TED STORY** ━━━━━

"One of the Wildest Places in the World"
—Jennie Turner Garlington

We lived on *Tenacious,* one of Dad's boats, down at Bannister's Wharf; all five of Ted Turner's kids and Jimmy Brown in one of the wildest places in the world at the time of the America's Cup. Jimmy would send my brother Beau up to the area where all the bars were, including one called the Black Pearl, to look for money that the partiers might have dropped on the ground. Beau always came back with pocketsful of money—twenties and fifty-dollar bills.

━━━━━━━━━━━━━━━━━━━━━━━━━

The July trials were more competitive. North and *Enterprise* had made some adjustments to their sails and strategy and we got off to a rough start. After losing the first few races I was able to secure a new jib for the final race and *Courageous* ended the trials with a head-to-head victory over *Enterprise. Independence,* though competitive, ended July looking like the third best boat in this three-way contest and now it would all come down to the final trials in August. There was intense pressure heading into the finals, and I decided to take a new approach this second time around. I made up my mind that this go-round I was going to have fun. I'd work hard, but I figured that the pressure was on the other crews and the way our team and boat were performing, staying loose and relaxed might even improve our chances of winning. Newport in the middle of an America's Cup summer was quite a scene and I made the most of it. My more fun-loving style continued to cause a stir within sailing circles and soon I was pegged with the nickname "Captain Outrageous." I was just being myself, of course, but all these things being relative I guess my behavior was pretty far outside the norm.

I continued to work hard and make sure my crew was well prepared, and in the final trials we sailed better than ever, getting off to a great start in the early races. Meanwhile, *Enterprise* performed poorly in her first few contests, and their syndicate, believing he had not made the necessary strategy adjustments to keep up with *Courageous*, replaced Lowell North. After eighteen total races, we had won nine, *Enterprise* five, and *Independence* four, and the selection committee decided they had seen enough. Led by none other than Commodore Hinman, they approached to give us the news. Three years after having to relieve me of my duties, George Hinman now had the pleasant task of informing us that we had been selected to defend the Cup. It was a tremendous thrill for all of us.

Courageous had been winning convincingly enough that the committee made their decision relatively early, giving us two full weeks to gear up for the Cup races. Meanwhile, the team from Australia—on a boat named *Australia*—emerged as the challenger. The Cup would go to the first boat to win four races, and in the first contest we started out even and for the first seven or eight minutes, we stayed that way. Our two boats were really feeling each other out and I remember Gary Jobson using his handheld compass to track *Australia*'s speed. He turned to me with a concerned look and said, "They're not slow." I grinned back at Gary and said, "Yeah, but they're not fast, either!"

Not long after that, I decided to get into a tacking duel and we found that with each tack we picked up a few seconds on *Australia*. These were long races—the course was just over twenty-four nautical miles— but they were generally pretty close, and every second you could add to your lead was important. We won the first race by nearly two minutes. The next three races were almost identical—close starts and a long, steady tacking duel leading us to victory. *Courageous* beat *Australia* 4–0. We were the America's Cup champions!

We had worked so hard that when that final horn sounded, we were ecstatic and the post-race celebration began immediately. Other boats that had been watching the final race came up to us with bottles of champagne and beer. As was the custom, when we reached the dock, we all either jumped or were thrown in the water and it was really cold. One of the guys from the Swedish team gave me a bottle of aquavit. We were having a great time when all of a sudden somebody said, "Time for the press conference!"

Celebrating with my teammates, I had completely forgotten the press conference. By this time I was more than a little tipsy and the crew had to practically carry me to the press tent. I hardly even remember the press conference but it was recorded for posterity and I must admit that it disappoints me that my slipping under the table to retrieve my bottle of booze remains the image a lot of people have of our victory. After the conference I ran straight to our boarding house. I didn't even have dinner— I just went straight to bed.

I was thirty-nine years old when I won the America's Cup. My life had been exciting up to this point but this was by far my most exhilarating victory. Our crew had performed brilliantly and I enjoyed the hard work, the success, and the recognition. As I flew home to Atlanta, and prepared to go back to work, my thoughts turned to what would come next.

13

Cable News Network

With TBS on the satellite I was convinced that in addition to being a lot of fun, cable programming was going to be an important business. As the operators invested in infrastructure and added new subscribers, the channels they carried generated additional revenue with few incremental costs. With a shared desire to grow our industry, the cable operators and I had a friendly partnership. I needed them to run more cable and to grow distribution and they needed me to create quality programming that would encourage people to sign up. I summed up this relationship one time in a conversation with Bob Magness, the founder of TCI and a cable pioneer. "Bob," I said, "you run the wires, I'll make them sing!"

By 1978 it had been several years since I first considered an all-news channel and still no one had done it, so I decided to consider launching one myself. But at the time, Turner Broadcasting didn't even have a news department. As an over-the-air station in Atlanta, WTBS was required by the FCC to fulfill basic requirements for news and public affairs programming. But with our limited budgets and our concentration as an entertainment service, we did as little news as possible, and we presented it in an irreverent fashion in the overnight hours. (Our anchor, Bill Tush, would on occasion read the news with a German shepherd sitting next to him, or he'd put a shopping bag over his head and call himself the "Unknown Newsman.") At a 1979 congressional hearing about the Super-Station, a panel grilled me about the way we presented the news. When Massachusetts representative Ed Markey asked me if it was accurate that we were airing news "at three or four in the morning," I answered, "That's accurate, and we have 100 percent share of the audience then!" News was treated as something we needed to do to keep our license, not as an important part of our business.

I was so busy that I rarely watched news on television. In the late 1970s, most newscasts were on only at 6:00, 7:00, and 11:00 P.M. I usually came home around 8:00 and since I got up so early in the morning I'd be asleep around 10:00. I wound up getting most of my news from newspapers and weekly magazines and I figured that my experience was not unique—there had to be other people whose work hours were not conducive to watching the evening news. I also knew of the success of all-news radio and if it could work on radio it would work on TV.

Because we were so small, this would be a risky undertaking, so I spoke to other people in the industry to make sure no one else was planning a news channel. It would have been a disaster to invest in a new start-up only to have to compete with a larger, well-financed competitor. One of the people I called was Jerry Levin. Time Inc. was now successful with HBO and as the publishers of magazines like *Time, Life,* and *People,* they seemed to be a logical company to move into cable news. Jerry let me know that they had studied the concept seriously but couldn't see how it would make financial sense. Their research showed that the news departments at ABC, NBC, and CBS were each spending between $200 and $300 million a year just to put on a thirty-minute telecast at night and morning shows like *Today* and *Good Morning America*. This led them to conclude that twenty-four hours of newscasts daily would simply cost too much. Jerry assured me that if we gave it a try, Time Inc. would not be a competitor, and as cable operators, they would do what they could to be helpful to our efforts. Another party rumored to be interested in a news channel was the Washington Post Company. They not only published *The Washington Post* and *Newsweek,* but also owned some local TV stations. But from what I heard they, too, were intimidated by the broadcast networks' news budgets and were not likely to move forward.

Clearly, the companies for whom the economics of twenty-four-hour news would have made the most sense were the Big Three broadcasters. They already had most of what was needed—studios, bureaus, reporters, anchors—almost everything but a belief in cable. The over-the-air broadcast business had been good to them and they gave this new technology short shrift. To me, network executives had become short-term thinkers whose primary focus was to have better ratings than the other two networks. While we pondered the future and were planning several years out, they spent most of their time thinking about which prime-time shows they should renew or cancel. I've often compared business strategy to a chess game, and when it came to Turner vs. the networks, they might have had more pieces on the board but they only thought about their next move while I was planning ten moves ahead.

As hard as it was for me to believe, all the evidence suggested that neither ABC, nor NBC, nor CBS was getting into cable news anytime soon. I decided it was time for us to try it ourselves, and if we were going to do it we had better move quickly. We were so much smaller than our competitors that the only way we could compete effectively was to take advantage of opportunities before they became obvious.

I'm often asked if we ever did any formal research on the viability of twenty-four-hour cable news and my answer is no. I had spent over five years thinking about it, and it was time to get going. Henry Ford didn't need focus groups to tell him that people would prefer inexpensive, dependable automobiles over horses, and I doubt that Alexander Graham Bell stopped to worry about whether people would prefer speaking to each other on the phone. If viewers liked watching news on television, why wouldn't they want the option to do it at any hour of the day? And wouldn't it be great to see breaking news live, instead of having to wait to watch it on tape at 7:00 or 11:00?

In addition to bypassing research, we also took a different approach to thinking about what it would cost to run such a channel. Instead of looking at what the networks were spending and adding to that number, we started with how much we could afford, then tried to back into a feasible plan at that level of expenses. The number we originally came up with was $30 million per year. This was about one tenth the annual costs of the Big Three news divisions, but even at that level of expenditure this venture would be a huge stretch for our company.

For years I had been selling off our billboard interests to help fund our expansion into television and to launch the SuperStation. I decided that if we moved ahead with news, it would be necessary to part with WRET in Charlotte, which we believed we could sell for around $20 million. Even with these proceeds it was clear that this business would never make it on advertising revenue alone. We needed commitments from cable companies not only to carry the service, but to pay us a per-subscriber fee as well.

As straightforward as the concept for an all-news channel was, I wanted to name the service before we marketed it. My family name had been on each of our businesses, but in this case, knowing how much we'd need the cable operators' support, I decided to emphasize "cable" and call it the Cable News Network—CNN. My reasoning was simple; using "cable" in the name would not only bring attention to this relatively new means of distribution, it would help motivate cable operators to carry us. After all, if someone signed up for cable, they'd have to assume that they would receive the *Cable* News Network.

With a name for the channel and a rough idea of expenses, I decided to test the waters at the annual Western Cable Show in December of 1978. Terry McGuirk and I arranged for a meeting with the board of the NCTA—essentially the heads of all the major cable companies—and there I described my plans for the Cable News Network. In addition to telling them how great this service would be for our industry I let them know that the only way we could make it work was to charge a fee of 15 cents per subscriber per month ($1.80 per year). At that point cable was only available to about 10 million homes so even if we were launched in each and every single household, our total cable fee revenue would be $18 million, not enough to cover our annual expenses.

We'd try to make up that difference in advertising sales, I explained, but that would be a very tough go in the early years. I told them that I wasn't asking them to risk anything—they didn't need to make an up-front investment with us, they simply had to pay us if we delivered the product. At the end of this fairly brief presentation I passed around copies of a contract and asked each of them to sign it. Essentially, it said that if I put CNN on the air, they would carry it and pay. Not surprisingly, they balked at signing a document like this on the spot with such short notice but I left with confidence, feeling that we would have the industry's support.

With little news expertise in house I had to go outside to find someone to run this operation. The SuperStation was still about a year away from turning profitable and resources were scarce (in fact, there were several within Turner Broadcasting who were lobbying me *not* to move forward with CNN for fear that it would bankrupt the company). Needing an executive who could run the operation on a shoestring, I couldn't look to the broadcast networks. Instead, I became interested in a small out-fit called the Independent Television News Association, or ITNA. They were in the business of supplying video news stories to independent TV stations across the country and had a reputation for producing a high volume of product at a low cost. I asked around about their president, Reese Schonfeld, who everyone said would be perfect for what I had in mind.

When I called and explained the concept of CNN to Reese, he got it right away and was really excited. He would have accepted the job right then but he had another year left to go on his contract at ITNA. Shortly after our initial call but well before his term was out, he agreed to come on board and began to contribute to our planning and development process on a part-time basis. During this period, Reese made our first full-time hire, Burt Reinhardt. Burt would serve as Reese's number two and not only was he a terrific guy, he was also a seasoned news professional who knew how to get things done. (Burt began his career at Fox Movietone News and served as a combat cameraman during World War II.)

We had held very preliminary conversations with cable operators for more than a year, but it wasn't until July 1, 1979, that I made the firm decision to launch CNN and we made our public announcement shortly thereafter. I was still concerned about competition and feared that once we made our intentions known, someone might come out of the woodwork, so I wanted to be sure that we pegged a start date that was not far into the future. I was also hoping to compete in the 1980 America's Cup and knew that the trials would occupy most of that summer. We settled on a launch of June 1, 1980, leaving us just eleven months to get on air.

One of our first priorities was to find a building. We were already packed tightly in our midtown Atlanta offices and we needed a studio and space for hundreds of new hires. Real estate and construction were not my specialties so I called my lifelong friend and sailing crewmember, Bunky Helfrich. Bunky was living in Hilton Head after a successful career as an architect in Savannah and I asked him to leave his comfortable lifestyle to come to work for me. His charge was to figure out how we were going to build facilities in time to meet our aggressive timetable. I'm sure this wasn't an easy decision for him, but fortunately for me he said yes.

Right around that time the Progressive Club, a Jewish country club in midtown Atlanta, had decided to sell their old clubhouse and move north of the city. An abandoned country club might not have been an ideal place from which to start a news network but it was right across the highway from our existing offices and it encompassed about ten acres. Bunky checked it out and while we knew we'd have to be creative, we figured that we could convert the first and second floors to offices and turn the gym and locker rooms in the basement into studio space. Behind the building, in addition to tennis courts and a swimming pool, there was quite a bit of open land (including some still recognizable Civil War bunkers). Reese Schonfeld had explained to me that we would need several satellite receiver dishes to collect incoming feeds and this would be the perfect place to put them. We decided to buy the property and it wasn't long before construction crews were at work converting a plantation-style clubhouse mansion into the home of television's first ever twenty-four-hour news service.

Another timing challenge we faced was the ordering of equipment. With no established news operations we had to start from scratch, purchasing cameras, lights, tape machines, satellite dishes—a huge amount of equipment. The lead times required for ordering some of these items were as long as nine months. We estimated that they would need about a month of rehearsal and run-through time before going on air, meaning that to make a May 1 rehearsal date, we had just one month to make estimates and order everything we were going to need. That huge task fell on the shoulders of our chief engineer, a calm and capable guy named Gene Wright. It was a frantic time but fortunately for us, Gene was up to the task.

Although I hadn't watched much television news, I did have some strong opinions about what I wanted CNN to be. While the networks and local news stations seemed to follow a "if it bleeds, it leads," rule centering their broadcasts on murders, car wrecks, disasters, and the like, I wanted us to do more serious journalism and to go deeper into the more important issues of the day. I also wanted to present the news in an unbiased fashion. At that time, some of the evening anchors, including Walter Cronkite, were injecting their own opinions into the telecasts and I just didn't like it. Schonfeld and I decided that on CNN, news would be the star, not our on-air people. (Speaking of Cronkite, we did at one point consider trying to hire him or some other name anchor. Each one declined, saying they were tied up with long-term contracts.)

Reese Schonfeld thought we would benefit from having at least one well-known and credible TV journalist and he convinced the well-respected Daniel Schorr to join our team. Schorr had had a great career at CBS but had left there after a dispute a few years before. He had been doing some stories for ITNA and had a good relationship with Reese. When I met Dan, his biggest concern was that I not tell him what to do or say on the air. He didn't want me forcing my opinions on him and he didn't want to be asked to make any commercial endorsements. After I made it clear that these requests were not a problem, Dan signed up with us and made several public appearances on our behalf as we attempted to sell CNN to cable operators and Madison Avenue.

CNN was still surrounded by skeptics and critics. Many "experts" thought we would never launch, let alone be successful. There was no way we could afford to do it, they claimed, and we certainly didn't have the journalistic expertise required to do it well. Several questioned the concept, saying there was already plenty of news on television and with print and radio news, consumers had access to all the coverage they could ever want. Some in the news establishment even had issues with our location. The network news divisions were all based in New York and they couldn't see how an operation like this could be run from a place like Atlanta.

When I'd hear that, I'd think, "Why not Atlanta? The biggest soft drink company in the world is based there. Procter & Gamble is the world's biggest soap company and they're in Cincinnati. Why does everything big have to be based in New York?" My standing with these media elites was just as it had been with the sailing establishment when I started racing, the baseball owners when I bought the Braves, and the

Hollywood studios when I launched the SuperStation. Just as it had in the past, my outsider status only made me want to work that much harder and to succeed that much more.

It was an exciting time. Still working hard to make the SuperStation work we were now adding an operation that was many times more complex and expensive. Once again I would need to be creative with financing the venture and in addition to working on the sale of WRET, I knew we'd have to figure out ways to borrow more money. On top of all that, my sailing career was still in high gear and I had a full schedule during the summer of 1979. In August, I took a break from the office and flew to the U.K. to compete in the world's most important ocean race—the Fastnet.

━━━━━━━━ A TED STORY ━━━━━━━━

"What Do We Do Now?"
—Bunky Helfrich

I was visiting Ted and Janie in 1979 for a celebration of their fifteenth wedding anniversary when Ted said to me, "Look, I think I'm going to start this news network. Why don't you come up and help me with it?" I said, "That sounds great, Ted, do you have any property yet?" He said that he didn't but toward the end of July he called me about the Progressive Club. He and I went out to look at it and while I thought we could make it work, getting it all ready to be on air by June of 1980 would be an incredible task.

My main contact on this project was Reese Schonfeld. We got a lot accomplished in a short period of time, despite the fact that he was under contract with someone else for our first few months together. I remember even having to meet him at the airport a couple of times. Ted had a vision for what he called an "open newsroom" for CNN—a setup where the audience could see everything going on to put the newscast together. A lot of people thought this would never work but Reese said that there was already a station in Vancouver that was using one. In August, he and I flew out there to check it out.

I knew that Ted was over in Europe

for the Fastnet race (I might have been on his crew had I not been so busy with CNN) but I was startled when the news station in Vancouver broke in with a story about it. There had been a bad storm. An unknown number of sailors had been killed and the word was that Ted Turner was one of them.

Reese looked at me and said, "What do we do now?"

And I said, "Damned if I know."

14

Fastnet

Just as our planning for CNN kicked into high gear it was time for me to go to Great Britain for a week of racing. By this point— August of 1979—we had assembled enough of the key CNN management team that things would move along in my absence. Plus, I really wanted to win the Fastnet Race.

The Fastnet is the final of a series of competitions known as Cowes Week, named for its home base of Cowes village, on the Isle of Wight, which is located on the southern coast of England. This is

the place where sailboat racing began—
the sport's equivalent to baseball's Coo-
perstown. I would be leading a crew on
Tenacious, an Olin Stephens–designed
yacht that I bought in the mid-1970s. The
Fastnet was a different kind of race from
the America's Cup. In Newport, you competed against a small number of boats in
a series of shorter races, but Fastnet was
a long 605-mile ocean race with a field of
more than three hundred competing yachts.
I had competed well here before but never
took home first prize. Winning the America's Cup and Fastnet would be compara-
ble to taking the Olympic gold medal in
both the marathon and the 100 meters,
and I was eager to win it.

I had great confidence in *Tenacious* and,
as always, I needed a strong crew. I couldn't
simply reassemble our America's Cup team
since that kind of match racing and open
ocean competitions like the Fastnet attract
different types of sailors. One guy who was
great at both kinds was Gary Jobson. Since
serving as my tactician on *Courageous,* he
had raced with me on *Tenacious* for the
last couple of years, but as Fastnet drew
closer, Gary decided he needed to skip it.

The full Cowes Week was a significant time commitment and my crews still had to pay their own way. But Gary and I had become a team and I really wanted him there, so as the event drew closer I decided to call him up and ask him one more time. I reminded him of the fun we'd had winning the America's Cup and explained that I didn't think I could win the Fastnet without him. Gary finally relented and agreed to come.

Working together, Gary and I put together a great crew. Two of the less experienced among them was my then sixteen-year-old son, Teddy, and a guy named Christian Williams, a newspaper reporter who was writing a book about me. Teddy was spending the summer working on various crews and Williams thought it might be helpful for his research to see me in action on a boat. Including me, there were eighteen men in the crew and one woman. (Jane Potts was the sister of one of our crew and served as our cook—a very important job in a multiday event like this!) Each one knew what he was doing and after just two days of practice we were ready for Cowes Week. We won enough races that week to be awarded the Queen's

Cup—a prize given to the best-performing boat in the series. With one day off before Fastnet, I took the crew over to Portsmouth to see *Victory,* which had been Lord Nelson's flagship. I wanted to visit it not only because I enjoyed maritime military history but I also thought it would give us all some great motivation going into what would be a long, hard race together.

———— A TED STORY ————

"Ocean Racing Isn't Baby-Sitting"
—Teddy Turner

Because of our family dynamic at the time—mainly the issues some of us were having with Janie—I got to spend a lot of summers on my dad's boats. Starting when I was about six I would go out with the crew and do a bunch of the deliveries—the trips you took when you had to get the boat from one race to the next. It was almost like "Turner Summer Camp" out on the water with an interesting bunch of young guys running a sailboat. In truth, I never got to spend much time with Dad because when he'd come in for the races, I'd have to get off the boat. He wouldn't let me race with him until I was fifteen and I was almost sixteen the first time I raced offshore. By then I'd already done thousands of miles on the ocean and he was comfortable having me aboard. His theory was that ocean racing isn't baby-sitting. He'd say that to put me on the crew, he'd have to take someone off and I couldn't go on until I was experienced enough to pull my own weight. So I started racing in the spring of 1979 and spent that spring and summer on and off the boat the entire time and ended up doing the Fastnet Race.

From the Fastnet Race starting line in Cowes, contestants sail in a southwesterly direction through the English Channel, and then turn to the northwest to cross the Irish Sea. Boats then circle Fastnet Rock, off the southwestern tip of Ireland, and roughly retrace the course back to the finish line in Plymouth, England. The entire course distance of 605 miles can, depending on conditions, take three to five days to complete. In 1979, 303 boats entered the race. Unlike the America's Cup where all the yachts are of roughly the same size, in Fastnet boats as small as twenty-eight feet competed against others as large as eighty feet. To balance the competition, the larger (faster) boats are given a handicap, with several hours added to their time.

In 1971, for example, I set a course record for Fastnet but still didn't win first prize. A smaller boat that finished after me was declared the winner after the handicap was added to my time. The start of the race was also staggered. Yachts were sent off over the course of an hour in six divisions at ten-minute intervals. These groupings were determined by boat length, with the larger boats placed in the rear and smaller ones in front. At sixty-one feet, *Tenacious* was toward the larger end of the scale. Our boat size would not only help us move quickly through the water, it would also give us an advantage should the conditions turn rough. At the start—1:30 P.M. on Saturday, August 11—the weather was fine, and while the long-range forecast called for some wind and possibly rain, conditions were not a concern.

As with all ocean races, we split into two watches, each one managing the boat for four hours at a time. Gary Jobson and I had been by each other's side in the America's Cup, but here he served as captain of one of our watches, while another good friend and experienced seaman named Jim Mattingly served as the other. We collaborated on tactical decisions as we took turns steering the boat. Because of the handicap system and the extended length of the course it's impossible to know precisely where you stand in an event like this, but forty-eight hours into the race, as we moved closer to Fastnet Rock, we knew we were doing well. The crew was working together and Jane Potts kept everyone happily fed. I was eager to break my course record and win the race, and halfway through the contest I thought we had a chance to do both.

Peter Bowker was our navigator and part of his job was to retrieve and interpret the weather updates we received over the radio. About the time that we were turning Fastnet Rock, Bowker relayed a report that a low pressure system was coming in from the North Atlantic and a major storm would hit us sometime that night. They were calling for Force 7 or 8 winds, possibly reaching Force 9 in some locations—hurricane conditions. In addition to considering what this meant for *Tenacious* and trying to prepare myself mentally for the storm, I couldn't help but think about the fact that there were more than three hundred boats in this race and some of them were far too small for a storm of this magnitude. While I felt we'd be all right, I predicted to my crew that twenty men would die that night.

Conditions were still moderate when we rounded the rock around 6:30 on Monday evening, but as night fell we could feel the wind building and the seas starting to rise. I told the crew to eat dinner and get their rest, as we were in for a long, tough night. Winds of the sort they were predicting are always dangerous, but in this body of water they would be particularly devastating. The Atlantic Ocean can reach depths of thousands of feet but in the Irish Sea, where we were racing, it shoals to just a couple of hundred feet. Shallow water causes waves to build up steeper and deeper. With proper sail management, you can usually handle the wind—it's the steep waves that pose most of the problems. There was no doubt that the weather was deteriorating by 8:00 P.M. when I handed the wheel over to Gary Jobson for the next four-hour watch. He did a great job during that stretch while I stayed below and tried to get as much rest as possible. I knew the situation could be very different by midnight when it would be time to change watches again.

────── A TED STORY ──────

"His Finest Moment"
—Gary Jobson

Ted had the watch from 12:00 A.M. to 4:00 A.M. and that was the absolute worst of the storm. I kept popping up from belowdecks to see what I could do to help and he kept telling me to get back down and get some rest. That was the way he liked to sail—he wanted the helmsman who was not on watch to take it easy because when it came time to take the wheel he had to be mentally sharp. But that night was never restful—it was hell down below. It was cold and wet—we were thrown all over the place and everybody was getting sick.

At one point, when the wind got really hard—like 60 knots—we had to get the mainsail down and Ted did let me come up and help with that. It was quite a feat of seamanship for us to get that sail wrestled, corralled, and tied down. With the mainsail down the sailing got a little easier. We used a small storm trysail—a triangular storm sail—and that worked well. During those four hours down below, Bowker was monitoring the radio. We heard Mayday calls all night—it was just bedlam on the radio—and we saw flares going off in the distance.

I came back up at 4:00 A.M. and Ted went below, completely exhausted. Handing the wheel over he said, "Don't let anybody else steer! You're the only helmsman!" On this next shift the winds started to die down, probably to about 50 knots, but the waves were still gigantic. In a storm like that, the wind makes you weary and the spray hurts when it hits you, but what separated Fastnet from anything else I've ever experienced were the short, steep waves. I can still remember these big thirty-five-footers breaking over my head and crashing into the cockpit and thinking, "How am I ever going to be able to describe this to anybody? How is anybody ever going to understand what this is all about?"

Ted was really tough that night. I was watching him and he was so strong that I didn't get frightened. I thought, "If he's all right, then things must be okay." The harder it got, the better he was. I think it was his finest moment.

Conditions were really rough during that midnight to 4:00 A.M. watch. After the race, some people said the waves were as high as forty feet. I'm not sure I ever saw any that high but I'd say they were averaging eighteen to twenty feet and some were probably thirty or thirty-five. The wind was blowing so hard that the top six to ten feet of some of these were breaking as if they were coming up on a beach. The watch crew clipped on their safety harnesses that were attached to a side rail where they would all huddle together. When the waves broke on us they were all but submerged. Despite the fact that *Tenacious* weighed about seventy thousand pounds, she was still thrown about twenty to thirty feet to leeward when the bigger waves hit. A couple of times we were knocked almost flat, but I had great confidence in the strength and integrity of our boat. (That doesn't mean something couldn't have broken. In fact, *Tenacious* was made of aluminum, with plates welded over aluminum ribs, and after the race we saw that several plates had broken and the front of the boat had to be rewelded.)

Visibility was poor. Not only were we sailing in the dark but the howling wind and rain made it hard to keep your eyes open, and down in the trough of one of these waves, the view ahead was nothing but black. During these early morning hours, the bigger boats had also made the turn and were sailing ahead of us, but most of the smaller boats were still making their way out to Fastnet Rock and that presented a challenge. When we rode up to the top of a wave we could briefly make out the red and green bow lights of oncoming boats and we had to make a split decision about which way to turn the wheel to avoid a collision. I knew that if we ever collided it would be a disaster. I don't think we ever came closer than two hundred feet or so to an oncoming boat, but with the limited visibility, it was quite a challenge.

As the storm made the sailing increasingly difficult, precise navigation had become impossible. Fastnet rules banned the use of some of the more advanced navigation technologies so the best we were allowed was a radio direction finder or RDF—a handheld device that uses radio signals to gauge the boat's location. Peter Bowker was responsible for using our RDF, and at one point, just as he stepped forward on the deck to try to get a reading, a breaking wave sent him flying toward the stern. He crashed so hard against the metal steering wheel that he bent it, and in the process the RDF was broken.

It was really scary that night, but as dangerous as things became for us, I refused to get too worried. If I had, I might have slowed up—there were eighteen other people aboard and as their skipper I had responsibility—but I felt that our boat was strong enough and I continued to press on. Even at the height of the storm, I was more concerned about winning than I was about dying.

By the time Jobson's watch finished at 8:00 A.M., the storm was starting to settle down. He'd had the job of steering us around the Scilly Isles, the final turn before heading back into the Channel and on toward the finish line at Plymouth. In good conditions, you try to make the turn as close to the Scillies as you can. With low visibility and lacking electronic navigation, we took a conservative approach and made a wide pass of the Scillies. We never saw the islands. I was disappointed by how far away we were from them— probably about ten miles and rounding wide cost us some time—but it was the safe thing to do.

By the end of that shift, around 8:00 A.M., the storm was pretty much over and we were able to get the mainsail back up. The rest of the race was uneventful and we crossed the finish line to Plymouth at about 10:30 on Tuesday night. Relieved to have successfully completed the course, we were hopeful that we'd sailed well enough to win. In contrast, most of the spectators were simply concerned about whether their friends or loved ones had survived. Rescue teams were being dispatched and it became clear that the night had been nearly as disastrous as I had predicted. In the end, nineteen people lost their lives that night—fifteen racers and four people from the crew of a pace boat. During the overnight chaos, all kinds of rumors were being spread, including one that *Tenacious* was among the boats that were missing. It turned out that when some of the rescue helicopters flew over the fleet, they didn't see our boat. They assumed the worst, and we were farther ahead than they realized and they didn't see us because they underestimated our speed.

—————— A TED STORY ——————

"Do Not Panic or You Will Die"
—Teddy Turner

Under the worst conditions, ocean racing can become a game of survival and the tougher the game is the more Dad likes it. One of the lessons he taught me is that in these situations, "You are in control of your own situation until you give up. Do not panic or you will die." And that night, he never gave up. I was watching my dad, not just because he was my father, but also because he was the skipper and it made a big impact on me to watch him not be scared.

We didn't know really how bad things had been for everyone else until early in the morning after the storm. We were having breakfast and listening to the radio—just a regular commercial station on the stereo—and they started talking about the tragedy of the night before. Everybody got very somber when we pulled into Portsmouth for the finish. The docks were crowded with thousands of people with pictures of their kids and their family since a lot of people knew that their child, husband, or family member was out there but they didn't necessarily know which boat they were on. They'd come up to you and say, "Have you seen this person?" Then the Coast Guard cutter came in and started unloading bodies. Needless to say, this was all pretty daunting for a sixteen-year-old.

When I woke up Wednesday morning, I was told that *Tenacious* had finished in second place. As had been the case in 1971, the winner was a smaller boat that came in far behind us but was declared the winner after handicap hours were added to our time. I was very disappointed. Meanwhile, because of the storm and the loss of life, Fastnet had become an international news story. As one of the race's well known competitors, many in the press wanted to talk to me. I did a live television interview with David Hartman on *Good Morning America* and spoke to other journalists from around the world.

During these interviews, I expressed disappointment with our second place finish and when asked about the disaster I explained my feelings that there were several smaller boats in the race that had no business being out there. They were too small to be on a course where storms like this can happen. Bad weather was part of the sport, I explained, and competitors need to be prepared. A couple of times I even commented that the British should be thankful for weather like this, explaining that it was a storm like this one in these very waters that helped keep the Spanish Armada from invading England in the sixteenth century. "If it weren't for this kind of weather," I explained to the British press, "you'd all be speaking Spanish!"

Looking back, I can see why I offended some people. From their perspective, a terrible tragedy had just occurred and they were expecting my tone to be more somber and subdued. From my perspective, my crew and I had just survived an epic race through terrible conditions. I'd barely had time to process everything that had happened and I was merely speaking my mind. These storms happen and sailors who enter these races should be prepared for them.

I was also frustrated that one of the smaller boats had managed to beat us on an adjusted time and I was preparing to go home when I was told that the judges had made a correction. The skipper of the smaller boat reported that they had never made it to Fastnet Rock—when they crossed the finish line at Plymouth, they hadn't even completed the course. *Tenacious* was now declared the winner! Because of the storm, this was not the same kind of celebratory situation we had at the Newport docks two years earlier, but this was a race I had always wanted to win and we had done it in the worst conditions imaginable.

Some good did come from the Fastnet tragedy. Several studies were conducted and papers written, resulting in new safety standards for the sport. While there have been fatalities in ocean races since then, including six deaths in the 1998 Sydney–Hobart race, yachting is a safer sport than it was prior to Fastnet, and I believe that my frank post-race comments helped stimulate some of the attention on eliminating unsafe boats from these competitions.

I would later learn that during the time when rumors spread that I was missing, CNN's newly signed anchor Daniel Schorr was making an appearance on our behalf at a cable trade show. The story of my possible demise was all over but people had no source for accurate updates as events unfolded. Eventually, word got out that I was okay, and when it did, Schorr turned the entire event to our advantage. He explained that when CNN was up and running as the first-ever twenty-four-hour news service, the Fastnet Race was precisely the kind of story we would cover. I liked Dan's style and I was eager to get back to Atlanta to keep our launch plans moving forward full steam ahead.

15

CNN Launch

When I returned home from the Fastnet Race we were just nine months away from CNN's launch and everyone was going 90 miles an hour to make it happen. Bunky was retrofitting the country club facilities while Gene Wright and his team of engineers were still making sure we secured and installed all our necessary equipment. Reese Schonfeld and Burt Reinhardt were making hires right and left and our salespeople were trying to sell cable operators and advertisers on this brand-new concept. It was an exciting time.

The CNN launch phase was particularly intense for me because I knew we were breaking one of the golden rules of start-ups—we were launching a business without sufficient capital to see it through to profitability. The problem was, I also knew I needed to move quickly and that there wouldn't be many lenders or investors out there who would advance this kind of money considering our lack of experience in news. My only options to raise funds were to sell even more assets (we had already been selling off the billboard and radio businesses to fund our expansion), sell stock, or borrow more money.

By this time, I had been in and out of banks for years and whenever I dealt with them it was a culture clash. Banks like businesses that are proven, steady, and predictable; they are less comfortable with the unknown and with unproven strategies. At one point, after we acquired WTBS and launched the SuperStation, we were seen as such a high-risk client that we were relegated to working with Citicorp's special division for highly collateralized, high-interest loans. Before that, we even had to work with a factoring company, to whom we paid a very high rate of interest and put up our receivables and inventory as collateral. They even made weekly checks of our books before giving us our cash. We had somehow survived it all and while it looked like the SuperStation was on a path to profitability, it was still losing several million dollars a year when we decided to move ahead with CNN. We felt the banks would not be receptive to this risky new venture, so I decided to mobilize with the resources we could generate on our own.

By this time, we owned both the Braves and the NBA's Atlanta Hawks (which I bought from Tom Cousins in 1977). Either one of these would have fetched a sizable price but they were too important to the SuperStation strategically for me to consider a sale. With our radio and billboard businesses already sold, our most valuable and least strategic asset that remained was WRET in Charlotte. Purchasing that station eight years before had cost me about $1 million. Now, with the improvements we had made and the growth of the television marketplace, the business was valued at about $20 million. We reached an agreement to sell to Westinghouse at that price, and once the deal closed and the FCC approved the license transfer, these funds would go directly toward CNN's launch. We would have enough money to get on the air, but nowhere near as much as we'd need to survive what was sure to be several years of losses before we made it into the black.

As a student of military history, I likened the CNN launch strategy to Irwin Rommel's desert campaign during World War II. On several occasions, the German general attacked the British when he knew he didn't have enough fuel to conduct an entire offensive. What he intended to do was strike when they weren't expecting it, overrun their lines, and then capture their fuel dumps. At that point he could refuel his Panzers and continue the offensive. My vision for financing CNN was similar. If we had enough cash to get on the air and could somehow get through our first year of operation, people would see that this was a viable and valuable service. Once the concept was proven, we would have easier access to capital. Even in the worst case, I figured that if we ran out of money after launching the channel and getting some distribution, we would have created a valuable asset that we could sell to a competitor. The key for us was to get started.

Shortly after making the decision to move forward with CNN, we negotiated a deal with RCA to reserve transponder space on SATCOM III, a new satellite they had built to meet the rising demand. Cable operators currently receiving SATCOM I, the satellite that was delivering the Super-Station and HBO, would be able to get a signal from SATCOM III without having to buy any new receiving equipment. A slot on SATCOM III was vital to CNN. No matter how hard we worked on our programming plans, advertising sales, or distribution deals with cable operators, without a transponder, we couldn't transmit. Yet despite the satellite's importance, I really didn't pay much attention to its launch in December 1979 as I assumed it to be a routine procedure. Then RCA called to tell us that SATCOM III had disappeared. They didn't know whether it blew up or what, but regardless, the satellite was gone, and unless we found a substitute, our plan for CNN was in jeopardy. Amidst all the efforts to get CNN on the air, it never occurred to me that something might go wrong with the satellite. The fact that RCA owned NBC—a potential CNN competitor—concerned me, but when I headed south for SORC races, I left feeling fully confident that our team would be able to work out a solution with RCA.

I was racing in the Bahamas in February when I got a call from Terry McGuirk. In short, he let me know that RCA did not have any workable solutions. We had asked them to free up an extra slot on SATCOM I, but the best they could offer was a transponder on one of their other communications satellites. This would not work for us since cable operators couldn't get the CNN signal without buying a second receiver. We were having enough trouble getting them to sign up for CNN, so there was no way they'd invest in a second dish just for our signal. If this was the best RCA could do, CNN—now less than four months from launch—was dead in the water.

I flew to Atlanta immediately while our team and outside legal counsel worked frantically on a solution. At first glance,

RCA appeared to hold the cards. After all, it was a large, well-financed conglomerate, while Turner Broadcasting was still small and highly leveraged. Making matters worse, our SATCOM III agreement guaranteed us a transponder *only* if the satellite had a successful launch—there were no backup provisions in the case of failure.

Our lawyers kept digging until one of them remembered a provision he had carved out in the deal we had reached with RCA a few years before when we sold our Atlanta uplink facility to them. This clause stipulated that whenever RCA allocated new satellite transponders, they owed Turner Broadcasting a right of first refusal. RCA had leased several transponders in the years since this agreement was signed and in every case they had overlooked this particular provision. While this contract had no direct bearing on the current situation (and the truth is, we wouldn't have needed these transponders had they been offered), they were technically in breach. It looked like we might have some leverage in our negotiations.

Our backs were against the wall, but that also played to our advantage. I'm convinced that one of the reasons I've been successful is that I've almost always competed against people who were bigger and stronger but who had less commitment and desire than I did. RCA was a huge company, but for Turner Broadcasting, this dispute meant everything. We had bet the future of our company on CNN and had already poured millions into it. Now, less than four months from launch, we were in jeopardy. We had to succeed.

Our team flew to New York to meet with the RCA satellite people at their plush executive offices. I decided that I had no choice but to play tough and let them know I was serious. I contended that we had been good partners for a long time and as such they should help figure out a way to get us a slot on SATCOM I. I also argued that our lawyers considered RCA to be in breach of our earlier contract regarding our first refusal rights and said that if they didn't sort this out quickly we were going to sue and take our case to the FCC. We had already invested more than $30 million in CNN and we would seek at least that amount in damages. I also made the point that it probably wouldn't look good to the regulators that RCA also happened to own NBC. These were senior executives—the top people in the satellite division—and I told them they better make it clear to RCA's top management that we would litigate if we had to.

We got their attention and left that meeting with the sense that the RCA people almost wanted us to sue them. Turns out they were in a bind because we weren't the only programmer with a SATCOM III slot reserved who now wanted space on SATCOM I. Since they had only two openings available there, if they granted a transponder to CNN, they would have no logical or legal explanation as to why Turner was taken care of while the others were not. Of course, if a lawsuit from us would actually do them a favor, we were more than happy to oblige. Our legal team worked around the clock and by the end of February, Turner Broadcasting sued RCA for breach of contract.

Within a week the court ordered an injunction. We were granted access to SATCOM I for the next six months, taking us beyond our June 1 launch date. Then in April, the FCC weighed in and ordered this access period to be extended through December. While this didn't give us all the security we would have liked, we could move forward with our plans and we were confident that between April and December we would come up with a long-term solution.

While we went to the brink with RCA, the business of building CNN continued and the atmosphere in Atlanta was chaotic. One of our biggest challenges was recruiting. Prior to launch we had to hire about three hundred people and attracting them wasn't easy. We did find some people in Atlanta, but in most instances, joining CNN meant a move from a different television market and taking a chance on a business that many in the industry viewed as a long shot. Oftentimes we made offers to people whose spouse also happened to work in television and for whom a move to Atlanta would mean sacrificing their job. Many local stations would not allow husband-and-wife teams to work together but we told them that was no problem at CNN. We didn't have these

My father, Robert E. Turner II.

My mother, Florence Rooney Turner.

An early picture of me in my favorite sailor suit.

My sister, Mary Jean, and me in 1942.

My favorite picture of Mary Jean, taken not too long before she became sick.

TED TURNER　　　　**BILL COOK**

Debaters Win Title
In State Tourney;
Turner Best Speaker

Bill Cook and Ted Turner, McCallie's affirmative debate team, won the state championship at the Tennessee Interscholastic Literary League finals in Knoxville last weekend. Turner was also named "best debater" in the meet, edging Cook by less than a point.

McCallie's debate team was great training and one of my first tastes of public success.

Shaking hands with Dr. J.P. McCallie on graduation day.

In my Coast Guard days.

Dad and me on the day of my wedding to Judy Nye.

After my father's death, duck hunting with Bob Naegele (second from right) at his property in Winnipeg, Canada. By this time Bob was a happy shareholder in Turner Advertising.

After acquiring the Tennessee Valley Billboard Company.

American Eagle's mast had broken the night before, but while the Coast Guard towed us in from the Gulf Stream, I still managed a smile and gave a "V" for victory.

Judy, with our baby
daughter, Laura Lee.

In the WTCG
studio.

I once helped
umpire a spring
training game,
just for fun.

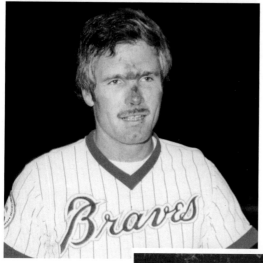

After pushing a baseball down the line with my nose, I bloodied my face but beat Tug McGraw by about six feet!

My young family. From left to right: Rhett, Beau, Jennie, Laura, and Teddy.

With my son Beau, a batboy for the Braves.

With Janie in Newport.

Gary Jobson and I taking our regular pre-race walk.

There were a couple hundred thousand people at the docks after we won the 1977 America's Cup, and I bowed to acknowledge their applause.

At the 1977 America's Cup press conference.

After the Braves clinched the 1982 National League West title on the road against the Padres, I invited the San Diego Chicken to join Skip Caray and me for the locker roomcelebration.

The Standard Club building in Atlanta, which became the original home of Cable News Network.

June 1, 1980, announcing the launch of CNN.

rules and we hired quite a few such pairs. An anchor's wife might be a producer at a different station or a camerawoman's husband might work with a competitor's studio crew and we'd just hire both of them. We wound up with so many spouses and family members on the CNN payroll that I joked the initials might as well stand for the "Cable *Nepotism* Network!" We did many things differently, and we managed to attract some great talent. We didn't often get people who were at the height of their careers but we did find some promising up-and-comers who were attracted by CNN and the chance to be on the ground floor of something new, ambitious, and exciting.

Along with hiring the staff, Reese Schonfeld also had to figure out how to fill a twenty-four-hour, seven-day-a-week news schedule, something that no one else had ever done before. He realized that we couldn't do it all with breaking news and felt we should hire a group of well-known people specifically to provide editorial commentary. I thought that was a good idea as long as we did our best to get people from across the political spectrum and we always identify their views as their own, not CNN's. We managed to sign Bill Simon, Bella Abzug, Phyllis Schlafly, Rowland Evans, and Bob Novak, among others. It was an impressive group, and combined with local anchors from around the country, Reese and his recruiters assembled a solid on-air team.

———————— A TED STORY ————————

"These People Are Nuts!"
—Lou Dobbs

(LOU DOBBS IS CURRENTLY THE ANCHOR AND MANAGING EDITOR OF CNN'S *LOU DOBBS TONIGHT*.)

In late 1979 I was working as a reporter and anchor at KING television in Seattle when I got a couple of calls from a headhunter trying to hire people for this proposed new news service in Atlanta. After I turned them down a couple of times, Sam Zelman, the CNN executive in charge of putting together the on-air team, gave me a call. When I let him know I wasn't interested he said, "Well you ought to at least come down here. You'll meet a lot of unusual people, if nothing else."

I finally made the trip in January of 1980. This was just six months before the announced launch date and when I walked into this old ramshackle, run-down Georgian colonial I thought, "These people are nuts!" It certainly did not meet my preconception of what an innovative new television news outlet might look like, but I stayed long enough to have dinner with a group of CNN people and they were great. Everybody was completely energized. When I met Ted he didn't know me from Adam but he greeted me like a long-lost brother. His enthusiasm was infectious and he was absolutely the definition of charismatic. He was in super sales mode and explained to me that CNN was going to be the greatest thing in the history of Western civilization! My visit didn't leave me feeling like this would be the case, but I was convinced that win, lose, or draw this would be a wonderful thing to be a part of.

At the time that we dodged the RCA satellite bullet, our all-important sale of WRET hit a snag. Our station manager in Charlotte had gotten into a dispute with representatives of a local African-American group called the Charlotte Coalition. They had been lobbying the station for more minority employment and the airing of more minority-related programming. And instead of being respectful and listening to their concerns, our manager got into a fight with them and ordered them out of his office. Following this shabby treatment, they filed a lawsuit against the station. The FCC was very attentive to potential issues of discrimination, and this claim was sure to hold up our license transfer.

Without this sale and the $20 million in proceeds, we were in big trouble. As this dispute dragged on we were forced to take out a $20 million loan at 25 percent interest, requiring us to make $400,000 interest payments every month. We couldn't afford to keep this up through a protracted legal process, so I set up a meeting in Charlotte with members of the coalition, and in addition to our lawyers, I asked

Hank Aaron to come with us. Hank was well respected in the black community and when he pointed at me in our first meeting with the coalition and said, "This guy isn't prejudiced," it was a powerful moment. Yet despite Hank's support, it was a tense series of negotiations.

In difficult situations like this, I try to be as straightforward as possible. I made it clear that I agreed that our manager had been in the wrong and as president of the company I took responsibility for his lousy judgment. I apologized for this behavior but explained that if they went forward with this suit, they wouldn't be punishing him; they'd only be hurting my company.

At one point in the negotiations I actually got down on the floor on my hands and knees and begged for forgiveness. I clasped my hands together and said, "You gotta let me sell this station or I'm a goner!" Somehow, between Hank Aaron's support and my demonstration of genuine contrition, we got the negotiations back on track and worked out a deal. They would drop the lawsuit if I agreed to make a certain level of donations to the United Negro

College Fund and some other worthy causes that they supported. With the lawsuit resolved, our license transfer was approved, and we completed our $20 million sale of WRET.

We were now just weeks away from CNN's debut. Practice and preliminary trials for the 1980 America's Cup had begun in Newport so my schedule was tight, but I wanted to be sure we put together a noteworthy launch that would let the world know that the Cable News Network was going to be something really important. We decided to hold a ceremony in front of our new offices—out on the lawn of the old Progressive Club. In addition to our own employees, we invited advertisers, cable operators, and members of the press. The network would begin satellite transmission at 6:00 P.M., so our event was scheduled to begin around 5:30. I flew down to Atlanta from Newport that morning.

We invited a combined Armed Forces Band, with top-notch musicians from the Army, Navy, Air Force, and Marines. They arrived a few hours early, as we were assembling bleachers and the viewing stand.

While they were rehearsing, I asked them to play "Nearer My God, to Thee," which I read was the last song played on the *Titanic* when she went down. We taped the performance so that in case the Cold War ever got hot and nuclear weapons were being launched, CNN could sign off its final broadcast with the Armed Forces Band and this recording. These were young service people and when they played this beautiful melody I had tears in my eyes. (By the way, as I understand it, this tape remains in CNN's library—but thankfully they've never had to air it!)

Once our guests arrived I kicked off the program with a few comments, then handed the stage over to our other speakers. In addition to Reese and other Turner executives, I invited NCTA president Tom Wheeler to say a few words to emphasize how important this new network was to the cable industry. When it came back to my turn, I discussed the important role I expected CNN to play in disseminating information and bringing people together. Finally, I read this statement, which had been prepared by our PR department:

**To act upon one's convictions while
    others wait,
To create a positive force in a world
    where cynics abound,
To provide information to people when it
    wasn't available before,
To offer those who want it a choice:
For the American people, whose thirst
    for understanding and a better life has
    made this venture possible;
For the cable industry, whose pioneering
    spirit caused this great step forward in
    communication;
And for those employees of Turner
    Broadcasting, whose total commit-
    ment to their company has brought us
    together today,
I dedicate the News Channel for
    America—The Cable News Network.**

Then the band played the National Anthem, as was the custom for television stations when they signed on and off each
day, and CNN went on the air. It was a
thrilling moment. We still had a lot of work
to do to make CNN a success, but we had
already cleared substantial hurdles and
had defied numerous skeptics simply by

getting on the air. As proud as I was and as much as I would have loved to stay for the entire reception, I had to leave a little early to catch my flight back to Newport and the America's Cup trials.

16

A Dagger Pointed at Our Heart

I decided to pursue the 1980 America's Cup with the same boat and largely the same crew we won with in 1977. With *Courageous* also taking the prize in 1974 we were asking her to win three cups in a row, a feat that had never occurred. Our competitors now had had six years to study her design and to use this information and the latest technologies to build a faster boat. I could have tried to build a new one as well but designing and building a twelve-meter yacht takes a lot of time, energy, and cash, and given everything else I had

had going on, especially getting CNN off the ground, I just couldn't do it.

Our prime competitor in the U.S. trials was Dennis Conner, my former crewmember and eventual rival in 1974. After skipping the 1977 event, Conner was now putting a tremendous amount of energy and resources into his 1980 campaign. In addition to financing and building a new boat—*Freedom*—he had hired Robbie Doyle to help with *Freedom*'s sails. Robbie was on our crew and made our sails in 1977 and was doing the same in 1980. The competition in 1977 could only guess about what sails we had and how to beat them, but with Doyle on two teams in 1980, Conner knew exactly what we were using and had the time and resources to make improvements. It was as if, before World War II, the British had a Messerschmitt 109 or the Germans got the Spitfire and they had three years to test their own planes against them. Dennis also spent a lot of time sailing and practicing with his team. In the twelve months leading up to the trials, he was on the water over three hundred days to our seventy. America's Cup yacht racing was becoming a full-time

sport and it was getting much more difficult to compete as an amateur.

From the first preliminary trials it was
clear that *Freedom* was the boat to beat.
They took eleven of twelve match races
and it was obvious that Conner's training,
testing, and investment in new technologies like Mylar and Kevlar sails were paying
off. It was a difficult time for the *Courageous* crew. In a sport like baseball, teams
go through losing streaks, but at least they
change cities every few days. At the America's Cup trials, you're in Newport all summer, and getting beaten day after day is
especially hard. The same guys who had a
great time winning together three years before were now struggling to keep their spirits up.

It was a difficult time for me, too. We
were sailing hard every day, and losing a
lot more than we won. After a long day on
the water, I'd shower, have dinner, and
then spend the evening on the phone
catching up on business in Atlanta. It had
been a real dash leading up to CNN's
launch and now that we were up and running, it turned out that our expenses were
nearly twice what we had budgeted while

our revenues were about half. The Newport trials would have been tough enough, but with CNN losses four times our projections, the pressure was excruciating.

One evening, as I stood in the shower after a day of racing, my body started to shake. I'd been stressed before but this was a first and I realized I was pushing myself to the brink. Once I managed to calm down I thought about the situation and realized that I was struggling to do three things well. I was trying to build a business, race boats at a world championship level, and of course, attempting to raise a family. Something had to go. Ignoring my family was not an option. My five children were getting older—the older two were nearly grown—and already knew I wasn't spending enough time with them. So it came down to sailing or business, and my decision became clear. In 1979, I became the first sailor to be named Yachtsman of the Year four times (I also received the honor in 1970, 1973, and 1977). I had already accomplished more in the sport than I ever imagined and it was hard to come up with any unmet goals that would keep me motivated. Quitting the company was a possibility—I probably could have sold Turner Broadcasting for hundreds of millions of dollars and never worked another day in my life—but unlike sailing, with my business career, I still had mountains to climb and I was excited about the future. In particular, CNN looked like it would not only be interesting, but also I believed it could have a major impact on the world. Then and there on that evening I decided that the 1980 America's Cup would be the end of my sailing career.

So it came almost as a relief when, at the end of the final trials in August, the selection committee's boat pulled alongside ours to tell us we were eliminated. I said my goodbyes and headed for Atlanta while Dennis and *Freedom* went on to successfully defend the Cup against Australia. In hindsight, we should never have entered the competition with such an old boat and with so little time to practice. The sport was moving in a different direction—with full-time participants and corporate sponsors—and it was passing us by. For me, retiring from the sport of sailing was bittersweet, but it was time to move on.

Turner Broadcasting would take every

bit of effort and ability I could muster. Keeping the business going while staying ahead of our creditors and competitors was hard work. CNN was off to a rough start. In addition to mounting losses that were well beyond our projections, media critics were taking shots at us. We had a lot of kinks to work out and some began referring to the network as "Chicken Noodle News." But often our coverage of a story would demonstrate that we were competent journalists and that the twenty-four-hour news concept was powerful. One such occasion was the MGM Grand Hotel fire in Vegas in November of 1980. Apart from the local stations, CNN was the only television outlet to follow this story from start to finish.

But despite these successes, we continued to confront institutional and competitive barriers that made our work difficult. In these early days, our crews were denied access to the White House pressroom and any other press pools organized to cover the president. We were told that only "the networks" (meaning ABC, NBC, and CBS) were allowed. When we responded, "But we *are* a network," it fell on deaf ears. The broadcast networks had no interest in CNN joining their exclusive club and the White House press people had no incentive to change policy, either.

CNN could not cover Washington politics adequately without access to the White House pressroom so we were forced to sue, and we went all the way to the top. In addition to ABC, NBC, and CBS, we also named in our lawsuit President Ronald Reagan, White House press chief Larry Speakes, and Reagan's chief of staff, James Baker. Our claim that CNN was unfairly being denied access placed the White House in a no-win situation. There was no way they could defend shutting out our journalists and once our case was made public, the issue was resolved in our favor.

CNN was still far from being a financial success but we were gaining attention and it wasn't long before we heard whispers about rival news networks being planned. The most persistent and logical rumor ultimately turned out to be true. Just over a year after CNN's launch, ABC and Westinghouse announced that they were forming a joint venture to enter the cable news business. This alliance made sense, as Westinghouse was operating an all-news radio station and ABC already had a full-scale television network news division. Their plan was to create two different channels and to launch them sequentially. The first, to be called Satellite News Channel, or SNC, would feature an eighteen-minute "wheel" of short news stories that they would update and repeat throughout the day. The second would be a longer-form news channel patterned directly after CNN. At the time of this announcement, we had already invested about $100 million in CNN and were still far from breaking even. Now, two multibillion-dollar corporations were coming at us with a dagger pointed at our heart.

I began to contemplate how we could combat such a competitive threat. I had purchased a 4,200-acre property in South Carolina called Hope Plantation in 1979, and it became a perfect place for the long walks I take when I need to clear my head and to think through strategic challenges. Sometimes I walk by myself and on other occasions I engage in debate with people whose opinions I value. One such person is Taylor Glover, my financial adviser and good friend.

—————— A TED STORY ——————

"He Was Driven"
—Taylor Glover

(TAYLOR GLOVER SPENT NEARLY THIRTY
YEARS WITH MERRILL LYNCH BEFORE
BECOMING PRESIDENT AND CEO OF
TURNER ENTERPRISES,
INC., IN 2002.)

In the late 1970s, Ducks Unlimited was
trying to bring a chapter to Atlanta
and I volunteered to help them out.
They were planning an auction banquet and I agreed to be in charge of
securing items to put up for bid. We
were hoping to get a set of season
tickets to the Atlanta Hawks and since
I'd heard that Ted was an outdoors-
man, I decided to call him directly. He
didn't know me at all but I got right
through and he put me on his speak-
erphone. He told me that he thought
Ducks Unlimited was a great organization and that he'd be happy to support them, so I asked him about
donating Hawks season tickets.

"No problem!" he said, "How many

do you need and which game do you want?" When I explained once again that I wanted season tickets, not just seats for one game, he said he couldn't give away that much. He told me that two season tickets were worth $700 and that was more than he could contribute. I tried to convince him that since they weren't selling out, it would benefit him to have some more fans in those seats, plus they'd buy beer, souvenirs, etc. I also challenged him about whether they were even worth that much and told him they'd probably only go for about half that amount, or $350 at the auction.

He didn't buy that argument so I finally proposed a deal. I said, "I'll tell you what. If you give us those tickets and they sell for more than $350, I'll personally buy four of your best tickets." He said, "Okay, you've got a deal. I bid $351, now you have to buy four seats down on the floor!"

I said, "No, no, no, you have to be present at the banquet to make a bid." So he asked me when it was and said he'd be there.

We sat together at the dinner and Ted wound up bidding high on everything, including guns, paintings, a canoe—he even bought two hunting dogs. One of the final items put up was a trip to a plantation owned by Rankin Smith, the owner of the Atlanta Falcons. When they announced this trip, Ted leaned over to me and said, "I own the best duck hunting place there is. It's over in South Carolina—a whole plantation—and since this is a duck function, I could have given a trip there."

I said, "Well, I'm in charge of prizes and you're in charge of your plantation, we could work out a deal right now." He agreed and a few minutes later I got up on the stage to describe this new item on our agenda and to try to get everyone excited. Of course I barely knew anything about it so Ted jumped up and gave me the hook. He got everyone so fired up about this place that it finally sold for a bid of $10,000.

I thanked Ted and on the way out he asked if I could bring everything he bought over to his office the next morning. So I left there with several shotguns in my car, two dogs, paintings, and a canoe sticking out the back—everything he'd won that night—and I drove over to his office the next morning. He invited me to go hunting with him on his next trip and it was then our personal friendship began. After that first weekend I knew that Ted was somebody really special. As a broker I'd worked with a lot of smart people but he had one of the brightest, quickest minds I'd ever been around. On top of that, he was driven way beyond anyone else I'd ever met. He was also very open about sharing his thoughts with me. He'd use me as a sounding board on everything from what he was doing in Washington to his strategic plans for CNN. He always did most of the talking but appreciated the questions I asked and the holes I tried to poke in his arguments.

I once again thought in military terms and reasoned that I could not afford to engage in a long, protracted war against opponents with such superior resources. I had to knock them out, and quickly. I viewed CNN as our beachhead, and I figured the only way we could keep them from taking this territory was to create our own headline service and fend them off. Around Labor Day of 1981 we decided to create CNN2, an all-news channel with a thirty-minute cycle of headline stories. With Satellite News Channel planning to launch in June of 1982, we announced that our new service would begin six months before theirs, on January 1. We had to get the new channel on the air in just four months.

Fortunately, we had purchased the Progressive Club property in part because it had plenty of land for expansion. Bunky Helfrich decided that for CNN2 we could take the space where the swimming pool had been and put up a Butler Building (this is essentially an aluminum Quonset hut). Launching CNN had been a more extensive undertaking, but with CNN2's compressed timetable the pace of our challenges was incredible. This was the greatest threat that our company had ever faced, and every one of us knew it.

One of the main reasons SNC was such a challenge was that its presence would make it more difficult for us to collect license fees from cable operators—and without these payments, CNN would never be profitable. At the time, we were charging 15 cents per month per subscriber for one service, but ABC/Westinghouse was going to offer both of their channels for free. Their plan supposed that the scale advantages—both in production and their ability to sell advertising—would allow them to make money without license fees. We realized this meant that SNC's distribution might surpass our own and that CNN might even get dropped from cable systems that would switch us out in favor of a free competitor.

While we couldn't give away both our channels for free, and I didn't like the idea of dropping our price for CNN, I thought we could win this battle if we kept CNN's rates where they were but offered CNN2 free of charge to those cable systems that carried CNN. As part of our sales plan, I also made every effort to remind cable operators that while ABC and Westinghouse were newcomers to cable, I had been there from the beginning. I was even featured in a promotional music video. The song's title was "I Was Cable When Cable Wasn't Cool," and it served as a pointed reminder to the operators of our long-standing partnership. In addition to circulating copies of the song we took out trade ads and even a billboard at the national convention in Las Vegas. I was standing there with my cowboy hat and guitar and everyone seemed to appreciate my spirit and showmanship and this campaign definitely helped us.

Another welcome opportunity presented itself in the form of a boast from an ABC executive shortly after their launch announcement. He told a newspaper reporter that this was going to be like General Motors going after Studebaker, and was quoted saying something to the effect of "we have deep pockets and Turner doesn't." This comment, coupled with the fact that they were coming after us with well-below-market prices, gave us a great case to accuse them of predatory behavior in violation of antitrust laws. This would be no small deal—in antitrust cases the aggrieved party can sue for treble damages, and since our CNN investment to date was upward of $100 million, we could sue for $300 million. Their executives claimed publicly that this threat didn't concern them, but privately we knew they were worried.

The battle became increasingly costly for both sides. Having learned our lesson from the SATCOM III disappearance, the minute we decided to launch CNN2 we focused on securing a transponder. Since none was on the market we had to work out a deal with Warner Communications, who had a lease on a transponder but with no immediate plans to use it. When we told them we couldn't afford to pay cash they came back and countered with the idea of taking over our ad sales operation. Essentially, they would merge Turner Broadcasting's sales team into their own and collect a royalty on the revenue generated from our networks. This was not a great solution for us—it's a very risky thing handing your sales efforts over to someone else—but we needed that transponder and we made the deal. (It would be another two years before we could unwind this relationship and once again took over the selling of our own advertising time.)

On the SNC side, their business plan had never contemplated the launch of CNN2 and now that we would be effectively splitting the market for a headline service, their losses would be larger than they anticipated. Struggling to gain distribution against CNN2, they had to pay up-front fees to cable operators in exchange for inclusion in the lineup. We countered with what we called our "$3 Plan." At 15 cents per month we were getting $1.80 per subscriber for CNN, and we told cable operators that if they carried both of our news services we would pay them back $1 per year for three years. This was a very costly exercise for us—effectively lowering our sub fee for both channels by nearly 70 percent—but it was an effective tool in slowing SNC's distribution efforts.

After CNN2 had been on the air for several months and shortly after SNC launched—and as all of our losses continued to mount—we heard that ABC and Westinghouse had decided to delay the launch of their second channel. With this development, Turner was now the company with two networks to their one. We also heard rumors that they might be open to settling our antitrust claim. I could sense that we were winning.

Our lawyers met with theirs to discuss a settlement. ABC and Westinghouse said they were willing to exit the cable news business if we agreed to pay them $25 million. We might have been able to win our antitrust case but that could have dragged on for several years. Twenty-five million dollars was a lot of money, especially on top of the other millions we had invested, but Bill Bevins, my top financial person, reasoned with me that fighting it out with SNC was costing us $4 million a month, so for the cost of about six months of more fighting, we could buy them out altogether. We decided to settle for the $25 million. It was a costly sum but a big win nonetheless, and it would be thirteen years before we faced another twenty-four-hour all-news channel.

CNN2, later renamed Headline News, went on to be a successful service and an important part of our overall business. Fending off ABC and Westinghouse, though expensive, was a huge shot in the arm for our company. I've told people that Turner Broadcasting's defeating ABC and Westinghouse in the early 1980s was like Luxembourg going to war with both the United States and the Soviet Union—and winning.

Launching the SuperStation and CNN and winning the America's Cup and Fastnet were major achievements, but this was my biggest win so far.

By the time I gave up racing, my children were well on their way to becoming adults. For their high school years, both Teddy and Laura went away to private school. Given the ongoing tensions between them and their stepmother, this made the most sense. After returning from Cincinnati, Laura went to a boarding school in Texas, before coming back to Georgia to attend Rabun Gap School, from which she graduated in 1979.

With Teddy away at McCallie, this left our three youngest children at home, and as they grew older, Janie and I became increasingly concerned about the public schools in Atlanta. Since we weren't sure that their grades would get them into Atlanta's elite private schools, Janie and I came up with an idea. Why not move our family to South Carolina and live at Hope Plantation? This was a beautiful property, about thirty miles from Charleston, and there was a good private school in Walterboro named the John C. Calhoun Academy that they could attend. I couldn't commute to Atlanta from there but I was spending so many nights sleeping in my office that this wouldn't change our routine and I could still make it home on weekends.

The move seemed to work well and having our home base near Charleston also wound up influencing where Teddy was to attend college. I believe in the value of a military experience, so when Janie pointed out that since it was so close by, Teddy should consider The Citadel, I liked her idea a lot. I knew it was tough but I thought it would be good for his development.

───────── A TED STORY ─────────

"I Can't Believe My Dad Sent Me to College"
—Teddy Turner

When people sometimes say to me, "I can't believe your dad made you go

to The Citadel," I say, "You've got it a
little wrong; I can't believe my dad
sent me to college!" He was so cheap
I actually wasn't sure if he'd pay my
tuition, but he did like the idea of me
going on from McCallie to get my military education in college. His father
was not a big fan of military colleges,
from what we understand, because
he wanted Dad to go to an Ivy League
school so he could have a higher
standing and stature both education-
ally and socially and Brown seemed
like a better thing to do for a successful businessman's son. But I think that
when Dad went to Brown he realized
that that might have been true in general but that it wasn't a place that
worked for him.

The Citadel was not an easy school
by any means but I had it a lot easier
than most kids. I grew up in a household that was a tight ship, then went to
McCallie, which, having just changed
from being military a couple of years
before, was still a tight ship, so the
environment at The Citadel was not

completely foreign. I felt sorry for kids who came there straight from home.

When Teddy came home for Thanksgiving his freshman year, the changes in him were remarkable. He went there with long curly hair and they cut it all off. He must have lost about thirty pounds and he sat bolt upright at the dinner table. He looked fabulous and every time we talked to him it was "Yes, sir" and "No, sir." He set a great example for his younger siblings. All three of my sons wound up attending and graduating from The Citadel.

———— A TED STORY ————

"He Makes You Want to Be Better"
— Beau Turner

Despite my two older brothers going to The Citadel, I still had trouble getting in. I had been diagnosed as dyslexic and was screwing off in high school. I could tell my dad was disappointed in me and I told myself I was going to get into that school. I kept trying to get a meeting with the colonel in charge of admissions but they kept throwing me out, saying I wasn't getting in. I finally literally barged my way in one time and when I sat down, I noticed that the colonel had a hunting bow on his desk, so I started up a conversation about hunting. He had heard about Hope Plantation and what a great place that was, and after we started to hit it off I asked if he would consider accepting me conditionally, essentially the same deal the athletes got, and he finally said yes.

Once I got in I really busted my butt and wound up getting good grades and making the dean's list a couple of times. Basically, I didn't want to disappoint my dad. He always has a way of making you want to work harder. Whether it's his kids or his employees, he makes you want to be better.

One of the reasons I like military schools was I wanted my boys to be tough and self-sufficient. I also tried to set a personal example for all my children when it came to hard work and appreciating the value of hard-earned money. My kids obviously saw the hours I put in at the office and at the height of my wealth I still drove around Atlanta in a Ford Taurus and bought my clothes off the rack. In fact, I was so thrifty that someone at the company once said, "Ted Turner could squeeze Lincoln off a penny!" During my sailing career and my time at Brown, I'd seen plenty of wealthy people's children who were spoiled and didn't have much of a work ethic. I didn't want to see my kids end up like that and while they certainly enjoyed some of the fruits of my success—whether that was my boys hanging out with Braves players at spring training or Laura and Jennie owning horses when they were teenagers—I made it a point to be sure that they didn't get too much handed to them on a silver platter.

―――――― A TED STORY ――――――

"I Did That for You Guys"
—Rhett Turner

I remember we would go duck hunting in South Carolina in December and January and my dad would drive us out in his Jeep. It had a cover and heating, but instead of using either of those Dad kept the top off and the windshield straight down. We had our jackets and warm clothes on but it was still really cold and he's up there shivering while he's driving the car and Beau and I are sitting there freezing, thinking, "Jeez, can't he at least put the windshield up?" I never understood why he did this until finally, several years ago, I asked him. I said, "Dad, when we were down at Hope Plantation I don't understand why you drove that Jeep with the top and the windshield down. Remember? You'd be freezing, with snot going down your mustache and gloves; you could hardly hold on to the steering wheel."

He said, "Son, I didn't do that for

me. I did that for you guys. I was working on making you tough."

It was never as bad as in *The Great Santini* but life with my dad was a little bit like being in the Meecham family from that book. Their dad was really tough, but no matter how hard he was on them they loved him. It's the same way with my dad. The hardness was difficult but the reward is he's made us very competitive to want to succeed in the world, whereas a lot of wealthy people don't raise their families in an environment that makes them competitive and they don't succeed on their own.

Whenever I was home, I tried to put my time with my kids to good use and while I might not have been there as much as some fathers, I was around enough to know that my children were coming along really well and I was very proud of them.

17

World Citizen

CNN had been on the air about eighteen months when we discovered that Fidel Castro was a viewer. We weren't distributing the channel to international markets at that point but our signal spilled into Cuba and when one of our crews went there they found that Castro had installed his own dish and watched us regularly. In fact, he was so enthusiastic about our service that he invited me to visit.

This gave me a lot to think about. My father had raised me to be distrustful of communists and this view was reinforced by the political climate of the times. I had been voting Republican for years and still considered myself a conservative, although I'd never been politically active. I had casually mentioned to people that I might run for president but this was never something I really considered seriously (and the only time I ever attended a Republican function was when I went to the Goldwater party in Atlanta but I was only there trying to meet girls).

Now that I was in the news business I wanted to become more involved in world affairs. I also believed that it pays to understand your enemy, and at that time, communists were our enemies. I joked that the invitation to Cuba might be part of a plot to have me kidnapped. But why would Castro want to kidnap me? (I was working so hard at the time that I remarked that a kidnapping might not be a bad thing—if they held me captive at one of their beach resorts I might even get a chance to relax.) But I also had some real concerns about the negative publicity this trip might generate. After thinking it over carefully and weighing the pros and cons, I decided to go. I accepted the invitation and flew to Havana for a week-long visit.

By the time of this trip—in February of 1982—Castro had been the target of more than twenty assassination attempts, and the itinerary we received was light on details regarding when or where I might actually see him. After touching down in Havana I was taken to the Riviera Hotel for lunch with the city's mayor, and during that short car ride I was struck by what I saw. My image of a communist state was one of tanks in the streets, soldiers with guns, people walking around with glum faces. Instead, the Cubans looked just as cheerful as anybody. They dressed in bright colors and had smiles on their faces. I knew that all my movements were being controlled carefully, but while heading to see a zoo that was under construction, our driver got lost. We were on a dirt road trying to find our way when we stopped to ask a villager for directions. I needed to go to the bathroom and the villager let me into his house to use his. When I got inside, there was a framed picture of Castro on the wall. After hearing terrible stories about poor treatment during Castro's regime, I was surprised by this admiration from one of his countrymen.

Later that afternoon I was taken to meet Castro himself. I learned before the trip that he liked baseball, fishing, and hunting so I brought as gifts a Braves cap and some fishing gear. This resulted in some unusual-looking luggage and his concerned guards gave my belongings a thorough once-over, but once they realized I carried nothing more threatening than some rods, reels, and tackle, the mood became relaxed.

Castro's charisma was apparent the instant he entered the room. He's a tall man and his eyes sparkle and dance when he speaks to you. We were clearly sizing each other up but our conversation was friendly and cordial. He appreciated the gifts and put on the Braves cap, but looking at the fishing gear he explained that he was a spearfisherman. I offered him a rod and reel demonstration and before you knew it, there I was, in the halls of Castro's palace, giving casting lessons to Fidel and his bodyguards.

When meeting someone with a completely different background and contrasting point of view, I've always found it helpful to start out by discussing things you have in common. In this case, we broke the ice by talking about baseball and fishing, and we developed a strong enough rapport that Castro invited me for a visit that weekend at his retreat on an island in the Bay of Pigs. There, I was able to watch him spearfish and we hunted ducks together. He was talented at both and being together in these natural settings was a great way to relax and get to know each other. As careful as those guards were that first day, when we went hunting, one of them handed me a 12-gauge automatic shotgun. I have to admit that there was a moment when I thought to myself, "Here I am, ten feet from Fidel Castro with a shotgun in my hand. I wonder how much the CIA would pay to be in this position right now?" We actually became so comfortable that during that night after dinner, when we had both had some rum and smoked cigars, our conversation turned to world affairs. At one point I leaned over and asked him, "Are you really interfering in Angola and Central America?" Castro looked me right in the eye and said, "Yes, and so are you. What makes you think that it's okay for the U.S. to interfere there but Cuba shouldn't?"

I said, "Because we stand for freedom and capitalism and you don't."

Castro replied, "So what makes you think that you're right and we're wrong?"

My mouth dropped open. I'd had ideological discussions with other people—McCallie and Brown University professors, for example—about the relative merits of capitalism, communism, and other systems, but these were always at a theoretical level. Now I was having this discussion face-to-face with an intelligent, articulate person who was leading a country and who was our sworn enemy. I had always been taught that ideas and opinions like his were of little value, and while he didn't convince me that his way was right, I must confess that experiencing the depth of his convictions first-hand, and his logical objections to U.S. policies, was a powerful experience. I barely slept that night, tossing and turning as I thought about our conversation.

After this eye-opening trip I flew home with a whole new desire to understand more about other cultures and political systems and to do what I could to increase communication and dialogue between nations. With this realization, and after seeing Castro's interest in CNN, I knew that we had a real opportunity to build an international news business. It wasn't long before we were having meetings with leaders from all over the world and working on distribution deals to make CNN not only the first twenty-four-hour news channel but also the first global television network.

I also began to expand my thinking about the kinds of programming that we would run on the SuperStation. Beyond movies, sports, and sitcoms, I realized that we could add documentaries to our lineup. As the networks chased viewers with increasing levels of sex and violence, I liked the idea of counterprogramming with high-quality documentaries that might do some good for society. John Denver had become a friend of mine—he was great guy and a passionate advocate for the environment. He let me know that Jacques Cousteau, the legendary oceanographer, had asked him if he knew anyone in the United States who might want to be his production partner. Cousteau had worked with ABC in the past but they were no longer interested in airing his shows. He had also worked with PBS and since that relationship had also come to an end, Denver suggested he speak with me.

I greatly admired Captain Cousteau. In my mind, if you had to pick a mother of the environmental movement it would be Rachel Carson, and if you had to pick a father, it would be Jacques Cousteau. When we met we hit it off immediately and I knew that airing his programming would provide a big boost for the SuperStation. We entered into an agreement through which TBS became Cousteau's television partner. Not only did Cousteau go on to produce some terrific shows for us, I became good friends with him and his son Jean-Michel. One of my most memorable experiences was spending a week on the *Calypso* with my two youngest sons, during the shooting of a seven-hour series on the Amazon. I was proud to underwrite these prestigious shows and being around the Cousteaus made me want to work that much harder to use my influence to expose more people to the important issues facing our planet.

Another important influence on me was a woman named J. J. Ebaugh, whom I met in Newport at the 1980 America's Cup. At that time, J. J. was dating a crewmember of one of the other boats but later we began seeing each other. J. J. was very bright—her father was a medical doctor and professor—and she had a real zest for life and for learning. She also had her pilot's license, and around this time I bought my first small, single engine plane and J. J. became my pilot. She was passionate about issues like world population, the environment, and arms control, and we discussed these and other important matters whenever we were together. On occasion, I'd sit in the co-pilot's seat while she flew the plane and we would discuss the important issues of the day. Over a very short period of time I developed relationships with people like Carl Sagan, Audubon Society head Russell Peterson, Lester Brown of Worldwatch, and former President Jimmy Carter. Going back to my high school debate days, I've enjoyed discussing topics with people who don't necessarily share my opinions. While getting to know these people, I often engaged them in interesting and stimulating conversations.

Being exposed to these big thinkers pushed me to consider how I might use our company's cable channels to improve the world, but there was not enough of an audience or advertiser base to fund this kind of programming. Then I thought, What if we put together a nonprofit entity, populated its board with a diverse group of world leaders, thinkers, and advocates, and produced programs paid for by the group's own fund-raising efforts? We could then air the shows on TBS and expose them to our growing audience. In addition to producing some interesting and provocative programs, gathering such a body of people might stimulate discussion and action on issues that could make for a better world.

I decided to create a foundation and named it the Better World Society. We announced the formation of this organization at a New York press conference in 1985 and I was able to attract an incredible board of directors from around the globe. We hired Thomas Belford as our executive director and our first four board members were myself, Jean-Michel Cousteau, Russell Peterson, and Lester Brown. I wanted to be sure that we built a group that had a majority of members from outside the United States, and in addition to former President Carter, we attracted three other former heads of state—President Obesanjo from Nigeria, Gro Harlem Brundtland of Norway, and Rodrigo Carazo of Costa Rica. Also joining the board were Dr. Georgi Arbatov from the Soviet Union, Dr. M. S. Swaminathan of India, Chinese government official Zhou Boping, Yasushi Akashi from Japan, former U.N. High Commissioner for Refugees Prince Sadruddin Aga Khan from Pakistan, and from the United States, former Secretary-General of International Planned Parenthood Julia Henderson.

Our statement of purpose was straightforward:

The Better World Society is an international nonprofit membership organization dedicated to fostering individual awareness of those global issues which

bear directly on the sustainability of human and other life on Earth. Beyond awareness, the Society seeks to instill in citizens of all nations a sense of common responsibility for the fate of life on Earth. As well as an understanding of the constructive actions we can take, individually and in concert, to redirect our nations toward sustainable progress and world peace. From this perspective, the society will focus chiefly on the issues of nuclear arms control and reduction, population stabilization, stewardship of the Earth's environment, efficient use of its resources, and fulfillment of the basic human needs of the world's peoples.

Meeting with these people was an incredible experience. I came to see those from other countries not as "foreigners," but as fellow citizens of the planet. I began to view the word "foreign" as pejorative and created a rule within Turner Broadcasting that the word could not be used either on air or in conversation around the office. Instead, the word "international" was to be

used, and while we did run into some occasions where the term was unavoidable,
as in the case of certain titles, like "Secretary of Foreign Affairs" or a named prize
like "Best Foreign Film," this was a rule we
took seriously and I think it helped our employees think about the world differently.
(One less serious moment came during a
Braves telecast shortly after I issued this
policy. One of our announcers, Skip Caray,
described a player stepping out of the bat-
ter's box to "remove an international object
from his eye." Most of our audience must
have wondered what he was talking about,
but Turner employees who were watching
got a chuckle.)

While the Better World Society featured
an incredible team and we financed and
aired some great programs, raising the
money every year took a lot of work, mostly
for me, and not once did we ever reach
our budget. I can remember flying to Chicago or New York to meet with wealthy
individuals or foundations, making our presentation, then flying back to Atlanta and
getting a check two weeks later for $1,000.
While this fund-raising was frustrating, the
intellectual stimulation we received from

the board was tremendous and this experience had a profound impact on me. Having spent my career using war analogies to develop business strategies and with military leaders as my heroes, I began to think more about people who made peace their life's objective. For many years, I had the busts of Horatio Nelson and Alexander the Great in my office and I decided to replace them with busts of Gandhi and Martin Luther King. My father had raised me with a "my country right or wrong" mentality. But as I thought through issues with more of an open mind, I began to question assumptions that I took for granted when I was growing up.

When we dissolved the Better World Society after six years of operations, I remember gritting my teeth and thinking to myself that the next time I do something like this, I'll have made enough of my own money that I won't have to be a fund-raiser. In the meantime, there was plenty of work to do if I was ever going to make that happen.

18

The Goodwill Games

I made my first trip to the Soviet Union early in 1984. I wanted CNN to become a global business and after my Cuba trip, I was hopeful that we could do business in the Soviet Union. When the driver who picked up our group at the Moscow airport drove us by a beautiful new facility, he explained, sadly, that it had been built specifically for the 1980 Olympics, the Games that had been boycotted by the United States in protest of the Soviet Union's war in Afghanistan. Throughout our visit it seemed like everywhere we went there was another reminder of those

Olympics and the more I saw, the sadder I was that our athletes had not been able to participate. Adding to my disappointment was the fact that the Soviets were thinking about retaliating by staying home during the 1984 Olympics later that summer in Los Angeles.

The situation was depressing. There was already so much distrust and so little communication between our two countries, and now both sides were deciding that they couldn't join each other and the rest of the world for an athletic competition. My first exposure to people from other countries was through sailing, and it occurred to me that elite athletes have more opportunities to associate with their peers from around the globe than just about anyone. When they do, despite the competition they usually get along. It's easy to hate people you don't know, but it's hard to hate people once you get to know them and recognize how much you have in common. The Russian people were more like us than they were different—they loved their families, they had pets, they enjoyed ballet and classical music, and they liked having a drink of vodka with their friends. This isn't to say that our political differences weren't significant—they were—but I felt that we'd never bridge these differences by simply shutting down communication and avoiding international gatherings like the Olympics.

After the Soviets made it official that they would retaliate with their boycott of the Los Angeles Games, I had an idea. Why not create a competition outside the Olympics that would allow American and Soviet athletes to compete? By 1986, it would be ten years since summer athletes from the two superpowers had competed head-to-head and I felt they would be eager for the opportunity. By this time, I had hired Bob Wussler from CBS, where he'd had experience producing large-scale sporting events for television. When I explained to Bob my idea, he grasped it immediately, and since he knew that I wanted this event to help bring our two countries closer together, we decided to call them the Goodwill Games. We loved this name, and though the original idea was to restrict the competition just to the United

States and the Soviet Union, as we thought about it, we decided to make these games as much like the Olympics as possible and to extend invitations to the best athletes from all over the world. Soviet officials embraced the idea and agreed to host the games in Moscow. We were off and running on another new and massive undertaking.

To make it work, we had to convince the various countries to send their teams, and at first the U.S. federations struggled with their decision. Their athletes were eager to participate and it became almost impossible for them to say no. For sports that don't have professional leagues (like track and field and gymnastics) the Olympic Games were the pinnacle, and since the boycotts had kept these athletes on the sidelines, they were eager to go to Moscow. Once the U.S. federations agreed to send teams to a Soviet-hosted event, the other countries followed. (We did have one disappointment. Just prior to the games Defense Secretary Caspar Weinberger told the handful of American athletes who were members of the U.S. military that they would not be allowed to participate.) The games would be held in the summer of '86 and we would televise them on TBS SuperStation. We negotiated deals with overseas networks to help us extend our reach and sell more advertising. To differentiate the Goodwill Games from the Olympics, we did away with preliminary heats wherever possible, making more of the competitions a final contest for the medal. I didn't get involved in the planning of athletic competitions other than making sure that yachting was included, as I never would have been able to live it down in the sailing community if it hadn't been! Ultimately, more than three thousand athletes from seventy-nine countries competed in eighteen different sports.

It was a couple of days before the Goodwill Games began that I first met Mikhail Gorbachev. Georgi Arbatov, my friend from the Better World Society board, set up the meeting and it was very heartening. Gorbachev expressed his hope that American leadership would focus on building an environment where our young people would be able to grow up to be friendly,

cooperative, and more tolerant of other
countries' political systems. He said it
was time to put the arms race behind us
and to move on to spend our time and
energy more productively. I encouraged
him to be patient with us because we had
a military-industrial complex with a vested
interest in continuing the arms race and a
free, privately owned media that also op-
erates in its own best interest. I told him
that while President Reagan might be inclined, it would be difficult for him to take
the lead in de-escalating the arms race
and that he—Gorbachev—was in a much
better position to make the first moves.
By doing that, Gorbachev might get the
ball rolling, bring an end to the Cold War,
and maybe even win the Nobel Peace
Prize in the process. It was a terrific meeting that would mark the beginning of a
lifelong friendship.

Going to Moscow also gave me a chance
to see my oldest son, Teddy. When he
graduated from The Citadel the previous
summer I encouraged him to consider
working at the CNN bureau in Moscow.

_____ A TED STORY _____

"A Great Experience"
—Teddy Turner

Dad was always very plain with all of us: "After graduation you have two weeks and your stuff better be out of my house." He was never into handouts. When I was in college I had a $25 a week allowance and I was traveling all over the country with The Citadel sailing team on an annual budget of less than $1,500. I learned how to live very frugally, thanks to Dad.

When I came home for Christmas my senior year he asked me what I wanted to do, and I said, "Well, I guess I'd like to come work for you." That's what I had always done. In addition to helping out with his sailing crew, when I was twelve I was one of the last family members to work for the outdoor advertising company before it was sold, and later I had summer jobs at CNN.

He said, "What area of the business would you like to work in?"

I told him I'd enjoyed my summers at CNN and thought that was really where the future of the company was going to be. When he asked me what kind of work I wanted to do, I said, "Well, I'm not an in-the-front-of-the-camera guy. I've got a great face for radio so I'd rather work behind the camera or in the studio." Dad thought that sounded great but when he asked me where I wanted to be located, it threw me for a loop because I'd always assumed it would be Atlanta. He explained that we really only packaged the news in Atlanta; it wasn't really "made" there. "There are only two places in the world at this time where real news is made," he said, "and that's Washington, D.C., and Moscow. As far as politics and the shape of world power go, those are the two cities."

I had never thought about it like that and since I figured I could go to D.C. anytime, I decided that Moscow would be a lot more interesting. So when I went back to school I tried to take Russian; they did have a small

Russian department at The Citadel, but you couldn't take 101 in the second semester, so right after I graduated I moved to D.C. and took three months of intensive language study there.

Gorbachev came into power the spring of 1985 and when I got to Moscow in September of 1985 the words "perestroika" and "glasnost" hadn't really come out yet. The timing couldn't have been better. I went to Afghanistan a couple times as the war there was winding down. Chernobyl blew up while I was in Russia so I went to Kiev a lot. We went down to a Soviet nuclear test site because there were big test ban things going on, and I was there in Moscow for the first Goodwill Games. It was a great experience and I really was able to do some pretty amazing things

---

By the time the Goodwill Games began, it was clear that they would not be a financial success, but seeing the athletes come together from around the globe I was convinced we were doing something worthwhile. The Soviet organizers put a lot of effort into the opening ceremonies and they were beautiful and moving. And Gorbachev's decision to attend in person added a lot of weight and credibility to the event. There were also many special moments throughout the competition. At the close of the swimming events, the American co-captains—one man and one woman—gave gifts to their Soviet counterparts and spoke brief words of peace that were translated into Russian over the loudspeakers. When I looked around the arena I didn't see a dry eye. Whenever medals were handed out to Americans or Soviets it was remarkable to see athletes from these two rival nations standing at attention and showing respect while the other country's national anthem was played. At the rowing venue, the Soviet army band of about one hundred musicians played the anthems live. Given the troubled state of our relations at the time, seeing and hearing them play "The Star-Spangled Banner" was incredible. At one point, after the eight-oared shells competition, four Soviets got into the American boat and four

from the U.S. team got into the Soviet boat
and they rowed back and forth together.

At the closing ceremonies, I was given
an opportunity to address the crowd and
the audience watching on Soviet television. The games were heavily viewed in
the Soviet Union and I believe that about a
third of their television households were
tuned in that night. Given the tenor of the
times, it was pretty surprising that they
would let me address such a mass audience live—for all they knew I could have
grabbed the mike and said, "Down with
communism!" but they let me go on without even asking what I had planned to say.
I used the opportunity to thank our gracious hosts and to express my hope that
these events might have helped advance
the cause of peace around the world. The
Goodwill Games really did live up to their
name.

We lost more than $25 million on those
initial Goodwill Games. Even though we had
the same events and so many of the same
athletes, these weren't the true Olympics
and in the United States we simply couldn't
draw anywhere near the audience that
NBC had for the Olympics. Undeterred,

we began planning for the next edition of the Goodwill Games, to be held in the United States. Seattle hosted the games in 1990 and did a great job, but by then the Soviets and Americans had both participated in the 1988 Olympics in South Korea, so boycotts were over. In '94, the Russian city of St. Petersburg served as our host and while the games continued to attract great athletes, they failed to deliver a large TV audience in the United States. (One of my personal highlights of the St. Petersburg games was meeting my greeter at the airport. The mayor of St. Petersburg had sent his deputy to pick me up and escort us to dinner. His name was Vladimir Putin. He told us that his wife had just been hospitalized after a serious automobile accident. I said, "Don't have dinner with us. Go home to your wife!" Putin was reluctant because entertaining us was his job but I talked him into going to the hospital. Years later, he told me he'd never forgotten that kindness.

We held two more summer games—1998 in New York City and 2001 in Brisbane, Australia, and in 2000, Lake Placid, New York, hosted the first and only Winter

Goodwill Games. By the time of the Brisbane games I was no longer calling the
shots at Turner Broadcasting and since
the Goodwill Games continued to lose
money, Time Warner decided that they
would be discontinued. After those many
events, our total losses on the games were
more than $100 million, but it's my belief
that these games, especially the initial
games in 1986, played a major role in helping thaw relations between the United States
and the Soviet Union and contributed to the
Cold War's peaceful conclusion.

The Goodwill Games may have lost
some money, but in my mind, they were an
investment toward peace that was worth
every penny.

19

CBS

I was learning very quickly that in television it was better to be big than to be small. The business was a lot like Monopoly, and to be the winner you had to own multiple properties around the board. By 1984 the SuperStation, CNN, and Headline News were growing into solid businesses but it was still a struggle for a company the size of Turner to battle with the traditional Big Three broadcasters for audience and advertising dollars. I was sure that the best way to compete would be to have a broadcast network and the cable networks under the same ownership.

The most logical move would have been for the Big Three broadcasters to diversify into cable. For the first time in their history, they faced competition from outside their ranks and while the individual audiences for cable channels were small, taken together they were gaining meaningful market share. But to my continued amazement, even after missing the twenty-four-hour news opportunity, the networks stayed on the sidelines and watched the launch of other cable channels like Discovery, USA, MTV, and Nickelodeon. They were worrying more about the previous night's ratings than the long-term future of their business. (ABC was a slight exception. They didn't create ESPN but they did acquire a minority position and exercised their option to purchase a majority stake years later when the channel was clearly a winner.)

A merger of Turner Broadcasting with a Big Three network made a lot of sense. First of all, there would be tremendous savings in news. CNN had built bureaus all over the world and so had the news divisions of ABC, NBC, and CBS. With a merger, consolidating facilities would result in significant savings, and when these were realized, spending could increase elsewhere. While the broadcast-only networks had four hours a day of news to program, we would have the forty-eight hours on cable (twenty-four hours for both CNN and Headline News). With fifty-two hours against which to amortize the costs, our company would leave the competition in the dust.

On the entertainment side, a network combined with the SuperStation could do a better job of maximizing the value of its prime-time entertainment programming. The networks had been so dominant that antitrust rules were created to prohibit them from being vertically integrated and producing this programming themselves. Instead, they licensed the shows from the Hollywood studios and generally paid for the rights to air each one just twice a year. A network like CBS would lease a show like *M*A*S*H* and spend money to build it into a hit, only to have the show's owner—in this case, 20th Century Fox—sell its reruns to local stations or cable channels. CBS didn't make a dime from this "off-network" syndication and in some cases the shows were sold to local affiliates of rival networks.

But if CBS and the SuperStation were part of the same company, we could negotiate a comprehensive corporate deal with Fox. After CBS built a show into a hit, TBS would have the option to air the syndicated episodes. By participating in both stages we could reap more value. Our leverage with Hollywood would be improved, and with the same sales force selling shows like M*A*S*H on the network and the cable channel, we could strike better deals with advertisers. As a bigger, more efficient company than our network rivals, we could channel our higher profits into bigger bids on high-profile sports rights like the NFL and the Olympics. The list of advantages was long and I was eager to explain my vision to the networks. I was confident that at least one might want to do a deal and join us.

But in the early 1980s, the Big Three networks were insular and didn't welcome an outsider trying to crash their party. In many ways, they behaved like a cartel. The headquarters of ABC, NBC, and CBS were all within two blocks of each other in midtown Manhattan. All three were profitable. They paid their executives well and when one of them was fired he was usually picked up by one of the competitors. The networks all signed the same contracts with their technical unions, and each one paid roughly the same prices to Hollywood studios for programming.

Relative to Turner Broadcasting, the networks were huge. In 1984, our revenues were just over $280 million while CBS's were nearly $5 *billion*. We managed to turn a profit of just $10 million that year. (CNN and Headline News were growing but still losing a little money—the Super-Station was driving our results with $177 million in revenue and $66 million in profits.) Wall Street recognized that we were improving and now that we were turning the corner to profitability our stock often traded at high multiples. Still, our market capitalization was in the range of several hundred million dollars, while the networks were all worth several billion.

Each of my meetings with the networks took place in their large, well-appointed offices in Manhattan. These were a far cry from what we were used to in Atlanta. At ABC, I met with Fred Pierce, who had recently been made that company's president. He told me that he had worked his way up through the ranks for twenty-five years and he wouldn't take a chance on losing control. His opposition wasn't based on whether it made sense for his company or its shareholders but rather because it might have a negative impact on himself.

I had hoped to speak with RCA's chairman, Thornton Bradshaw, regarding NBC but I was instead handed off to Robert Mulholland, the network's chief operating officer. He understood the synergies I outlined and to illustrate one of my points, described NBC's deal for the hit miniseries *Shogun*. He said that they purchased the right for three airings but only had time in their schedule for two. I said, "That's a perfect example, Bob. If we were part of the same company, we'd take that third run on the SuperStation and generate another million dollars in ad revenue without spending a penny more for the program!" As obvious as these opportunities were, Mulholland still told me to forget it. "RCA will never go for a merger with you," he confided. "They just don't take those kinds of risks."

That left CBS, whose president was Tom Wyman. He was a likable guy and our discussions were cordial. He said he admired what we were doing with CNN and the SuperStation and he seemed to be enthusiastic about the benefits of a combination between our two companies— enough so that he said he would discuss the idea with his executive committee.

I left Tom's office feeling upbeat but a few weeks later he called to let me know that the CBS executive committee had rejected the idea. I was never told exactly what their concerns were but I'm sure my case wasn't helped when *The New York Times* quoted me saying some things about William Paley, CBS's highly respected founder. They ran a piece in which I took the networks to task for all the sleazy programming and I specifically condemned Paley for letting the "Tiffany Network's" standards drop so far. Unfortunately, I accentuated my point by saying that Paley had turned CBS into a "whorehouse." I still tend to speak my mind, but back then I really used to get carried away, and I'm sure this exaggerated analogy didn't help my chances with CBS's executive committee.

For their various reasons, all three networks turned me down. But I refused to let the idea of a network-Turner merger die. If they wouldn't entertain a friendly deal, I'd have to find another way. I'd been an operator my entire career and didn't know much about unfriendly takeovers but during that time—it was now the fall of 1984—they were happening left and right. I always try to learn from the best, and the most prominent guy in the world of takeovers then was T. Boone Pickens. We hadn't met but when I called him he appreciated my vision, and agreed to a meeting.

My corporate financial people and I flew to New York to meet secretly with Pickens at a suite in the Helmsley Hotel. He was tall and thin with bright eyes. He was also very smart and engaging and we got along quite well. His experience was largely in the oil business but he grasped the potential of our plan right away. He said he'd think about it and get back to me.

About a week later Pickens called and said he wanted to move forward and that RCA should be our primary target. He asked me to fly down to his winter vacation home in Florida for another private meeting to work through the details. During these discussions, Pickens explained his belief that RCA's assets were significantly undervalued, and that after an acquisition he could make money selling their nonbroadcast assets (they still owned Hertz Rent A Car, for example) at a profit. Turner Broadcasting would end up with the NBC network, their owned-and-operated stations, and RCA's satellite business. (Given my history of struggles with transponder access, I really liked the idea of owning my own satellite company.)

Pickens and I agreed that we would work out the mechanics of our takeover strategy and line up the money. He had connections with Drexel Burnham, one of Wall Street's top investment banks at that time, Carl Icahn, and others, and in those days these guys would get together and go after companies aggressively. My role would be to help him put a value on the television properties and to use my experience and contacts in Washington to sort out the broadcast regulatory issues that this deal would present. It was a promising start but, unfortunately, after a handful of discussions over the course of the next few weeks, Pickens got tied up in a take-over bid for Unocal and told me that he just didn't have the time or resources to simultaneously pursue RCA. I was disap-pointed, but I learned a lot from the pro-cess and remained determined to keep trying.

Around this time a nonprofit organiza-tion called Fairness in Media announced its intention to try an unfriendly acquisition of CBS. The group included North Caro-lina senator Jesse Helms and they said they were frustrated with what they felt was a liberal bias at CBS News. They encour-aged all their members, as well as other conservatives around the country, to pur-chase CBS stock with the goal of building a large enough ownership stake to dictate policy. (At one point, when asked why he wanted control of CBS, Helms responded simply, "So I can be Dan Rather's boss.")

I had met Senator Helms before and he was happy to see me again to explore the possibility of working together. At CNN we were trying to air the news in an unbiased fashion and develop a good reputation with people on both sides of the aisle. (Incidentally, I must really have kept people guessing about my political views in those days. The Fairness in Media discussions coincided with the planning stages for the first Goodwill Games, and on one of my trips to Washington I went straight from Jesse Helms's office to the Soviet embassy!)

While Helms was most concerned about network news content, I told him that I really wanted to do something about all the sleazy, violent entertainment programming that they ran. These shows drew a large audience and that's all they cared about. (I remember saying in a speech one time that 70 percent of network programming was trash, and at the cocktail party afterward, a network programming person confronted me about it. I asked him what percentage he would put on it and he said 50 percent. I said, "Well, when I went to school, 50 percent was a failing grade, so based on even your own estimates, you guys get an F." Another network person once said to me, "You know, Turner, you've criticized us network executives for our sleazy programming but I want you to know that in our personal lives, most of us are very upstanding, fine family people." I told him, "That's what the Nazis said at Nuremburg!")

I explained to Helms that it would be impractical to walk in and cancel all these shows of questionable taste. Instead, my idea was to keep the shows, but change their tone. One of CBS's big hits back then was *The Dukes of Hazzard,* a show in which the Duke brothers were always driving their cars like maniacs and walking away from crashes like nothing happened. My idea was to have an episode where one of the guys hits a telephone pole and is almost killed, and when he's in the hospital he decides it's time to make a change. Instead of driving the sheriff and the mayor crazy, he and his brother decide to run for mayor and sheriff and turn the town around. I'd have all the bad guys and negative role models in all the shows change their ways and become good guys!

On *Dallas,* another popular CBS show, the lead character, JR, was a conniving, womanizing oil tycoon. I was tired of seeing businesspeople portrayed as evil money-grubbers and thought it would be great if JR woke up one morning and decided to turn his life around—to become an honest business owner and a faithful family man. To some, my stance may have been surprising coming from someone who was himself struggling in a second marriage, but I always believed that television is such a powerful medium that broadcasters have a responsibility to air programs that featured positive role models.

I think Senator Helms liked what I had to say but after a couple of meetings I decided a partnership with him wouldn't work. Friends of mine in Washington, including Senator Tim Wirth, cautioned me against becoming too closely aligned with someone as controversial and polarizing as Helms, especially given my involvement with CNN. CBS eventually sued Fairness in Media, claiming that their activities in pursuit of CBS were in violation of laws restricting the political and business activities of nonprofit organizations. While I didn't follow through with Helms, our discussions only heightened my interest in CBS, and I concentrated on figuring out a way to pursue the network on my own.

In the midst of this activity—March of

1985—came the surprising announcement that ABC was being acquired by Capital Cities Communications. This was big news. At $3.5 billion it was the largest non-oil merger in U.S. history and the deal marked the first time that ownership of a major broadcast network had changed hands. Capital Cities was a much smaller company than ABC and unlike the deals I was contemplating, this merger was friendly. Several important ABC affiliates were owned by Capital Cities and the companies were longtime partners. Also, rather than having to resort to any exotic financing, Capital Cities' management secured $500 million of the cash that they needed to complete the deal from investor Warren Buffett. (Incidentally, Fred Pierce, the executive with concerns about losing his position after a merger with Turner, was removed from his post after their deal with Capital Cities closed.)

I needed to act quickly. ABC was off the market and speculation was rampant that NBC, a subsidiary of RCA, and CBS were prime targets for takeovers. RCA was too big for me to take on and it's practically impossible to make a hostile bid for a subsidiary. That left CBS but I was in a tough spot—on my own without big money behind me. I went to Hope Plantation to take some long walks and formulate a plan. I had come to know Drexel Burnham's Michael Milken and months before he had spoken to me about using high-yield "junk" bonds to raise money for a run at a network. On one of my walks, a new thought occurred to me—what if we offered the junk bonds directly to CBS shareholders? These instruments were very much in fashion but no one had ever tried swapping them directly to shareholders. This would definitely be a unique approach but I thought it might work.

I would need an investment bank to put this all together so I met with the management at Robinson-Humphrey in Atlanta, the same firm that represented Jack Rice when I bought Channel 17. They were also a subsidiary of American Express and I knew the company's CEO, Jim Robinson, when he lived in Atlanta and I used to try and sell him billboard space. This would be a major acquisition—probably in the $5–$6 billion dollar range, and the bank fees would be substantial.

When the Robinson-Humphrey people presented the proposal to Shearson Lehman, the division of American Express in New York that was best suited for a deal of this magnitude, they were interested. We paid them a million-dollar retainer and after an intense few weeks working on a plan they invited me down to their executive committee meeting in Boca Raton, Florida. I had hoped that we would use these meetings to map out our strategy and the next steps, but instead I was kept waiting outside the discussions, only to be told they had ultimately decided to pass on working with us. At least they returned our million-dollar check.

Shortly before this Florida meeting, word got out that Shearson was working with us. We heard that the story was leaked on purpose. I soon realized that the bankers who turned us down were not staying away from this deal for financial reasons. Instead, they feared the strength of CBS's news division, and particularly the clout of the show *60 Minutes*. The takeover business was controversial then and none of these guys wanted to back a hostile bid for CBS only to find Mike Wallace and a camera crew knocking on their door to do an investigative piece on *their* company. It was eye-opening for me to see the powerful influence the networks had.

Eventually, E. F. Hutton agreed to work with us and we began an intense period of mapping out a deal. This was no simple matter—we had to not only work out the mechanics of our debt offer but also sort through the complicated regulatory issues our acquisition would face. In addition to the usual issues related to the FCC approving station license transfers, in many markets CBS owned television and radio. The FCC allowed them to maintain this cross-ownership even after the laws were established that outlawed the practice. While CBS had been given this grandfather clause, if and when the company ever changed ownership, the buyer would have to sell either the radio or the television stations in these markets to come into compliance.

In addition to a financial adviser, we needed extensive legal help, and when word got out that we were working with E. F. Hutton and moving forward with a bid, CBS hired numerous New York law firms that specialized in takeovers, making it practically impossible for those firms to work with us. Ultimately, we were able to hire a firm in Los Angeles named Latham & Watkins and they did a good job.

It was complicated but stimulating, and by the middle of April 1985, we were prepared to announce our bid. Our offer valued CBS shares at more than $175. As recently as February, CBS stock had been trading around $75 per share but after Capital Cities bought ABC at a premium, CBS's price topped $100. In sum, we were offering CBS shareholders the opportunity to sell their CBS stock to Turner Broadcasting in exchange for high-yield bonds. While CBS shares had provided them with dividends of around $3, our notes would have paid close to $22 annually. We would pay these notes off using the company's operating profits and also through the sale of the CBS record division, which was worth about a billion dollars, and the book publishing division (Simon & Schuster), which was worth about $500 million.

It was an intriguing deal that had a lot going for it, but one thing it didn't have was cash. Prior to my proposal getting off the ground, Ivan Boesky, a prominent arbitrageur at that time, purchased 8.7 percent of CBS's stock for $240 million. I tried to enlist him in our cause but it was too late—with all the speculation swirling around CBS he stood to make a handsome profit just by sitting on his shares. I also spoke with Bill Simon, a well-respected and wealthy former secretary of the treasury, and Bill McGowan, the chairman of MCI. Simon was an on-air contributor to CNN at the time and MCI had been one of our most supportive advertisers. I was hoping that they would make a major investment in the deal, but after some promising conversations, they both passed.

After working with Fairness in Media, hiring E. F. Hutton, and all the speculation around which network would sell next and to whom, by the time I came to New York to announce our formal offer, the press attention was tremendous. I stayed at the Waldorf Towers (I liked it there because they were one of the first hotels to get cable and I could watch CNN and the Super-Station), and so many reporters were hanging out in the lobby that I used the service elevator to sneak in and out. Eventually though, they figured out which floor I was on and I remember looking out through the peephole of my door one morning and seeing that there were reporters camped out in the hall outside my room. When I made the twelve-block walk from our lawyers' offices to the Park Lane Hotel where our press conference was set up, I was surrounded the entire way by a pack of reporters. When I walked into the hotel ballroom, so many flashbulbs went off you would have thought it was a Hollywood premiere.

The press coverage was tremendous. It was a crazy and chaotic time and I enjoyed it. Throughout the buildup to the deal, some of my own executives tried to talk me out of all this activity, saying it was too costly and that it wouldn't work. Deep down, I knew our bid was a long shot but so was just about everything else in my career. Between legal and banking fees, the whole venture would cost us about $20 million, but the way I saw it, we were getting at least that much value back in publicity. And in the process, we were tying one of our major competitors in knots trying to fend us off.

CBS, of course, did everything they could to kill our deal. Their initial comments were the ones we expected—they had no interest in selling the company, our bid was too low, and there was no cash in it. But when we refused to go away, they stepped up their efforts, including personal attacks against me. To make a case that I was unfit to run a broadcast network, they found various groups to talk about comments I had made in the past that they claimed were disparaging of various ethnic or religious groups. They even hired a private investigator to follow me. I admit that I was different from the executives running CBS, but there was nothing in my private life that they could hold against me. Besides, given the low quality of so much of their own programming, they were in no position to be making judgments about other people's character.

CBS also tried making appeals in Washington. Tom Wyman was a friend of Missouri senator Tom Eagleton from their college days together at Amherst and he was able to convince him to try to help him out. Unfortunately for CBS, I also knew a lot of senators and when Wyman and I went to Washington to testify at hearings I had a sympathetic audience and more than held my own. CBS also tried to work with the legislature in the state of New York to have them introduce new laws banning hostile takeovers. Fortunately, I had met Governor Mario Cuomo through CNN and was able to discuss the matter with him. He told me that given all the investment banking activity in New York, he was not inclined to change the laws but said, "If you buy CBS and move the company to Atlanta, I'm going to look pretty foolish!" I made it clear to him that I had no intention of taking the company out of Manhattan and that sealed his support.

The months following our April announcement continued to be tumultuous. Every time CBS made a move or a claim against us, we would try to counter. At one point, they were reported to have worked with General Electric on a "friendly" merger but that fell through. (Incidentally, GE would go on to buy RCA and thereby own the NBC network the following year.) As the pressure continued into July, CBS wound up having to resort to what is known as a poison pill to keep our proposal from getting to their shareholders: they agreed to take on significant debt and to spend almost $1 billion to buy back up to 21 percent of their company's stock, valuing their shares about $150. This deal would take CBS debts to levels that our proposal couldn't support. The final nail in the coffin was that these new securities that they would sell to CBS shareholders included covenants that put a ceiling on the amount of leverage the company could take on.

While we made some counterclaims and talked about the possibility of fighting on, everyone now knew that we no longer had a reasonable shot at getting CBS. But what they didn't know was that I had spent the past few weeks discussing an entirely different merger. MGM/UA owner Kirk Kerkorian had been following my efforts to purchase CBS and decided to give me a call. He said that he was considering selling MGM and wondered if I was interested. I was. After putting so much effort into our hostile bid for CBS, it was refreshing to deal with a willing seller. I quickly concluded that having a movie studio in the hand was better than a network in the bush.

After months of battling it out in New York, I bought an airline ticket to Los Angeles and headed west, to Hollywood.

20

MGM

In the early 1980s, about the same time that I began my exploratory meetings with the executives at the broadcast networks, I also considered combining Turner Broadcasting with one of the movie studios. As a small, independent programmer I was concerned that our access to quality entertainment product would be vulnerable. Like the networks, the SuperStation relied on Hollywood suppliers for most of our series and I could easily foresee a time when the studios, under pressure from the broadcast networks, would either hike our license fees so high that we would no longer have a profitable business or start cable networks of their own and compete with us using their own programming. If we could merge with a preexisting studio, we'd at least guarantee a steady supply of product from our partner.

My most promising discussions along these lines were with Kirk Kerkorian, who owned control of MGM/UA. Kirk was based in Los Angeles, and he was curious enough about my company to fly to Atlanta for our initial meeting. I liked him. He was an astute, clever businessman who seemed to have the Midas touch when it came to investing and trading in industries ranging from airlines to entertainment to hotels (he was one of the most visionary and successful developers of Las Vegas). Kirk understood how Turner Broadcasting would benefit from a guaranteed supply of entertainment programming and I showed him the benefits we could provide to MGM. Our combined company could create an instant advantage over our competitors by using unsold advertising inventory on our cable networks to promote MGM's new releases and home videos. Since so many people who watched the SuperStation were movie fans, it would be a particularly effective promotional platform for new MGM releases. His 50 percent stake in MGM/UA was of roughly equal value to my 80 percent of Turner Broadcasting, so I proposed that we form a 50/50 partnership and run the new company together.

I thought our initial meetings went great, but in later years Kerkorian confided that he wasn't sure what to make of me. He thought I seemed a little young (I was in my early forties, and he was in his late sixties) and others had apparently warned him that I might be a little brash and unpredictable. These concerns led him to politely pass on doing a deal at that time. It wasn't until the subsequent months—when he observed my handling of our run at CBS—that he decided that I might be someone with whom he could do business.

In late July 1985, just as CBS was formulating its poison pill provisions, Kerkorian called to tell me he had changed his mind about doing a deal with me. He said he wanted to stay in the movie business on a smaller scale and intended to keep United Artists, but all of his other assets, including MGM, were on the table. He had retained Drexel Burnham to prepare to sell the company at auction with a target date of August 6. The asking price would be $1.5 billion—nearly double what these assets were trading for on the open market—but if we submitted an offer before then, we could stop the auction and keep the deal private. We had just two weeks to make a deal and the price was high, but I decided to go for it.

I hadn't given up on CBS at this point, but I knew that it was going to be an uphill and expensive battle against a company that was determined to fight me off. Now I had the willing seller of a studio on the line. And MGM wasn't just any studio. In addition to ongoing production capacity, they also owned the largest movie library in the world, home to some of the greatest films ever made, including classic musicals like *Meet Me in St. Louis* and *Singin' in the Rain,* epics like *Doctor Zhivago,* family titles like *The Wizard of Oz,* and my all-time personal favorite, *Gone With the Wind*. In addition to the historical output of MGM and United Artists, Kerkorian also owned the RKO library (which included *Citizen*

Kane and the original *King Kong*) and all the Warner Brothers films released before 1948, including *Casablanca* and *The Maltese Falcon*. Taken together, the library controlled by MGM/UA accounted for about 35 percent of all the feature films ever made, and even though most of MGM's movies were pretty old, no other single studio had more than about 10 or 12 percent.

On top of their feature film collection, they also owned about a thousand theatrical cartoons, including MGM's *Tom and Jerry* series and Warner's pre-1948 *Looney Tunes* (such as *Bugs Bunny* and *Porky Pig*). They even controlled the rights to the TV special *How the Grinch Stole Christmas.* Other buyers might have looked at this library and placed a value based only on syndication and sales of home videos, a new and growing category but one that was driven by newer releases. But these assets were worth far more to me. The SuperStation had a huge appetite for movies and cartoons and MGM's collection would give us critical mass. I also believed that if I controlled enough programming I could launch a second entertainment channel and charge subscription fees (the SuperStation's revenues came solely from advertising, as FCC rules still did not allow us to redistribute the WTBS signal, let alone charge a fee for it). Different from MGM's other likely buyers—the other studios— Turner Broadcasting generated profits and created asset value by building networks. For us, this was truly a one-of-a-kind opportunity.

There was one other reason that I saw more value in this deal than did the other potential acquirers. Years before, I had met with a couple of entrepreneurs who were seeking investors. These two had developed a technology called "colorization" that could add color to old black and white films and television shows. I thought it was a great idea. By this time, everyone had color TVs and programming in color was simply better. I passed on investing at that time, explaining that while we ran a lot of black and white programming, we didn't own any of it. Instead, I suggested they speak to people at MGM and the other studios with old libraries. But I followed their progress in the trades in subsequent months and figured that if we ever controlled a library like MGM's, we could create value by colorizing the old black and white movies.

This was a great opportunity and I didn't haggle about the price. Instead, I focused on the terms and tried to get the deal done quickly. I needed a banker, and the only firm that could raise this much money for us this quickly was Drexel Burnham. As I noted, I had gotten to know Michael Milken well and had been a keynote speaker at one of the gatherings that he regularly put together in Los Angeles.

Drexel was already representing the other side, but we hired them anyway. There was potential for conflict but I trusted Michael and, besides, Turner Broadcasting and MGM/UA executives would deal directly with each other on the broader deal terms while Milken and his team would figure out the mechanics of the financing. It's hard to imagine this kind of scenario taking place today but in the mid-1980s this was in keeping with the times. Unconventional deals were fairly common. I guess it's pretty clear I never had any issue with doing the unconventional.

So, after months of exhausting work on

trying to take over CBS, I ordered our team to do an about-face and now focus its energies on MGM. Bill Bevins, my top financial person, and George Vandeman, our legal counsel, whom we had hired to help us with CBS, led the team that went to Los Angeles and worked around the clock to hammer out the details. Everyone put in a tremendous effort and on August 6—just under the wire—we signed a purchase agreement. The deal was complicated. Turner Broadcasting would acquire MGM/UA for $1.4 billion, then immediately sell United Artists back to Kerkorian, for $480 million. This would have brought our overall acquisition costs below $1 billion but we also assumed $700 million worth of MGM debt, pushing our total tab to roughly $1.6 billion. We planned to work out the remaining details and get shareholder and board approvals to close the deal by the spring of 1986.

I was elated. We had reached an agreement to buy one of the premier studios and the world's greatest film library, but the dose of reality was that we still weren't sure how we were going to pay for it. We had been prepared to take on significantly

Posing for our ad campaign, "I Was Cable When Cable Wasn't Cool."

With Fidel Castro, on my first visit to Cuba.

With Jacques
Cousteau.

My first meeting
with Mikhail
Gorbachev, just
prior to the start of
the 1986 Goodwill
Games. Bob
Wussler is seated
to my right and
Georgi Arbatov is
to Gorbachev's
left.

Standing by
the entrance to
MGM in 1986,
during the brief
period that I
owned the
working studio.

With my family in my office, sometime in the 1980s. From left to right: Rhett, Beau, Janie, me, Jennie, Laura, and Teddy.

With Jimmy Brown at Avalon.

Being named TIME Magazine's "Man of the Year" capped off an eventful 1991.

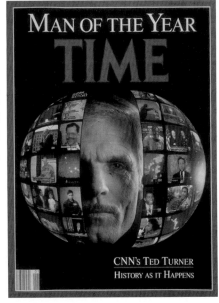

My mom, in her later years, with a picture of me.

Jane Fonda and me, relaxing with Rosalynn and President Carter, and Tom and Ann Cousins.

My favorite picture of Jane and me, taken at the Flying D.

On location at the *Gettysburg* shoot, with director Ron Maxwell.

Enjoying a Braves playoff game with Jane and our other guests.

After winning the 1995 World Series. The trophy is heavier than it looks!

With Jerry Levin, announcing our merger in 1996.

Mikhail Gorbachev with my old friend Harry the Magpie at the Flying D.

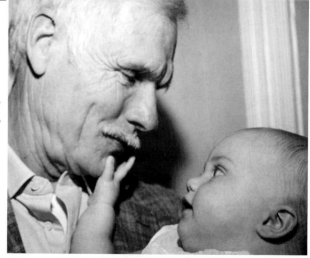

With my granddaughter Riley.

In 2001 the United States was still struggling to pay down its full debt to the United Nations, so I presented this check for more than $31 million to John Negroponte, to the delight of UN Secretary-General Kofi Annan.

This picture was taken after the AOL merger had been announced but prior to my being pushed aside. From left to right: Bob Pittman, Terry McGuirk, Jerry Levin, Dick Parsons, me, and Steve Case.

George W. McKerrow Jr. is my operating partner running Ted's Montana Grill.

A picture of me with the heads of three of my philanthropic organizations. From left to right: Sen. Timothy E. Wirth of the UN Foundation, me, the Turner Foundation's Mike Finley, and Sen. Sam Nunn of the Nuclear Threat Initiative.

Warren Buffett has been a great supporter of the Nuclear Threat Initiative, but here I tried to steal his entire wallet!

Nothing relaxes me more than a good day on a trout stream.

more debt to acquire CBS, but that company had tremendous cash flow that we felt we could immediately improve. MGM was different. We didn't have overlapping operations between our companies, and given the extremely unpredictable nature of the movie business, their profits were usually low during good years and nonexistent in bad ones. Adding our junk bond debt to the obligations already on MGM and Turner Broadcasting's books, our total borrowings were going to run to about $2 billion.

You could say we had a tiger—or maybe Leo the Lion—by the tail, and the weeks and months following our purchase would be among the most stressful, tumultuous, and exciting of my entire career. I remember flying out to Los Angeles for meetings at the studio shortly after the deal was announced. The MGM people had offered to send a car to meet me at LAX but when I saw how much they paid their drivers, I thought that was crazy so I rented a car instead. If you've ever driven a car around Los Angeles, you know how easy it is to get lost and that's what happened to me when I tried to drive to the MGM offices in

Culver City. I hate being late (my father always said, "You can't always be right, son, but you can always be on time"), and the more turned around I got the more frustrated I became. Finally, I got close enough to be able to see the MGM sign on the building in the distance. When I turned down the next street I was only a couple of blocks away, but I was going the wrong way down a one-way street and a policeman pulled me over. I apologized and said, "I'm sorry, officer, but I'm running late for a meeting at MGM." When he asked me what business I had at the studio, I answered, "Well, I bought it last week!" He let me go with just a warning.

━━━━━━━ A TED STORY ━━━━━━━

"I Bet You All Think That I'm Crazy"
—Roger Mayer

(IN 1985, ROGER MAYER WAS EXECUTIVE
VICE PRESIDENT OF ADMINISTRATION
FOR MGM.)

We had been hearing rumors about Ted Turner circling around our company and first thing one morning about ten of the top executives got a call from Frank Rothman, our chairman of the board. We were asked to come to the boardroom for a meeting at noon. We suspected that it might have something to do with Turner Broadcasting but we weren't given any details.

When we gathered around the board table, not one but two chairs were open at its head. Just as we started making nervous jokes about why that might be the door opened and in walked Frank Rothman and Ted Turner! They sat down and Rothman said very graciously, "We want you to know that Turner Broadcasting is acquiring our company and Ted really wanted to meet all of you."

After a few more opening comments Rothman turned the meeting over to Ted, and his opening line was, "I bet you all think that I'm crazy." To our credit, we all nodded yes. We knew better than anyone that MGM was a problem company and from what we had heard that Ted was contemplating paying, it seemed to all of us like a lot of money.

He continued, "You probably want to know why I bought this company and I'll tell you why. You own my two favorite movies: *The Wizard of Oz* and *Gone With the Wind*." We waited for the other shoe to drop and he then pointed to his mustache and said, "Don't you think I look a little like Rhett Butler?" Of course he does, so once again we all nodded yes! It was quite an introduction.

Shortly thereafter, in one of our first individual meetings together after the deal was made public, I told him that I wanted to walk him around the lot and casually introduce him to people. "They don't know who you are or what to expect, and it would be a great management tool for you if you would just walk around and take a tour." He told me that sounded like a great idea and asked how much time we would need. I told him it would probably take two hours; the main lot was about forty-two acres at that time and we would do a lot of walking.

We went into every department and talked to everyone we saw. People were startled by these unannounced visits and would say, "Oh, hello Mr. Turner!" and he would always respond, "Call me Ted!"

He must have said "Call me Ted" two hundred times that day. It was quite a tour. Ted seemed to be most enthusiastic and impressed by what he saw and people were very excited to meet their charismatic new owner.

After signing our deal and while we were waiting to close, MGM released a string of movies that flopped, one after another. The industry in general was having a tough summer and the slate that MGM produced was performing particularly poorly. We knew what was in their pipeline from our due diligence but it was difficult to know that this list represented one turkey after another (including *Year of the Dragon,* starring Mickey Rourke, and *Code Name: Emerald,* a World War II drama with Max Von Sydow). MGM released about one movie every month and on average, each title was losing about $15 million. (It got so bad by the following summer that when

Paramount was touting a much anticipated summer release, I joked, "They have *Top Gun,* and we have *Bottom Gun!*") People who had already been critical of the high price we paid for the studio were now speculating that Kerkorian knew he had bad movies in the can and was wise to sell when he did. That may be, but in fairness to Kirk he showed us the list and let us make our own judgment. He never warranted that they would perform at a certain level, just that they would be released on certain dates and supported with specific marketing budgets. I wanted MGM's current production, but my interest in the studio was largely centered on the library. It was hard for me to believe that they would run up about $100 million in losses from these movies over the next twelve months but they did—making a difficult situation that much harder. As early as October of 1985 we felt we would have to make serious changes to our deal if we were ever going to close. Some suggested that we find a loophole and pull out of it, but I felt we could find a way to make the deal work.

The word was all over Hollywood and Wall Street that I had overpaid and it wasn't long before we were in discussions with other companies about transactions that might help us pay down our debt and stay afloat. Viacom, which owned Showtime and the Movie Channel, expressed interest in buying half of MGM but those discussions never went very far. In addition, around the same time, NBC began talking to cable operators about starting their own news channel, possibly trying to take advantage of our difficult financial situation. Fighting off Satellite News Channel had cost us $100 million and we were in no position to take NBC on at that time.

I decided to negotiate with NBC directly, and we began discussions about their buying 50 percent of CNN for close to $300 million. That activity sparked interest from Rupert Murdoch at News Corporation and the management of Time Inc., but they both wanted to buy all of CNN, not a minority position. The NBC discussions grew fairly intense but they insisted on full editorial control and I wasn't willing to part with it. Our talks broke off, but the cable operators stood by me and didn't embrace NBC's plans for a CNN challenger. It would be several years before they entered the cable news business.

We also discussed a straight corporate merger with Allen Neuharth of Gannett, a TV station and newspaper company with good cash flow. Al and I liked each other a lot. He was a big fan of our news operation and said that CNN helped give him the idea for *USA Today*—which he saw as a print equivalent—in 1982. Our talks were serious but I had too many concerns about the future of the print business to move forward with him.

With Milken's help, we reduced the cash component of our deal by issuing new shares of preferred stock in Turner Broadcasting System, Inc. to Kerkorian and the other MGM/UA shareholders, and by the end of March 1986 we officially closed our deal. That was the good news. The bad news was that the terms stipulated that we pay off our $600 million in junk bond debt by September, just nine months away. MGM was operating at a loss (having just released more box office failures, including *9 1/2 Weeks*) and Turner Broadcasting was barely squeaking by even *before* we layered on these additional commitments. In fact, I don't think we expected our *revenues* to exceed $600 million over those upcoming three quarters. Making matters worse, Kerkorian's new preferred shares carried dividend obligations and our debt covenants prevented us from paying these in cash until our bond obligations were taken care of. In the absence of cash, we'd have to use Turner common stock.

The situation was dire and the only way to raise $600 million in cash was to sell assets. As much as I loved the idea of being in the movie business, I would have to live without a studio. The one thing I absolutely insisted that we keep was the library. Following this directive, the Drexel team went to work and by early June we sold the production company, the home video business, and the rights to the MGM logo back to Kirk Kerkorian for $300 million and the studio lot and film laboratory to Lorimar for $190 million. Meanwhile, we managed to keep the RKO and pre-1948 Warner Brothers libraries—and the rights to one of my favorite TV series, *Gilligan's Island*.

We did the best that we could do but it was painful giving up MGM. (I never even had a chance to use a casting couch!) As I mentioned before, when I entered the TV business, I'd never watched much TV and I wasn't a fan of network news before launching CNN. But I had enjoyed movies since I was a kid, and I was sorry not to retain the studio. But we had still managed to acquire the world's greatest movie library and now it was time to make the acquisition work. As Scarlett O'Hara said in a movie I now owned, "After all, tomorrow is another day!"

When the dust settled on our deal, Kirk Kerkorian was praised for profiting handsomely by simply selling assets to me at a high price and buying them back for less. Some have speculated that he took me to the cleaners, but I thought he was honorable throughout the process and we've remained friends. But friendly or not, I owed him a lot of money and while our core businesses continued to perform well, we had lost money on the Goodwill Games that summer and it was becoming clear that it would be difficult to pay Kerkorian without refinancing. Otherwise, we'd have to compensate him with newly issued stock, greatly diluting my Turner Broadcasting holdings. If we weren't careful, control of the company could shift from Turner to Kerkorian.

Once again, my back was up against the wall. I needed capital but where could I turn? Who would have an interest in helping me stay both afloat and independent? It didn't take me long to conclude that the cable operators would be my best bet.

—————— A TED STORY ——————

"You've Got to Do Something!"
—John Malone

I was asleep one morning at my home in Denver when the phone rang and it was Ted calling. He and my wife, Leslie, have an interesting relationship because she likes him but she also gives him a hard time about all the dating he does. At any rate, it was about 5:30 A.M.—he'd forgotten the time zone difference from Atlanta—and Leslie picked it up and she kind of gave me the elbow and said, "It's that asshole friend of yours, Turner!"

I took the phone and he says, "You've got to do something! You've got to do something!"

"What have I got to do, Ted?"

"You've got to do something or else CNN will become KNN!"

"What the hell's KNN?" I asked.

"The KERKORIAN NEWS NET-WORK!"

He asked for my help in figuring everything out and that set us out to raise the money to restructure the debt and get Kerkorian off his back. It was one of those deals where Milken was financing both sides and had gotten Ted into one of those escalating interest deals and it would force him to make the payments in stock if he couldn't afford to pay in cash.

By the end of 1986 it was clear that if I didn't do something soon I'd begin having to transfer Turner stock to Kerkorian within a couple of months. John Malone understood my situation and he and I set to work immediately, knowing that if we didn't successfully change the company's ownership structure, within five quarters I would lose control of Turner Broadcasting.

21

The Cable Operators

Calling on John Malone turned out to be the best thing I could have done. Not only did he have a strong grasp of financial issues and an incredible knack for deal making but he also had a burning desire to see us all in the cable industry succeed. TCI didn't yet have an investment in Turner but John already considered us to be on the same team. Our collective fight was against the broadcast networks, and while our immediate issue was losing control of a Hollywood studio, John could envision our assets eventually flipping to a Big Three broadcaster; and if ABC, NBC, or CBS added strong cable channels to their portfolio, their leverage over the industry would be enhanced significantly.

As hard as it might have been for me to have outsiders own a significant stake in the company, I did believe that TCI and the cable companies would be good partners. I listened to my father's advice about getting to know your customers and in the ten years since we had launched the SuperStation, nearly all of them had become friends. For example, that past summer I had flown the group over to Moscow for the Goodwill Games and we had a fabulous time together. The industry was full of solid businessmen and while our negotiations were always challenging, we knew we needed each other. My sense was that if they also had a direct financial interest in our success, we could work collaboratively on new networks and we'd have a much better chance of launching these channels with distribution and subscriber fees. If there was ever a group that I'd welcome into our company as investors and directors, this was it.

━━━━━━ A TED STORY ━━━━━━

"We Didn't Want to See Him Swallowed"
—John Malone

When I first looked at Ted's deal for the MGM library, it seemed to me that it was a great asset but that Ted had gotten himself in trouble—not necessarily that he paid too much but he took his leverage too high and the structure of the leverage was a problem. So we had to raise equity for him and I became the junior investment banker to get this done.

It was critically important to keep Ted independent. We didn't want to see him swallowed by anybody, especially a broadcaster. So what we were trying to do was preserve a major independent programmer for our own enlightened self-interest and for the good of the industry—and of course that also went parallel to Ted's view of the world at the time. We set out to raise about $550 million for 35 percent of TBS, Inc. I became the guy raising the money and we came up with half of it ourselves and then we went out to syndicate it. Early on, we thought we had Viacom, which was run at the time by Terry Elkes, and we had the Cox guys and we had the Times Mirror guys, and that was our team.

We deliberately wanted to keep it away from Time Inc. As much as we liked their CEO, Nick Nicholas, we knew they had great aspirations to control CNN and we wanted people who would be supportive and passive, not ones who would try and take it over from an editorial point of view. That was Ted, too—he didn't really want to run the risk of losing editorial control of his baby. And so that's how we set out to raise the money. Well, at the last minute Viacom gets taken over by Sumner Redstone. Sumner's not interested in playing team ball so he pulls out. So in order to replace Viacom we ultimately have to turn to Time Inc. Then, both Times Mirror and Cox say that if Time Inc. is in, we're out. So then we ended up having to put it together with just us and our affiliated companies and Time Inc. and with a series of other, smaller cable operators.

John's first discussion with the other cable operators began in January of 1987. By June, the deal was in place and more than thirty cable companies invested a total of $565 million for 37 percent of Turner Broadcasting System, Inc. For a number of reasons, we felt that this was a good transaction for Turner shareholders. I still controlled a majority of the company's voting shares, we raised the capital we needed, and we had a dream team of industry partners invested in our company. As part of the deal, seven of our fifteen board seats went to representatives of our larger cable investors, including TCI, Time Inc., and Continental Cablevision. I liked the idea of having smart cable operators on our board so much that I filled one of my eight seats with Brian Roberts of Comcast. (Comcast's investment wasn't large enough to earn a seat but I wanted him and his company to be involved.)

While they didn't own a majority of our voting shares, our new investors did attach strings to the deal. For example, TBS could not make expenditures of more than $2 million without board approval. But with that first restriction came a second. Both Time Inc. and TCI each had the right to veto any of these activities, so for any meaningful strategic moves or acquisitions, we had to get the approval of both TCI and Time Inc.

By the time we got to negotiating these finer points, not only did we not have a whole lot of leverage with our prospective investors, but both Bill Bevins, my vice president of finance, and I were exhausted. Between the planning for CBS, then negotiating to buy MGM, selling it back in pieces, and now this new arrangement, we were simply burned out. (Bevins, in fact, had a mild heart attack in my office and wound up leaving the company shortly after this deal was finalized.) Handing over veto power to Time and TCI would ultimately become one of my greatest regrets.

I'd been working with a board of directors for many years but these first meetings with this new group were an eye-opener. Not only had my authority been limited, I was now presiding over a board that included successful, strong-willed entrepreneurs who were also our biggest customers. It was a collegial group, but we all knew that there was some real competition and tension across their various companies. Recognizing that our arrangement was unusual, everyone worked hard to make sure we were acting in the best interest of our shareholders and trying to avoid conflicts of interest.

──────── A TED STORY ────────

"Not at All Shrinking Violets"
—Brian Roberts

(BRIAN ROBERTS IS CHAIRMAN AND CEO OF COMCAST CORPORATION.)

Back when I was a sophomore in college my father took me to the NCTA convention. At one point I walked by a room and saw a sign about the launch of a new network. I looked inside and there was a handful of people and there's this guy Ted Turner up there talking about this new thing that was going to change the world. He was discussing the launch of CNN and at first I thought the guy was crazy but I realized that the business was changing from just transmitting broadcast signals to delivering original programming. It was going to make cable very interesting.

Years later, I was working for the company full-time and had been assigned to be the person at Comcast who worked most closely with the programmers. When John Malone came around looking for investors in Turner I thought it was a great opportunity and recommended to my father that we put in $100 million. He couldn't see the benefit of such a big investment for a minority stake, so we wound up putting in about $5 million. Our investment was too small for a board seat but a little while later, Ted called up and asked me to join his board as one of his directors.

So there I was, in my late twenties, sitting on this board that was full of very strong-willed entrepreneurs who were very colorful characters—not at all shrinking violets. It was not a textbook Harvard board but it was a great education for me and the dynamics were fascinating. I used to joke that our meetings themselves would have made a great cable channel!

At our first board meeting I pushed hard for us to develop a new entertainment channel. My idea was to compete directly with the networks with original programming and while the SuperStation relied primarily on reruns and sports, this channel would make original movies and pursue big, high-profile events. Our management team, led by Gerry Hogan, put together a list of the top one hundred events on television— everything from the NFL to the Olympics, the Oscars, the Emmys, Miss America, and Wimbledon. This collection became our shopping list and we used it in sales pitches to advertisers and cable operators to give them an idea of how ambitious we planned to be. Filling out the schedule would be movies, series, and cartoons drawn primarily from our library. Because we would target the networks directly, when deciding on what to call the channel I felt we should use the word "network" and came up with Turner Network Television, or TNT. We planned for this channel to be dynamite!

Advertising revenue alone would not be enough to finance such an ambitious channel. We needed subscription fees as well and we targeted 15 cents per month. While 15 cents might not seem like much, when you multiply that by twelve months and spread it across millions of subscribers, the numbers get big pretty quickly, and these revenues would provide a strong, steady foundation for our continued investments in original, high-quality programming. CNN had gone on the air in 1980 with about 2 million subscribers, but cable penetration had grown dramatically since then, and with our operator owners in agreement with our plan it looked like we would launch TNT with much wider distribution.

In addition to high-profile events and original programming, I envisioned TNT as a vehicle to maximize the value of our newly purchased libraries. We continued to invest in the preservation and colorization of our older films. In fact, the first step in the colorization process is restoring the original print to the best state possible. Colorizing movies was not inexpensive—it cost about $2,000 per minute or about $200,000 for the average length film. But updating these older titles helped us earn new syndication revenues, especially overseas, where many television stations had stopped buying black and white product. It also gave us the opportunity to "premiere" these newly colorized classics on TBS and TNT.

The publicity we generated from colorization was tremendous. It was more controversial than I had anticipated and when we announced our colorization plans, there was backlash from the Hollywood community. Some directors and producers—everyone from Martin Scorsese to Billy Wilder—were outraged that we would colorize classic films without input from their original creators, who were mostly deceased. We were accused of "cultural vandalism." Woody Allen said that what we were doing was "criminal" and showed "a total contempt for film, for the director, and for the public."

I was undeterred. It was okay for people to write negative things about me just as long as they spelled my name right—and I really didn't think we were doing anything wrong. After restoring original black and white prints the colorization was done on a duplicate video copy, so the originals themselves weren't altered, and by breathing new life into these old movies we attracted audiences that wouldn't have seen them otherwise. Besides, movies had been altered ever since they were first shown on television. To fit a square television, widescreen feature films had to be squeezed and clipped, and they were edited for content (such as removing nudity or obscene language), and some were even sped up or slowed down to fit precise time slots on TV station schedules. What we were doing wasn't any worse than what had been going on for the past thirty years and besides, if a viewer *really* didn't like these changes, he could turn down his TV's color knob and watch it in black and white!

The colorization controversy grew so great that Roger Mayer, the MGM executive that I had put in charge of managing the movie library, was asked to go on shows like *Today* and *Good Morning America* to defend our position. Roger had an excellent reputation in Hollywood but that didn't keep people from getting angry. Eventually, we even had to make our case before Congress, and every time we were challenged, the laws were interpreted in our favor because we owned the films' copyrights.

These victories were reassuring to me as they supported one of my fundamental beliefs about running a business: when you own an asset, your job is to maximize its value. For Turner Broadcasting, that might mean using unsold billboards to promote our radio stations, airing the Braves on the SuperStation, or disappointing some film purists by updating old movies. Our competitors had more resources than we did and we had to do everything we could to get the most out of what we had. While colorization wasn't accepted in certain circles, TV audiences responded well. We

had run *Miracle on 34th Street* on the SuperStation at Christmastime for years, and
when we first showed the colorized version it did nearly *six times* its average rating (and when we added color to Santa's
outfit we had a high degree of confidence
that we were getting it right!).

Over the years, the colorization debate
quieted down, and ultimately our extensive film preservation work earned the approval of even our staunchest critics. Nearly
twenty years later, partly in recognition of
these efforts, Roger was given the Jean
Hersholt Humanitarian Award from the
Motion Picture Academy. The prize was
presented during the 2005 Oscar telecast,
and the man who volunteered to introduce
him and did so with the highest of praise
was none other than Martin Scorsese.
No one deserved that award more than
Roger, and it was a proud moment for all
of us.

TNT debuted on October 3, 1988. We
signed on with my favorite movie, *Gone
with the Wind,* and our signal reached an
amazing 17 million households, making
TNT's launch by far the largest in cable
history. We didn't charge a subscription

fee for the first three months, but in January of 1989, we began collecting a monthly rate of 15 cents per household. By spring, we were up to 24 million households and by TNT's first anniversary it was carried in 50 million homes and generated nearly $100 million in subscriber revenue alone. It would be a while before we landed any of the targets on our "Top 100" list but we did produce some great original movies—a first for basic cable—and viewers and advertisers responded well to the channel. TNT would eventually become home to telecasts of the NFL, the NBA, Wimbledon, PGA Golf, and other major events, and today it remains one of television's most valuable channels.

While TNT was a major success, due in large part to cooperation from our cable operator partners, they did stop me from pursuing another cable channel that I really wanted. By 1988 the Financial News Network (FNN) had been on the air for a few years and was headed toward bankruptcy. FNN was an independent channel that delivered twenty-four-hour business news. They struggled to build an audience and were now threatened by NBC's plans to launch a rival service named CNBC. Word got out that FNN could be purchased for as little as $100 million and I wanted it badly.

We already carried business news on CNN and extending that coverage on a twenty-four-hour channel would be easy. The cost efficiencies of such an acquisition were compelling and I thought that if we moved quickly to purchase FNN and strengthen the channel, CNBC would be dead on arrival. Unfortunately, the board did not agree, and for the first time since investing in Turner, they kept me from making a deal I really wanted to make. While they raised questions about the viability of the concept of twenty-four-hour business news and had concerns about the fact that NBC was planning a competitor, I think they worried that I was trying to do too much. This troubled them not only because it might cause us to become stretched too thin but also because we were growing too powerful. I was very disappointed. NBC wound up purchasing FNN in '91, which, after changing its name to CNBC, has been a success ever since.

The final years of the eighties were exciting for our company and we enjoyed tremendous growth. With cable distribution expanding rapidly and the industry supporting subscription fees, our businesses were sailing along. And while my cable operator directors frustrated me on occasion, in general our arrangement worked well for everyone and their investment in Turner Broadcasting was paying off handsomely. From the time between the stock market crash of 1987 and the end of 1989, our stock price went up by more than 500 percent, and while I owned a smaller percentage of the company, the value of my holdings had skyrocketed. Heading into the nineties, my Turner Broadcasting stock was worth more than $1 billion.

While I had never been in business primarily for the money, when I became a billionaire, it did feel good. My pleasure came not only from a sense that this was a measure of achievement, but also because I'd reached this point while still young and feeling like there were plenty of opportunities ahead.

22

Meeting Jane Fonda

I didn't set out to become a billionaire. I wanted to be a success, but learning from my father—whose life reached its crisis point at the very height of his net worth—I didn't set my goals in monetary terms. But many people do keep score this way and when you become well known for achievements in business, people often ask, "What's the secret?"

In addition to luck, there were a number of different factors and personal behaviors that worked in my favor, but none of them is really a secret. For one thing, I've always had a lot of energy. Ever since I was little, my mind and body were active and I couldn't stand sitting around. Even today, I'm constantly moving. Purgatory for me would be spending twenty-four hours with nothing to do but to be alone with my thoughts. I do a lot of thinking when I'm out walking, riding horses, or fishing, and at mealtime debating and discussing ideas with others. (This might explain why I used to have a problem with the popular view of heaven. Sitting around on a cloud playing the harp all day always seemed more like hell to me!)

I also keep my sights set on the future and don't spend much time dwelling on the past. I've had some tough experiences as a child and have had my share of business and personal setbacks, but sitting around thinking about them isn't going to change anything. Someone once said that I was a good winner but a better loser. When I have a setback, I put it behind me as fast as I can and keep moving. I don't play golf but I compare the way I respond to disappointments to the way a golfer does after he hits his drive into the water. He doesn't walk down to the pond, dive in, dig out his ball, examine the ball, and ponder what happened. Instead, he takes another ball out of his bag, tees it up, and keeps on playing. After a disappointment I always try to bounce back and I've no doubt that this has helped me tremendously. I also have a strong work ethic. From my earliest days pulling weeds in the yard to working for my dad out at the billboard company, nothing was handed to me; I always had to work for it.

There probably are some ways that I work and live that might be a little different from other people you come across. For one thing, I go to great lengths to be efficient with my time and try to make the most of every minute of every day. When I run meetings, they start on time. A lot of that came from my father and punctuality was stressed at McCallie and the Coast Guard. For much of my career, I didn't even waste time getting to and from work. There were long stretches when I spent most of my weeknights sleeping in my office, and later, when I could afford to, I built an apartment on the top floor of CNN. So when millions of Atlanta drivers were wasting their time sitting in traffic, my commute was nothing more than walking up a flight

of stairs, and I had that much more productive time to work every day.

My desire to use time wisely has even
extended to what I wear on my feet. For
most of my adult life, I've never worn lace-
up shoes. Most of my shoes are slip-ons,
so instead of spending time stooping over
tying my shoes, I do something else that's
productive.

Another way I save time is by managing
information efficiently. A lot of people become inundated with paper and e-mails,
but I make a point to keep a clean desk. I
never let things pile up. I couldn't do this
without a great executive assistant and for
the last twenty years, it's been Debbie
Masterson. She is invaluable, and in addition to keeping me on track and on schedule, I've always counted on her to screen
out correspondence that I don't need to
see. (Incidentally, Debbie handles all my
electronic correspondence—I don't use
e-mail myself.) The volume of mail I receive
is tremendous—from business reports, so-
licitations, and so forth—but over 90 percent never makes it to my desk. For most
requests, Debbie knows how to respond.

The 10 percent that makes it to my desk still amounts to a lot and I try to answer it all that day so that I don't get bogged down with unanswered messages.

Some of my passion for efficiency comes from my experience in sailboat racing. Races are won and lost by picking up a second here and a second there, and I learned a lot about how small things matter. Racing also contributed to my skill at delegation, an ability that's been of vital importance to my business success. Once you begin racing bigger boats, it becomes impossible for one person to do it all. Instead, you have to have good people, assign them responsibilities, and then let them do their jobs. As skipper, you steer the boat, plot strategy, and issue orders.

Basically, I ran my company the same way I ran my boat. I found the best people I could to run our businesses while I stepped back to keep an eye on our overall strategy and what our next move should be. A lot of entrepreneurs and company founders have trouble leading as their company grows. Part of the problem is that they become so used to having their hands in everything when the company is small that they find it difficult to delegate success-fully once the business gets big. I stayed on top of key issues relating to our indi-vidual businesses, but I let my managers manage. This gave me time to focus on the big picture.

Another quality that worked to my ad-vantage was my ability to create a fun, exciting environment. Everybody worked hard, often for less pay than they might have made elsewhere, but at Turner Broad-casting there was always a sense that we were the underdogs and we were motivated by the opportunity to prove the naysayers wrong. I certainly had a temper and there's no doubt that I yelled at people on occa-sion, but I was good at putting those dis-putes behind me and the next time I saw the person I'd been angry with, we usually shared a laugh and a pat on the back.

Unfortunately, I was better in business and sailing than I was in marriage. With Judy Nye, we were impulsive people who barely knew each other when we were married. Still, we managed to stay together for three years and had two great children together—Laura and Teddy. My second marriage, to Jane Smith, lasted more than twenty years and was quite a bit more complicated. We had three children in four years—Rhett, Beau, and Jennie—and with Teddy and Laura joining us unexpectedly, home life was chaotic. In my mind, Janie never could treat my two older children as if they were her own and there's no doubt that I was resentful of that. I was away racing and working a lot and that clearly didn't make things any easier, and she probably took out on Teddy and Laura some of the frustrations that were really aimed at me.

I've tried to be the best person that I could be, both at work and in my personal life, but monogamy for me has always been a struggle. As noted earlier, from an early age my dad told me "real men run around," but as I've reflected on his philosophies I no longer think he had it right. Maybe it's too late for me to change my ways but as my children have grown I've encouraged them to follow my advice and not my example when it comes to being in committed relationships.

Janie and I both tried to make the marriage work but when our kids were little, we were both too exhausted to think about much else than being good parents. After our children grew older, Janie and I weren't on the same wavelength when it came to thinking about the big picture and as I became more involved in working on global issues, we had less in common.

When I met J. J. Ebaugh, things were completely different. Not only was J. J. concerned about world problems, she also challenged me to think more about them myself. It was a better partnership than any I'd had before.

By the late 1980s, I'd been seeing J. J. on and off for about six years. Our relationship had become more serious—and more public—and with my children now grown, Janie and I separated. My wealth had increased a great deal during our marriage and my lawyers expressed concern that Janie may try to get a substantial sum in alimony. The way I looked at it, she deserved it. I never made things easy for her but she still hung in there with me through a lot of ups and downs. Divorce is always difficult but in this case the settlement negotiations were fair and went smoothly. We'd been drifting apart for the last few years so when our final arrangement was completed in October of 1988, it was a sad, but not completely sudden, end. Our marriage was never easy, but Janie and I had a lot of good times together and when we officially went our separate ways, our children were fine young adults. I'll always be grateful to her.

An *Atlanta* magazine cover once described J. J. as "The Woman Who Tamed Ted Turner," and many assumed that as soon as my divorce was final, she and I would be married. She certainly did have an impact on me and we've had some great times together. Among other things, she helped me understand the value of getting counseling during times of stress. I'd had some problems with mood swings when I was a kid—probably because of being sent away at such a young age and the anxiety that my life produced. I remember at the age of nine or ten just deciding on my own that I was going to accentuate the positive and eliminate the negative—just like that song suggested—and that helped me a lot.

Still, in the 1980s a doctor diagnosed me with bipolar depression and put me on lithium. I took this medication for a couple of years but I couldn't tell that it made much of a difference. When I switched psychiatrists, I had a thorough interview that led to a completely different diagnosis. My new doctor asked me questions like whether I ever went for long stretches without sleep (only when I was sailing, I told him), and whether I ever spent inordinate amounts of money. (We both got a chuckle out of that one. I'd been known for spending a lot of money at the company but he decided that this spending was never made out of the irrationally poor judgment that bipolar people often display.) He concluded that while I definitely had an uncommon drive and still do struggle with occasional bouts of anxiety, I don't have depression, and he canceled the lithium.

J. J. was a supportive partner throughout and we did consider getting married. But the more intimate we were, the more difficult our relationship became. J. J. also discovered that she was wrestling with some of her own psychological issues, and while we still cared about each other (and remain friends to this day),we realized that a long-term relationship just was not in the cards.

After parting with J. J., I went back to dating and during this time I read in the paper that Jane Fonda was getting a divorce from her husband. Instantly, I thought to myself, "Jane Fonda is someone I'd like to go out with!" Jane and I had met briefly several years before at a screening in Los Angeles and I had come to admire her over the years. During the Vietnam War mine was still very much a "my country, right or wrong" mentality, and I disapproved of her stance against the war. Over time, however, I changed my views and felt that the people who spoke out against the Vietnam conflict were right and courageous. I also admired what she had accomplished, first with her movies and later with her exercise videos. When VCRs came along, she was one of the only people—outside of the porn industry—who could sell videocassettes in big numbers.

—————— A TED STORY ——————

"I Think I'm Going to Call That Woman Up"
—President Jimmy Carter

The first time I was really alone with Ted and had a chance to talk at length with him was one weekend when Rosalynn and I went down to visit him. We were out in a little boat fishing in his hundred-acre lake—one of the best bass lakes on earth—and Jane Fonda had just announced that she was going to divorce.

Ted said to me, "I think I'm going to call that woman up and ask her for a date." (I didn't have a very favorable opinion of Jane then but I've changed my mind dramatically in the years since I've come to know her—she's one of the finest people I've ever met.) Anyway, I was there when he first had the thought.

——————————————————————

I asked my assistant to find Jane Fonda's number and when I called I got right to the point. I told her that I'd read that her marriage with Tom Hayden had ended and I wanted to see if she'd like to go out with me. She was taken aback and told me that her divorce had just gone through—she said she was flattered by my interest but that she needed six months before she thought she'd be ready to date again. I told her I understood and after a few more brief words, we hung up. I've always believed that if you really want something, hard work is important and so is follow-through. In this case, I really wanted to go out with her, so when she told me she needed six months, I made a note to call her back then. When the day arrived, precisely six months after our first phone conversation, I called her again. I said, "Hi, it's Ted Turner. The six months are up. Will you go out with me now?" She must have appreciated my persistence because she said yes and we agreed to see each other for dinner during my next trip to Los Angeles.

I picked her up at her home in Santa Monica and I was taken with her the moment she met me at the door. From meeting her before and watching her in the movies I knew she was attractive, but as we talked through our dinner date I was surprised by the strength of our connection. Knowing that a lot of people assumed I was a male chauvinist and a greedy capitalist, I was up front with her. I let her know that my dad had raised me without a lot of respect for women and that this was something I'd been working hard to change, especially with my most recent girlfriend. And knowing of Jane's political leanings, I even bragged to her about how many friends I had who were communists, including Castro and Gorbachev! I always tend to talk a lot when I'm excited or nervous and that night I was really excited.

Before our date I'd done research on Jane and while a lot of people saw us as an unlikely couple, we really did have a lot in common. We both had difficult, complicated fathers and we both had a parent commit suicide (Jane's mother killed herself when Jane was just twelve years old). I could tell right away that she was very smart and a hard worker. My sense was that, like me, she had a difficult upbringing that contributed to her drive to be a super achiever. Jane and I also figured out very quickly that we cared about a lot of the same issues. Our first date together ended with a hug and I told her that I was smitten. I knew that Jane Fonda was someone I wanted to get to know better.

It took a little persuasion but I convinced Jane to come visit my ranch in Montana that I had purchased a year before. I'd already acquired quite a bit of property but by this point not much in the West. In addition to Hope Plantation, in the late 1970s I purchased St. Phillip's Island (near Hilton Head, South Carolina) and I owned an 8,000-acre plantation near Tallahassee, Florida, called Avalon. I also owned a beautiful piece of land and house on the coast of Big Sur, California. (I bought this when I was dating J. J.) I'd spent most of my recreation time on southern plantations or on the high seas, but I quickly fell in love with the beauty of Big Sky Country. Not only was the scenery spectacular (and there were a lot fewer biting bugs than in the Southeast), I discovered that fly-fishing on a mountain stream calms my nerves and is a delightful pastime. Since I was no longer sailing, fishing and hunting became my main sources of relaxation.

My Montana ranch was beautiful, covering four thousand acres and with access

to tremendous trout streams. Since it was
the best property I'd seen out there, bar
none, I decided to name it the Bar None
Ranch. I remember how excited I was when
I first went out there as a landowner. I went
into the local store and bought a couple of
pairs of stiff new jeans, western boots, and
a cowboy hat. Walking out of the store I
looked like a city slicker—I think I still had
the price tag on my hat—and I'm sure the
locals on the street got a good laugh!

Jane accepted my invitation to spend
the weekend in Montana and we shared
an incredible few days. Being out there together was a special time for us. It was a
great chance to get to know each other
better and by the end of that trip I was
thinking that Jane was someone with
whom I could spend the rest of my life.

Unfortunately, Jane wasn't quite there
yet, and shortly after she returned to Los
Angeles, she let me know that she was
dating an Italian soccer player turned ac-
tor who was seventeen years her junior.
For Jane, I was a "younger man," too—she
had me by eleven months. I'd jokingly refer to him as her "Italian Stallion" and asked
why she insisted on discriminating against

older guys like me! I wouldn't give up, and I continued to stay in touch—I'd call, send flowers, anything I could think of to help her realize that I was still interested.

Finally, in January of 1990, her sister-in-law called to let me know that Jane had broken up with the "Italian Stallion" and was ready to go out with me. It was a great beginning to what would prove to be another eventful decade.

23

"Give Me Land, Lots of Land"

After buying the Bar None Ranch and spending increasing amounts of time in Montana, I fell even more in love with the area. When I enjoy something, I have a tendency to overdo it, and when I was told that a larger ranch was coming on the market, I was interested. Jane and I were still getting used to the scale of the Bar None when I told her that now I was going to look into a property that was many times larger. The Flying D Ranch is more than 119,000 acres, situated between the Gallatin and Madison Rivers. It's a beautiful property with good trout streams and it had a lot of pasture that would be perfect for a large bison herd. Jane thought I was crazy but for $21 million (or about $200 an acre) it seemed like it would not only be a great place, but also a terrific investment. I bought it in 1989.

Like most large ranches, the Flying D contained a lot of signs of human impact, like power lines and poles and barbwire fences. One of the first things I wanted to do was get rid of all this junk and barbed wire. My goal was to restore the property to what it would have looked like 150 years earlier, before the white man came. It was a lot of work, but we removed just about every sign of human disturbance, save the dirt and gravel roads.

Part of my desire to own this land was to make sure that it was never developed. Conserving this property for future generations seemed like the right thing to do, especially with so much development happening in that part of the country. I worked out a conservation easement with the Nature Conservancy that guarantees that the Flying D ranch will remain open space. I also began work to repopulate the property with bison, an animal that I'd been fascinated by for years. I'd purchased my first bison back in the 1970s—a bull and two cows—and kept them at Hope Plantation (where I also enjoyed raising and breeding bears, cougars, and other animals that had been native to that area in earlier days). I knew that the bison population had once numbered in the tens of millions before dropping to below a thousand, and for the Flying D to look like it looked hundreds of years before, we needed a large herd.

———————— A TED STORY ————————

"A Giant Environmental Canvas"
—Russ Miller

(RUSS MILLER IS VICE PRESIDENT AND GENERAL MANAGER OF TURNER ENTERPRISES, INC.)

I first met Ted in 1989 when he bought the Flying D. He invited ranch manager Bud Griffith and me up to the porch of the Spanish Creek house and we sat on the deck surveying the view shed in front of him. Ted had a book of prints by Karl Bodmer open on his lap. As we all sat there, Ted would look down at the print and up at the view shed, down at his lap, back up at the view. Finally, he looked at Bud and me and he said, "You see all that stuff out there?"

And we said, "What do you mean?"

"The haying equipment, the farm equipment, all of the buildings, all of the fences, all of the power lines, and the cattle, they're all gone, because I want the landscape to look like these Bodmers."

It was apparent to me then that Ted was a romantic artist and he saw the landscape as a giant environmental canvas.

Then, about a week later, Ted invited some of the leaders of the bison industry up to the Spanish Creek house again to talk about the prospect of raising bison on his ranches. After grilling them at length about the details of the prospective income and expense associated with bison he grinned at me and said, "Not only are we going to run bison, we're going to make more money than cattle ranchers!"

At that point I knew that Ted also was an astute businessman and that he saw the landscape as a compelling spreadsheet. About three years later Ted asked me to go to New Mexico to go and look at the Ladder Ranch, which he was considering buying. When I reported back to him that his happier bison would roam in Montana and not in New Mexico, he reminded me that the Ladder Ranch was home to three kinds of indigenous quail. In this conversation I realized that Ted also saw his land as a haven—a safe haven for native species. Now all three of those vignettes came together eight years and ten ranches later at our ranch manager's conference. All of us who worked for Ted knew what his land ethic was firsthand. We'd lived and breathed it for the last ten years. But Ted joined us because he wanted to formalize that ethic in a mission statement, which was to manage Turner lands in an economically sustainable and ecologically sensitive manner, while promoting the conservation of native species. That to me captures what Ted's land ethic is. Bison are the common thread that runs through all the ranches, but there are others as well. The thread of native flora, the thread of native fauna, and all woven together they create a rich tapestry that's unified, diverse, and strong.

During my early years of ranch ownership, my enthusiasm did lead me to make some mistakes. For example, the Flying D had hundreds of miles of barbed wire fencing and I had every bit of it removed, thinking this would allow the bison to roam free on about eighty thousand acres. I learned that when you do this, the animals tend to overgraze certain areas and undergraze others, and we had to bring back some limited fencing—not barbwire, I might add.

The Bar None and Flying D gave me so much pleasure that I decided to buy as many large properties as I could reasonably afford. By the end of the 1990s, I had purchased two more ranches in Montana, three in Nebraska, one in Kansas, and one in South Dakota (they're used primarily for bison ranching). Then between 1992 and 1996, I bought three large ranches in New Mexico. The biggest, Vermejo Park, is nearly 600,000 acres, and together these three ranches cover more than one million acres. They are also used for bison ranching, as well as hunting and fishing, and Vermejo sits on top of valuable natural gas that is being extracted by an energy company that has the rights. They do this work very carefully, extracting the gas while protecting the ranch's beauty and wildlife.

I've also enjoyed working on the return and protection of threatened and endangered species. In addition to bison (of which we now have about 45,000 head), we've worked to reintroduce about twenty other species. These include gray wolves, red-cockaded woodpeckers, and black-footed ferrets. These were all challenging projects so I looked for the best people I could to help manage the properties. I hired Russ Miller in 1989 and he's been with me ever since, doing a terrific job as general manager of the ranches. In 1997 I created the Turner Endangered Species

Fund, recruiting Mike Phillips (who led the effort to bring back the gray wolf to Yellowstone) to run the organization, along with my son Beau, who studied wildlife management at Montana State University after graduating from The Citadel.

In Montana, I learned to love fly-fishing. It's one of the few things I do that's not only interesting and challenging but also relaxing. Unfortunately, it's not a sport you can enjoy during a Montana winter (except on rare occasions), but I learned that there are rivers and areas in the Patagonia region of Argentina that are similar to those in Montana. Since South America is counter-seasonal to the United States, I could fish there during the North American winter. In '97 I purchased a nine-thousand-acre ranch in Patagonia named La Primavera, and in 2000, a 93,000-acre property named Collon Cura. I also bought a 24,000-acre ranch and fishing lodge on the island of Tierra del Fuego. These three properties all feature great fly-fishing.

Subsequently, I acquired two more ranches on the Great Plains of Nebraska and one in Oklahoma, primarily for raising bison. Today, with over 2 million acres, I'm the largest individual landowner in the United States. We operate our ranches responsibly from an environmental viewpoint and also have an outfitting business that allows hunters and fishermen to use our properties on a limited basis. With revenues from bison sales, some controlled forestry, energy leases, and private hunting and fishing, the ranches turn a small profit.

Owning the properties has given me tremendous pleasure. My connection to nature goes back to my early childhood when I spent hours outdoors either alone or with Jimmy Brown. I'd fish, gig for frogs, or just observe the wildlife around me and these times helped me through a lot of my loneliness and gave me great peace of mind. Being outdoors is my chance to unwind, clear my head, and think. The time I spend in nature refreshes and recharges me and reminds me how much raw beauty exists in the world—and how careful we should be to preserve it. The ranches are also great places for me to spend time with friends. On nearly every trip I make in the United States or Argentina, I invite friends and family. I've also hosted business colleagues and world leaders. (I'm proud to say that three Nobel Peace Prize winners have been among my houseguests—Mikhail Gorbachev, Jimmy Carter, and former UN secretary-general Kofi Annan.) I also enjoy observing and interacting with nature and it's a special feeling to be part of the natural environment.

One of my favorite experiences involves a bird I befriended several years ago at my Snow Crest Ranch in Montana. It was a baby magpie that had fallen out of its nest and was lying on the ground. My house staff and I pulled together a box, some paper towels, and an eyedropper, and gave it food and water. The little magpie responded and we pulled him through. In the process we bonded, and I named him Harry. We bought a traveling cage for him and took him with us when we moved from one ranch to another. He learned to talk and wound up providing great entertainment. We would let him out of the cage during the day and he'd follow me around. When I'm at a ranch I get a FedEx package from my office of the previous day's mail. With Harry, I'd sit on my couch reading my mail and once I was through, I'd crush the pages into a ball and throw them on the ground for Harry to play with. He charmed everyone (including Gorbachev—he sat next to his coffee cup one morning at breakfast and gave him a couple of light pecks on his famous forehead). Harry became a little too feisty and ran into trouble when he started dive-bombing people and we were concerned that he might put someone's eye out. We decided we had to take Harry to the Beartooth Nature Center in Red Lodge, Montana. He still lives there, and to this day, whenever I see magpies flying overhead, I think of my old pal Harry.

I'm proud of the work we've done to preserve and protect the properties and I've tried to do everything I can to make sure that they're maintained after I'm gone. With my passing the properties will be protected by conservation easements. In certain parts of the country, my rancher neighbors have grown suspicious of me and created theories about ulterior motives I might have, going so far as to speculate that I might be trying to tie up and control water rights for entire regions. None of this is true. As long as the conservation laws of the United States remain in place, the land will be protected from development in perpetuity (and we've taken similar measures with the Argentine properties).

I'm often reminded of Scarlett O'Hara's father in *Gone With the Wind*, who told her, "Why, land's the only thing in the world worth working for, worth fighting for, worth dying for, because it's the only thing that lasts." I've realized this to be true, and I'm proud to know that I've done what I can to make sure that my land is protected.

24

The Gulf War

Sometime around the middle of 1990 I realized that CNN needed some new leadership. Burt Reinhardt had done a terrific job since taking over after Reese Schonfeld's departure (Reese and I had differences over his management style and we parted company in 1982), but by this time Burt was well past retirement age. I learned that Tom Johnson, who was a respected career journalist, was available due to a restructuring at the Times Mirror Company. We met and he agreed to join us as president and CEO of CNN.

A TED STORY

"He's Still Got the Job if He Wants It!"
—Tom Johnson

(TOM JOHNSON WAS CEO OF CNN FROM AUGUST 1990 TO JUNE 2001.)

When I heard that Turner was looking to hire someone new to run CNN, I asked my friend Jerry Lindauer if he thought Ted might consider me. Jerry was chairman of Prime Cable and had known Ted for years. He said he didn't know but would give Ted a call and put in a good word. After having been president and publisher of the *L.A. Times* I'd recently been "elevated" to the position of vice chairman of the parent company, Times Mirror, and I was looking for a change. Ted told Jerry he'd be interested in a meeting and on his next trip to Los Angeles I met with him at his office in Century City. The meeting was on a Thursday at 10:00 in the morning and I figured it would run about two hours or so. Instead, it lasted about seventeen minutes and was interrupted four times by phone calls. I think two of those were from Jane Fonda.

At one point Ted said, "Tom, would you take the job as president of CNN?"

I said, "Ted, you need to know more about me and I need to know more about the job and about you."

And he said, "Well, can you let me know by Monday?" If you take out the time for the phone calls, the amount of actual conversation time with Ted was about three minutes, and now he was asking me to let him know Monday morning if I would take the job.

When I got back to my office at the *L.A. Times,* I got a call from Bill Shaw, who worked for Turner. "Did Ted offer you the job and did you accept?"

I said, "Mr. Shaw, I'm not sure."

Then Bill said, "Let me tell you a story. Ted once offered a baseball player a contract for a million dollars and told him he needed to know right away if he would accept. A few days passed and when Ted was told the guy hadn't made up his mind yet, Ted said, 'Tell that goddamn guy if he can't make up his mind he has no place in our organization!' and he withdrew the offer." Bill followed that story by telling me he looked forward to working with me. I told him I still had to do some due diligence on the opportunity and suggested they do some on me, too.

Over the next few days, I called a number of people to get their thoughts on Ted, CNN, and the opportunity I had before me. From President Carter to Roberto Goizueta at Coca-Cola to Bill Moyers and Walter Cronkite— everyone I spoke to was enthusiastic. But the one quote I'll never forget came from Jane Fonda, whom I had recently gotten to know. "Tom," she said, "he's the most remarkable man I've ever met."

To seal the deal completely, my wife, Edwina, and I offered to have dinner with Ted and Jane Fonda at a restaurant out on the Pacific Coast Highway, up in the Santa Monica hills. We met at Jane's house and Edwina drove the four of us to the restaurant in her white Jaguar. The first mistake I

made was when I suggested that Ted
sit in the front passenger seat next to
Edwina and I would sit in the back with
Jane. It was a mistake for two reasons. First, Ted sure as hell didn't want
to be seated anywhere except next to
Jane Fonda—he looked at me like I
was crazy—but he did it anyway. The
second problem was that I tend to get
carsick when I don't ride in the front.
Riding in the back with Jane, by the
time we got to the restaurant, I was
feeling pretty awful.

So we get to the restaurant and the
purpose of the meal was really to talk
about the job, what kind of working
relationship we were going to have,
and those sorts of things. But throughout the dinner, Ted could not keep his
hands off Jane and she couldn't keep
her hands off him. Edwina and I felt
like we were watching a couple of
teenagers! For my part, I don't know
if it was nerves or the car ride or both,
but I got progressively sicker through
the dinner and had to go to the bathroom to throw up three different times.
Needless to say, we didn't talk much

about the job before it was time to head home.

For the return trip back to Jane's house I got in the front seat and let Ted and Jane take the back. I told Edwina, "If I say 'pull over,' please pull over because I am really sick." A few minutes later, I did just that, and we pulled over on the side of the Pacific Coast Highway and I got out and was dry heaving by the side of the road. I told her to take Ted and Jane home and come back to get me. From the back seat window, Ted said, "Don't worry, we're not going to leave you here, pal!" but I insisted—I was so sick I didn't want anyone to see me. There I was, on a concrete slab next to the PCH, and as Edwina pulled away, I could hear Ted yell out to her in that loud voice of his, "Tell him he's still got the job if he wants it!"

Tom Johnson's first day at CNN was August 1, 1990. On August 2, Saddam Hussein's Iraqi army invaded Kuwait. It was trial by fire but fortunately for Tom,

CNN had, by this time, a very solid infra-structure. Even through the years when the network was losing money, we contin-ued to invest in our newsgathering capa-bilities and worked hard to develop strong relationships around the world.

As we expanded CNN, many govern-ments hesitated at the idea of bringing "American" news into their country. So, to demonstrate that we were open to a wide range of views, in 1987 we started a pro-gram called *World Report*. We set aside time on CNN for news reports produced from around the world and aired them just as they would run on their own stations. It was a unique approach that demonstrated to our global partners that we operated with a spirit of fairness and openness and it gave viewers in the United States the opportunity to see how other countries viewed world events. We also held an an-nual *World Report* conference in Atlanta that was attended by representatives of each of the participating countries and networks. It was a great opportunity for these people to get together, to share ideas, and to get to know one another.

Among the participants was a delegation

from Iraq, including Tariq Aziz, one of Saddam's closest lieutenants. The relationships we developed within Iraq's communications infrastructure would prove to be helpful later. As the Kuwait standoff continued and war looked increasingly likely, journalists began to pour into that region. Largely due to the trust and personal relationships that we had developed, CNN crews continued to gain access to key decision makers and physical locations in Iraq that were off limits to our competitors.

As the fall of 1990 progressed, we sensed that Operation Desert Storm could be a defining moment for CNN. We had set out to be the world's news leader and covering this war would be our opportunity to prove it. Televising an international story of this scope would not be inexpensive, and even though our ratings were sure to grow, our advertising revenue would not. It's very difficult to interrupt war coverage with commercials and even if we did, most advertisers wouldn't want their products associated with armed conflict.

Still, we welcomed the opportunity. If we did our jobs right, the long-term value to CNN would be immeasurable and I wasn't going to let short-term financial concerns distract us. (That said, I did pitch the cable operators on our board the idea of a "war tax," in which they'd increase the subscription fees they paid to CNN by 5 cents a month to offset our costs. I thought this could be positioned as a public service since our coverage would be so unique and important. They didn't go for it.)

Tom Johnson had been thrown into the deep end but he was a capable manager and he inherited a terrific team, from more senior journalists like Ed Turner (no relation to me), who was his number two, to very talented younger people like Eason Jordan, who was in charge of our international newsgathering. As they prepared a range of plans to ramp up coverage, Tom and this team presented me with various scenarios of spending increases, from $5 million up to $35 million in incremental expenses.

When they were finished, Tom said, "Ted, what am I authorized to spend?"

These expenses would all fall straight to the bottom line, but it was still an easy call for me. "You spend whatever it takes, pal," and that was the end of our meeting. Tom looked surprised—I don't think he was used to this kind of quick approval of major expenditures from his years in the newspaper business—but with a green light to spend $35 million, CNN rushed to improve existing facilities and establish new ones throughout the Gulf region, including Baghdad, Tel Aviv, Jerusalem, Saudi Arabia, Cairo, and Amman, Jordan.

Tensions grew in that region as Saddam continued to ignore deadlines for withdrawing his troops from Kuwait. In October Bernard Shaw scored a coup when Saddam Hussein sat down for an interview. People around the world watched, hoping that Saddam might offer some words to de-escalate the situation. He didn't, and we took a lot of flak from officials in Washington, who accused us of letting Saddam use CNN as his "mouthpiece," but I held to the view that it was our job to deliver the news from all sides and if the leader of a country with whom we were about to go to war wanted to give an interview, we couldn't turn him down.

Wars usually start when the talking stops. We weren't in any way endorsing

Iraq's position; we were simply providing an opportunity for the airing of positions from all sides of the conflict. It was in this spirit that in January, with war tensions reaching new heights, CNN received a request from Saddam's officials for another interview, and they specifically asked that it once again be with Bernnie Shaw. Bernie was a terrific journalist but for many years he had been an anchor, not a reporter, and now he was being asked to leave his desk in Washington to fly to the most dangerous place in the world.

Given the safety concerns, this couldn't have been an easy decision for Bernie, but he decided to go. Many again hoped that Saddam would use this interview to announce a plan for withdrawal from Kuwait and de-escalate the conflict. Instead, after Bernie had made the trip to Baghdad, Iraqi officials now told CNN that Saddam Hussein had changed his mind and would not be doing the interview. His decision to cancel was seen by many as a "last straw" and it was no longer a question of if the coalition would strike, but more of a matter of when and where. Having flown all that way for an interview, Bernie now found himself staying at the Al-Rashid hotel in the heart of Baghdad, a city on the brink of war.

Tom Johnson had excellent contacts in Washington and several of these, including White House Press Secretary Marlin Fitzwater, CIA Director William Webster, National Security Council Adviser Brent Scowcroft, and Joint Chiefs Chairman Colin Powell, called to ask him to move our people out of Iraq. Eventually, Tom even got a very serious call from President George H. W. Bush. The president expressed his appreciation for our thorough reporting but also voiced concerns that Saddam was using CNN to get his message out. Bush also made it clear that war was imminent and, according to Tom, he said, "Tell Bernie not to stay in Baghdad."

During his tenure at the L.A. *Times,* Tom had lost two journalists—one was killed in Iran when the Shah was overthrown and the other died covering the war in Nicaragua. Tom seriously considered ordering our people to leave Baghdad, but he knew this was something he'd have to run by me. He presented me with three options.

One was to move all CNN personnel out of Iraq and back to Amman. The second was to relocate them to the outskirts of Baghdad, and the third was to have them stay in place at the Al-Rashid.

Tom's personal recommendation was to get out of Iraq, and then try to move our people back in once the initial attacks were over. To me, these people were war journalists and I felt strongly that we had to leave the decision up to them. I said that those who wanted to stay could stay and those who wanted to leave could leave. I also made it clear to Tom that if anyone was killed or injured, I and I alone would take full responsibility. Peter Arnett, Bernard Shaw, John Holliman, and the crew, led by producer Robert Weiner, all decided to stay.

Hostilities began on the evening of January 16, 1991. I was in Los Angeles watching CNN at Jane Fonda's house and I'll never forget it. Bernie, Peter Arnett, and John Holliman delivered gripping coverage as the bombs began to fall. For the first time in history, a war was being televised live from behind the lines. I grabbed the remote. While CNN's team provided

riveting coverage and our lead anchor compared being in Baghdad to experiencing
"the center of hell," CBS's Dan Rather was
sitting at his desk in New York talking about
the attack. When I flipped to ABC, Peter
Jennings was also behind a desk, talking.
NBC and Tom Brokaw? Same thing.

Turning back to our live coverage, I
smiled. CNN scored the journalistic scoop
of the century.

━━━━━━ A TED STORY ━━━━━━

"You Are Making Things Very Difficult for Me"
—Tom Johnson

The night the bombs first fell I was
convinced that our crew would not be
alive by morning and none of us in
Atlanta slept a wink. It was particularly tense the few times when our
audio transmissions were interrupted.
To this day, most people don't realize
that all we had was audio coming out
of there. We were basically doing radio
with Holliman, Arnett, and Bernie with
different graphics and maps on the
screen. It was wild in the control room

and I remember looking up at the monitors we had tuned to CBS, NBC, ABC, PBS, the BBC, local affiliates—you name it, every single one had switched over to CNN's coverage. They hadn't asked for our permission, they just took it, so I called Ted and he said, "Just let them have it for a while." Before you knew it, we had faxes and phone calls coming in from all over the world from television outlets that wanted to become CNN affiliates and share footage of our broadcast. It was an incredible night and somehow, to our great relief, everyone made it through.

As we geared up for the second night of bombing, Eason Jordan told me that NBC News in Baghdad and Washington had hard information that the Al-Rashid hotel "was on the target list" because of a belief that there was an underground bunker in which Saddam could be hiding and because of all sorts of Iraqi antennae on the roof of the hotel. I didn't have time to waste so I decided go straight to Colin Powell. I was in the middle of a hectic newsroom and to be sure no one could overhear the call, I made it while crouched down beneath our International Assignment Desk.

When I explained that I had been told that the Al-Rashid Hotel was on the target list for that night, he almost took my head off over the phone.

"First, we warned you to get your people out of Baghdad. Their presence is complicating our mission. Second, target lists are secret [profanities omitted]. Now, do you think I would strike a hotel in which my friend Bernie Shaw is staying?"

With an eardrum throbbing, I thanked him and advised our personnel to stay in the Al-Rashid.

The creation of CNN is the business achievement of which I'm most proud, and CNN's coverage of Operation Desert Storm was the network's proudest moment. By being there—live and in person—we gripped viewers around the world. Bernard Shaw, John Holliman, Peter Arnett, and our crew showed incredible bravery and did a fantastic job. Here in the United States our ratings skyrocketed and there were nights when our viewership surpassed the broadcast networks'. Just over ten years after launching and being ridiculed as "Chicken Noodle News," CNN had established itself as the most capable, trusted news outlet in the world.

The ground phase of the Gulf War would last just one hundred days, and events—and ratings—at CNN returned to normal as the year progressed. By that summer, the big news in Atlanta was the Braves. Prior to 1991, the team had finished in last place three years in a row and hadn't had a winning season since 1983. I remember after one particularly bad year I got a call from Rankin Smith, who was then the owner of the Atlanta Falcons and a friendly rival. "Ted," he said, "I have to ask you. What does it feel like to lose a hundred games in one season?"

"Well, I don't look at it that way, Rankin," I responded. "The way I see it we won sixty-two games and that's more than the Falcons have won in the last ten years!"

The truth is that over the course of the years we did a pretty poor job of running the ball club. Among other bad decisions, within a four-year period I managed to fire two of the greatest managers of all time: Bobby Cox and Joe Torre. Fortunately, Cox agreed to return to the team partway through our dismal 1990 campaign and then we hired John Schuerholz from the Kansas City Royals to be our new general manager.

At last, in 1991, we turned it around. The Braves went "from worst to first" in one year, surging to a National League pennant and electrifying the city of Atlanta. Jane Fonda and I had a great time at the games, and after so many years of watching the Braves lose, it was an incredible thrill to participate in the World Series. Even though we wound up losing to the Minnesota Twins in a tense, seven-game series it was a lot of fun.

When Jane and I first began dating, we didn't think much about getting married. We'd both been divorced twice, and I didn't want to make the mistake of rushing into another marriage. But Jane and I were really getting along well so I said to her,

"Let's make a rule that we live together for two years and if things are still going well we can discuss marriage then." She thought that was a good idea and it's just what we did. After two years had passed we were still doing great so I raised the issue of marriage. Jane was still hesitant so I suggested, "Here's the reason I think we should get married. I've got five children and you have two. They're all getting to marrying age and we ought to show them we believe in the institution of marriage to try and encourage them not to be afraid and to show them that marriage can work. We've been getting along great and there's no reason why we shouldn't get along just as well if we're married." Jane thought about it and agreed. We planned a quiet ceremony at Avalon plantation in Florida. The guest list was small—just our closest friends and family—and it turned out to be a wonderful event. Jane's son Troy walked her down the aisle and she looked stunning. I was overjoyed that this wonderful, intelligent woman would now be my wife.

Unfortunately, my mom was too ill to attend, but when Jane and I flew to Montana for our honeymoon we stopped in

Cincinnati to see her. I knew it made her feel good to see the two of us so happy. A few days after our visit, she was interviewed for an article in *The Cincinnati Post* in which she told them how proud she was of me. She passed away the next day.

My mom was a beautiful, dignified, and gracious woman. She had some tough times with my dad and even more difficult struggles caring for my sister but she remained strong throughout. My sadness at my mom's passing was tempered by the fact that she had been able to enjoy her grandchildren and some of my success.

———

At the conclusion of '91, I was named *Time* magazine's Man of the Year. The recognition came in large part because of CNN's emergence as the world's news leader following its Gulf War coverage but the article also gave me credit for my past success as a yachtsman and my other contributions to the communications industry. It was a long way from selling billboards in the South, but I knew that I wasn't finished yet.

25

Movies and Cartoons

Moving into the 1990s my basic strategy for our company was clear. I wanted to own as much programming as possible and to air that product on the networks we owned and controlled. My continued hope was that one of these networks would be ABC, NBC, or CBS, but it didn't look like my directors from Time Warner (the name of the company formed after the 1989 merger of Time Inc. and Warner Communications) were going to allow that. But cable continued to grow and the success of TNT encouraged me to look for more opportunities to launch new entertainment channels.

I'd always had an interest in cartoons. When we ran them in the early days of WTBS they got good ratings and the early Warner Brothers and MGM cartoons that came with our acquisition of the MGM library performed very well on the Super-Station and TNT. Kids were attracted to cartoons and I got the idea that we should make one that would teach them about the environment. I thought it would make a lot of sense to reach children early and help them understand their role in taking care of our planet.

To do this I pulled a small team together, including Barbara Pyle, the head of our in-house environmental team, and we came up with a concept called *Captain Planet*. Working with the animation company DIC Entertainment, we produced a series where the superhero and his team of helpers ("The Planeteers") battled villains (they had great names like "Hoggish Greedley," "Venomous Skumm," and "Duke Nukem"). Because this was a new kind of show and since the subject matter was something that many in Hollywood really cared about, we attracted some stars to do voice-over

work, including Tom Cruise, Whoopi Gold-
berg, and Jeff Goldblum. The show did
well on our networks, but most importantly,
it really did teach kids a lot of valuable lessons. Today, when I speak to younger,
college-age audiences, I ask them to raise
their hands if they watched *Captain Planet*
and I'm amazed that so many hands go
up. It was gratifying to make a series that
kids enjoyed while also learning valuable
lessons. *Captain Planet* made me that
much more interested in being a bigger
player in children's programming.

In 1991 I heard rumors that the animation
company Hanna-Barbera Studios might be
for sale. They were owned by Cincinnati-
based Great American Communications,
which had bought the company as part of
its deal for Taft Broadcasting in the late '80s.
Hanna-Barbera's founders—Bill Hanna and
Joe Barbera—met each other in the '30s
when they worked together at MGM. When
that studio closed its animation business in
the late '50s, Bill and Joe started an independent production company and achieved
great success through the '60s and '70s.

Using a "limited animation" technique,

they were able to produce animation at a cost that allowed for series production, as opposed to one-off theatrical shorts and full-length features. But after a string of hit shows, including *Huckleberry Hound, The Flintstones*, *Scooby Doo*, and *The Jetsons*, the studio hit harder times in the '80s as other animation companies entered the series marketplace. Hanna-Barbera didn't do as good a job managing their library as had rival firms like the Walt Disney Company, and with Great American facing financial problems, a sale of Hanna-Barbera to a more strategic buyer was a logical step.

The most obvious of these was the Walt Disney Company. Disney knew how to market animated characters and adopting Fred Flintstone, Scooby Doo, and Huckleberry Hound into the same family as Mickey Mouse and Donald Duck made good sense. Hanna-Barbera's library could also support the Disney Channel. Word got around Hollywood that Disney CEO Michael Eisner did get the first crack at making this acquisition, but fortunately he balked at the asking price of $312 million and submitted an offer rumored to be about $200 million.

With Disney out of the running—at least temporarily—I decided to move quickly. If we could buy Hanna-Barbera and combine their library with the Warner Brothers (*Bugs Bunny, Daffy Duck*) and MGM (*Tom and Jerry*) animation that we had acquired when we bought MGM, we'd own about two thirds of all the cartoons ever made. Our plan was to use those shows to start a channel that ran nothing but cartoons, twenty-four hours a day. True, the Disney Channel and Nickelodeon ran some animated shows, but no one was doing nonstop cartoons, and with this great animation library this would be as much of a no-brainer as twenty-four-hour news had been. Just as it never made sense that people could only watch the news at 6:00, 7:00, and 11:00 P.M., why should kids have to wait until Saturday morning for cartoons? I also liked the fact that Hanna-Barbera's shows were all wholesome and family-friendly—not full of all the violence that seemed to be working its way into kids' animation in those days. For a little over $300 million

I'd be buying the opportunity to launch a unique and valuable cable channel.

Once again, I needed approval from my board but on this occasion, it turned out not to be a problem. They had kept me from buying FNN out of concern that we would become too powerful in news, but the kids business would be a new growth opportunity for us, and as cable operators they probably liked the idea of a competing channel giving them negotiating leverage against Nickelodeon and Disney. Time Warner could have objected or even gone after Hanna-Barbera themselves, but Turner Broadcasting owned Warner Brothers' pre-1948 library—including the bulk of their classic animation—and that made the deal far more logical for us. We'd still have to figure out how to handle the financing but the board gave me the green light.

I knew Great American's CEO, Carl Lindner. We had always gotten along well so I called him up directly. After the usual formalities I got right to the point. "I understand that you're considering selling Hanna-Barbera, is that true?"

"Yes it is, Ted," he replied.

"And I heard you're asking $312 million for it?"

"That's right, Ted."

And I said, "I'd like to offer you $312 million. Would you accept cash?"

"Yes, Ted."

"I'm hereby offering you your asking price of $312 million cash at closing."

And he said, "Well, Ted, you just bought yourself Hanna-Barbera!"

Sellers dream of getting a call like this but once again this was an asset that would be extremely valuable and I wanted to get it off the market right away. We scrambled to work out the financing and made a deal with the Apollo Investment Fund, run by former Drexel banker Leon Black. We each put in $50 million in cash, Apollo helped raise the rest in debt, and we closed on the deal in December '91. (We later bought out Apollo's 50 percent.)

I was really excited (it felt great having both Fred Flintstone and George Jetson on the payroll) and we started planning to launch the new channel. We played around with different names for the business but we decided that such a powerful, simple

concept—twenty-four-hour cartoons—
needed a simple name. We settled on calling it Cartoon Network and I told Scott
Sassa, the dynamic young executive who
I had put in charge of our entertainment
businesses, that the channel would launch
on October 1, 1992, at high noon.

Cable distribution was particularly tight
at this time as the broadcasters had been
provided with "must carry" rules handed
down by the FCC. This regulation put pressure on cable operators to carry the signals of local broadcasters. If the local
station exercised its "must carry" rights,
they would be put on the cable lineup but
they were not owed a subscription fee.
Their other option was to negotiate for "retransmission consent," meaning they could
try to extract a subscription fee for their
signal. When it became clear that the latter option probably wasn't viable, the bigger station groups did a smart thing. They
decided to create their own cable channels and told the cable operators that they
wouldn't haggle over carriage of their
over-the-air stations if they went along and
launched their new cable channels. This
was how Scripps launched the Food Net-

work and Home and Garden Television, and ABC and Hearst, part owners of ESPN, gained carriage for ESPN2.

I didn't like these rules because they were intended to protect the broadcasters. They didn't need the help, and it resulted in filling cable systems with channels that wouldn't have been there otherwise. (We would later challenge these rules in a lawsuit that went all the way to the Supreme Court. In 1997, in the case of *Turner Broadcasting vs. the FCC,* we lost by a 5–4 vote.)

These retransmission deals slowed the Cartoon Network's distribution but we knew it was just a matter of time before we were carried everywhere. Not only did we manage to collect subscription fees for the service but also our ratings were boffo. From my days at Channel 17, I'd learned that a good show—old or new—could compete and the classic Hanna-Barbera shows still were popular. Since some of our younger viewers hadn't seen these programs before, they didn't even know they were old. We produced new shows as well, and used Hanna-Barbera's production capabilities to make hits like *Dexter's Laboratory, Johnny Bravo,* and *The Powerpuff*

Girls. They also helped us revive the *Captain Planet* franchise by producing *The New Adventures of Captain Planet*.

In short, the Cartoon Network was a huge success. Several years after the launch, I was with Michael Eisner. He leaned over and said, "Do you want to know the biggest mistake I ever made?"

And I said, "No, Michael, what was it?"

"Not buying Hanna-Barbera when I had the chance—I should have never let you get it."

In addition to launching new channels, I was still eager to make sure that TBS and TNT continued to have access to new and better programming. It was good to have libraries but without a studio I worried that we might get cut off from new content. It would be like the United States having its oil supply cut off—we could survive for a while but pretty soon we'd be in big trouble.

When Martin Davis was exploring selling Paramount, we had conversations but they never went anywhere. He knew that I had spending constraints and he suspected correctly that my board didn't want me to buy a major studio. This was frustrating for me, as I thought it was obvious by then that owning production and distribution capabilities made sense. I think most of our board members knew it, too. I was convinced that Jerry Levin and the other Time Warner directors would say that they didn't want us to buy a studio because it was too expensive, too risky, or too distracting, but that what *really* concerned them was that we'd end up competing with Warner Brothers. The terms of their investment in Turner gave them the right to veto such deals, but it bothered me when I thought they would use their veto against the best long-term interests of the Turner Broadcasting shareholders.

I was determined to obtain production capabilities and if they wouldn't let me buy a big studio, perhaps I could go after a couple of smaller ones. Around that time, I got a call from Alan Horn at Castle Rock Entertainment, a successful production company he had founded in the late '80s along with a talented team of producers and executives, including Rob Reiner, Glenn Padnick, Andrew Sheinman, and Martin Shafer. They had produced a string of very good movies (including *A Few Good Men, City Slickers,* and *When Harry*

Met Sally) and also had experience producing TV series (including *Seinfeld,* which was about to become a huge hit).

───────── A TED STORY ─────────

"We Bonded Right Away"
—Alan Horn

(A FOUNDER OF CASTLE ROCK ENTERTAINMENT, ALAN HORN IS NOW PRESIDENT AND COO OF WARNER BROTHERS.)

I had spoken with the investment bank Allen and Company about selling our company and had been fishing around with some potential buyers but we weren't getting traction with anyone. My wife, Cindy, knew Jane Fonda from some work they had done on environmental causes and I had met Ted Turner years before when I was working for Norman Lear and he and I visited Ted on one of his properties. I remembered him from that time as being great fun and I decided to invite him and Jane over for dinner to talk to him about selling our company.

So Ted and Jane came over to our house and as they walked around and saw my collection of western art, Ted said, "Hell, you're buying western art and I'm buying the West!" We bonded right away. Ted was very straightforward about his interest in buying our company and very quickly thereafter we worked with his financial people on the subsequent details and had all the deal terms in place.

Another company I set my sights on was New Line Cinema. Run by its founders, Michael Lynne and Bob Shaye, New Line began by producing low-budget films for the college market. Their success grew with *Nightmare on Elm Street* and they had another hit with a live-action version of *Teenage Mutant Ninja Turtles*. The films they made weren't always my cup of tea—especially the horror movies—but they were the right size and I liked Bob and Mike a lot. I liked the fact that they were entrepreneurs who understood how to be successful with limited resources. If we could merge them into Turner, increase their budgets, and allow them to make bigger films, we could grow them into the kind of studio that we were being prevented from buying.

—————— A TED STORY ——————

"I'm Acquiring You Guys"
—Michael Lynne

A close friend of mine named Roy Furman headed up an investment firm that concentrated heavily on the media business. Roy would periodically meet with key people in the industry to talk about ideas and early in 1993 he had a meeting with Ted. Roy had a list of about ten items he wanted to discuss with Ted and around number nine he mentioned New Line. The only reason we were even on the list was because Roy had been involved with our initial public offering—we had absolutely no interest in doing a transaction at that time. But when our name came up Ted zeroed in and

New Line became the only thing he wanted to talk about!

So Roy called up afterward and spoke to Bob Shaye and me about the talk with Ted and said, "You're not going to believe this but Ted Turner is very eager to meet with you."

At the time we didn't know Ted at all but in thinking about it, if there was one person we might be open to talking to it was Ted Turner. He's an iconoclastic guy. He's not a bureaucrat and we weren't bureaucrats. If anybody could understand us and if there was anybody out there we might be able to work with, he could be the guy. We still didn't want to sell but if nothing else we figured it would be great to meet him, so with enormous skepticism we flew down to Atlanta. When we got up to his office Ted showed us all his Oscar statuettes from his MGM acquisition and Civil War memorabilia and then he went on with the meeting as if he had already done a deal with us! It was like someone turned on a switch in him and he said, "I'm acquiring you guys and you're going to come in here and make more money than your business has ever made before. We're on the same wavelength. You formed your business and are still running it, I formed my business and I'm still running it." He just went on and on and it was really overwhelming in a funny and bizarre way.

We had a lot to think about as we flew back to New York. Bob and I had always enjoyed being independent and emotionally we weren't ready to sell our company. But in many ways Ted was right—we were on the same wavelength. We had very similar business experiences and were in many respects similar kinds of people.

New Line and Castle Rock were solid companies run by great people and we quickly negotiated deals with them. I didn't know if the board would approve one, both, or neither but it came down to a vote at the board meeting in the summer of 1993. We were meeting in a room at the St. Regis Hotel in New York, and Bob Shaye and

Mike Lynne from New Line and Alan Horn from Castle Rock each had to make presentations directly to the board. This was an unusual practice and it turned out to be an unusual meeting. I remember the Time Warner directors being particularly difficult. To open the questioning of Michael Lynne and Bob Shaye, Michael Fuchs, at the time the head of HBO, asked, "Isn't it true that you guys just make B movies that most people really aren't that interested in?" It was a tough way to start, but Bob and Mike answered by explaining that they didn't think of movies as A or B but instead tried to produce ones that would be profitable.

The discussions continued to be contentious and right up to the vote it wasn't clear which way it would go. During a break in the meeting someone asked for individual vote counts, so we went around the table and one by one, the three Time Warner directors made similar statements filled with legalese like, "I have not consulted with my colleagues on this but I've studied the film business and believe that its risky nature will add to the volatility of Turner's earnings." They all said pretty much the same thing but instead of voting against the deals or exercising their veto right they claimed a possible conflict and abstained.

The way it wound up, we needed one more vote from an outside director and it all came down to Brian Roberts from Comcast. His company was not in the film business so he wasn't conflicted. Brian said that we were doing a good job running Turner, and that these film companies seemed to make good strategic sense to our company, and he enthusiastically supported the deals. (To this day, when I see Brian I thank him for letting me get into the movie business.) After being denied the chance to go after a major studio, for about $600 million we had acquired two smaller ones and I was determined to make our new programming ventures succeed.

At the same time, I was pushing TNT to produce more and better original movies and miniseries, and the one I was most excited about was *Gettysburg*. I had always had great interest in the Civil War, and one of my favorite works on the subject was Michael Shaara's *The Killer Angels,* which won the Pulitzer Prize in 1975. Ron Maxwell adapted the book into a screenplay and would also serve as the director of the project, which we had originally designed to be a miniseries for TNT.

Gettysburg would be our most ambitious original production, and Maxwell's terrific script helped attract an incredible cast including Martin Sheen, Jeff Daniels, Tom Berenger, and Sam Elliott. The National Park Service allowed us to shoot on the Gettysburg battlefield and as the dailies started coming in I knew that this miniseries was going to be great. I got so excited about the production that Maxwell asked if I wanted to make a cameo. I let them cast me as Colonel Waller T. Patton, a Confederate officer. There I was in full uniform and makeup out there in the fields with a huge battalion of Civil War reenactors. When it came time for my part, Maxwell yelled "Action!" and I led a charge only to be shot down. (Years later, I also made a cameo in *Gods and Generals,* a follow-up to Gettysburg, but curiously, neither of these performances led to any more acting offers!)

I was so impressed with the quality of this production that it gave me an idea—before it airs on TNT, we should release it in theaters. The first, obvious objection I received was that the movie would be way too long. Even if they edited aggressively, it would be hard to bring it in under five hours.

"No problem," I joked, "at five hours, we could charge double!"

I thought that *Gettysburg* had a chance to become a classic epic in the tradition of *Lawrence of Arabia* and *Gone With the Wind* and I figured that a theatrical release would only add to the title's value when we aired it on TNT and released it on video. I tried to get the New Line and Castle Rock people excited about it but they kept saying it was too long to play in theaters. I explained that we were working hard to shorten it and they'd understand my enthusiasm if they'd just take a look at it.

Alan Horn at Castle Rock had given me a particularly hard time about the movie's length and during a trip to Los Angeles I called to tell him I had a version I wanted him to see. When he said he could do it that afternoon I asked him what time.

"I can probably do it some time after lunch, say around 2:30. Would that work?" he said.

"Well, that depends on what time you're planning to have dinner!" I answered.

In the end, Maxwell and his team managed to get the film down to four hours and fourteen minutes—still making it the longest American movie ever distributed—ten minutes longer than *Cleopatra*. When I saw the final version, complete with Randy Edelman's beautiful score, tears welled up in my eyes. It was a proud moment for me to see this heroic story told so beautifully. New Line agreed to be our distributor and while it did prove difficult to get such a long movie into theaters (they had only half the chance to sell tickets as they would for a two-hour feature), we got some great reviews and wound up doing a little more than $10 million at the box office. That was far below the film's $25 million budget but it wound up doing very well on TNT and has had very strong home video sales over the years. *Gettysburg* continues to be shown in classrooms, and to this day it remains the film production of which I'm most proud.

By the end of '93, the Cartoon Network was clearly a winner and despite the board's initial objections, we were also in the movie business. As TNT aired more contemporary product and sports like the NBA, I wanted to make sure we continued to get value out of our classics library, too. But rather than license the movies to a competitor like American Movie Classics, we decided to start another channel of our own—and in April of '94 we launched Turner Classic Movies. Kicking off with a splashy event in the heart of Times Square (I got to flip the switch right in front of the JumboTron), the network struggled for distribution at first but when people saw the channel they fell in love with it and it became a moneymaker within a couple of years.

The early 1990s were a period of tremendous growth for us but I still wanted one more jewel in our crown. Even as we added new libraries, production companies, and cable channels, I worried that when I died, my tombstone would read, "Here Lies Ted Turner. He Never Owned a Broadcast Network!"

26

Networking

Even though I felt that Time Warner would continue to block my attempts to buy a network I still thought that merging with one made strategic sense, so I kept discussions quietly going with ABC, NBC, and CBS. My hope was that if I could negotiate an attractive deal I could get Jerry Levin to change his mind or maybe even convince him to cash out Time Warner's stake in Turner and clear the way for us to move forward.

ABC was off my radar screen for several years after Capital Cities Communications bought it in 1985. But in '92, when it came time for the networks to pursue the broadcast rights to the 1996 summer Olympics in Atlanta, we did have encouraging discussions with Capital Cities/ABC over the possibility of a joint bid. We reasoned that if we could create the most value—and therefore justify the highest bid—if we aired higher profile prime-time events on the ABC network while also offering daytime coverage on ABC's ESPN and Turner's TNT and TBS. Because we already had so much production infrastructure in Atlanta, it made sense for someone to partner with us. But we never did get to the point of putting forth an offer (and NBC wound up getting those rights). Yet through the course of these discussions I got to know Dan Burke, Capital Cities' CEO, and as we looked at the advantages of a joint Olympic bid, the conversation naturally went toward the synergies we could create if our two companies were combined.

I liked the Capital Cities people a lot. Dan Burke and Tom Murphy, the company's chairman, really understood the business. They had built their company by buying up TV and radio stations as well as newspapers and magazines and operating them efficiently. They were also straight shooters who always treated people with respect. (That said, our executive styles were definitely a little different. One time, during a closed-door meeting in Burke's office, my voice got a little louder than they were used to hearing on that floor. When I said something about how cable would eventually "strangle" the networks, Burke's secretary thought I was threatening her boss personally so she called security! Dan and I had a good laugh when security knocked on the door to make sure that everything was okay and that I wasn't trying to kill him.)

When Dan Burke retired from the company in '94, Tom Murphy moved back into the CEO position, and Bob Iger, who had been running the ABC network, was promoted to become the parent company's COO. One night when Jane and I went out to dinner with some friends in New York, we were seated at a table next to Bob and his wife, Willow Bay, whom I also knew since she was an anchor at CNN.

─────── **A TED STORY** ───────

"He Just Couldn't Let It Go"
—Bob Iger

(BOB IGER IS CURRENTLY PRESIDENT AND CEO OF THE WALT DISNEY COMPANY.)

Willow and I were out to dinner in New York and Ted and Jane were seated at the very next table, with Ted and I sitting back-to-back. When he saw us, he got really excited and said, very loudly, "We ought to figure out a way to merge our companies!" This was a crowded New York restaurant but Ted was practically screaming and people could definitely overhear him. He might as well have banged his fork against his glass and said he had an announcement to make. I asked him to keep his voice down but he just couldn't let it go and was talking to me more than he was the other people at his table. I finally told Ted I'd be happy to come down to Atlanta to talk about it some more in private.

When I did go to meet with him at his office I was shocked by his physical energy. He couldn't sit still and as we talked through how a merger might work, every time we agreed on something he'd give me a high five! And honestly there really was a lot to agree on. Combining ABC News with CNN made a lot of sense and we could have used Ted's animation content for the network's Saturday morning lineup. ESPN and Turner Sports would also work well together and with our ownership stake in Lifetime we probably could have found synergies with TBS and TNT. A merger between Capital Cities and Turner really would have been an exciting combination of assets, and after I briefed Tom Murphy on my conversation with Ted we set up a follow-up lunch in New York to begin more formal negotiations.

Bob Iger and I hit it off and since he was fairly new to his job I assured him that if we merged the companies, I'd recommend that he continue to run the ABC portion. When it came time to take the negotiations up a level, Tom Murphy set up a lunch in New York. He invited Warren Buffett, a longtime investor in Capital Cities, to attend and I invited John Malone. These were two great deal makers, and since a merger couldn't happen without their agreement, it made sense to involve them early. As Bob Iger and I discussed how the meeting might go, he cautioned me not to say anything about trying to buy a Hollywood studio. It looked like Sony might be ready to sell Columbia Pictures and I'd told Iger I wanted to go after it. "Murphy and Buffett hate the movie business," Bob cautioned me. "This might be something we could consider down the road after the deal is done but this meeting will go a lot better if you don't mention it." I understood, and we had plenty of other issues to discuss, so I didn't expect this to be a problem.

The lunch was at Capital Cities/ABC's Manhattan headquarters and the discussion was cordial and positive. Everyone around the table understood the benefits of merging the companies. Then, as we talked about ways we might expand the business down the road I mentioned that Sony might be willing to sell Columbia and exclaimed, "As soon as the ink dries on this deal and the merger is approved we should try to buy a studio." I was really taking a chance by bringing this up but if we were going to be partners, I felt I needed to be honest with them. Unfortunately, Iger's prediction was right, and immediately, Buffett said, "I don't like the motion picture business. I'm a director at Coke and when we owned Columbia it was a disaster."

I said, "Well, movies might not be a good business for a soft drink company, but if you're in the broadcasting business it makes all the sense in the world! If you don't want to be in the movie business, you don't want to be in the television business because this industry is going to go vertical. The first network and studio merger will have the first mover advantage and the company that gets there last is going to be playing catch-up."

When Tom Murphy joined in, agreeing with Warren, I could tell that the meeting had taken a bad turn. It might have been different if I'd backed right down but I couldn't. "The reason we're all here," I continued, "is because our industry is moving quickly and we want to anticipate the future.

I'm telling you now about my interest in a studio because I want us to have a harmonious relationship and I want you to sign off on this because it's the last piece of the big puzzle that we really need."

The conversation remained polite after that, but their enthusiasm dropped when they saw how serious I was about acquiring a studio. Iger called me a few days later to tell me they'd decided not to move forward. While Murphy openly disagreed with me in the meeting, I thought that Warren Buffett was the one who really killed the deal. Ironically, it was only about a year after that lunch that Capital Cities was bought by the Walt Disney Company. Today, every single broadcast network is aligned with a studio (ABC with Disney, NBC with Universal, CBS with Paramount, and Fox with 20th Century Fox). Sure enough, the industry did go vertical—I just wish I'd been able to convince them do it with me, first.

At NBC I stayed in regular contact with Bob Wright, the CEO. I'd known Bob from all the way back in the late 1970s when he ran Cox Cable in Atlanta. In 1980 he was among our invited guests at our CNN launch ceremony, and at one point, when CNN was having financial struggles, I spoke with him about the possibility of Cox making an investment with us. Bob and I had also been hunting together and we'd become pretty good friends.

─────── A TED STORY ───────

"You Shot My Deer!"
—Bob Wright

(BOB WRIGHT SERVED AS PRESIDENT AND CEO OF NBC FROM 1986 TO 2007.)

Ted invited my wife and me down to his place in South Carolina for a weekend to go hunting. I had shot a gun before and had killed some birds but this was deer hunting and I really didn't know anything about hunting. So it's in the fall, it's cool, and on the first morning there we go out and it's like 5:00 and Ted sits me in this tree. "This is your tree," he says. "You've got to climb up the tree and sit in that stand."

So I do it, and I'm sitting up there with my rifle and I've been there just ten minutes and I look down and there's a deer—not seven hundred yards away but right below me. I said to myself, "That's a pretty big deer!" So I take the gun out and I point it down and shoot the deer. This wasn't exactly the way I pictured it would be, but less than an hour into the trip I've shot a deer. About five minutes after my gun went off, one of the Jeeps we'd driven out in comes rolling around. Ted's in it and he sees me standing there looking at the deer and he says, "I've been hunting that deer for two years! You shot my goddamn deer!"

"How do you know it's your deer?" I asked.

"Look at it—it's a ten-point buck!"

So I said, "You mean those things on the top?" and I counted them—one, two, three, four, five, and said, "Yeah, there are ten."

And he yelled again, "You shot my deer!" He was really upset.

So we go back to the house and

have something to eat and he's all wound up about this deer and says, "I want to go back out and do some more shooting."

I said, "Shooting what?"

"Wild hogs! We're going to shoot wild hogs!"

So my wife, Suzanne, and I get in this big Jeep. We're sitting in the back and conveniently I don't have a rifle but Ted has two. So we get out a ways and he stops the car and these huge hogs are coming through this high grass and he starts shooting away! They're really big and they're all around us and he's shooting them and they're running, running left and right. One's coming at us, shoot 'um. One's going away. He's getting them every which way. The changing rifles, the smell of smoke is all over the place. He clearly had to go after these hogs to get that deer off his mind!

With his background in cable, Bob Wright seemed eager to diversify NBC beyond the broadcast business. They owned

CNBC but as far as cable networks were concerned that was it, and many of the same synergies that would have existed with a Turner-ABC deal were also there with NBC. There were different ideas floating around about how a merger with NBC might work, ranging from Turner Broadcasting being acquired directly, to NBC being spun out from GE and merging with Turner to form a new, separate entity. Either way, valuations, structure, and responsibilities were issues to be resolved. Conversations grew serious enough for Bob to fly down to Atlanta with his boss, General Electric CEO Jack Welch, for a meeting with me.

We met in secret at a suite in the Ritz-Carlton in the Buckhead section of Atlanta—myself, Bob Wright, and Jack Welch. I knew Welch by reputation but didn't really know him personally and I looked forward to meeting with him, but from the beginning of this conversation, I was disappointed. It seemed clear to me that Welch either didn't understand or appreciate our business or he hadn't done his homework for the meeting. Whenever he referred to a valuation of our company it was very low and when it came to corporate structure and reporting lines I could tell that if we ever were to do a deal I'd be just another employee of General Electric.

──────── A TED STORY ────────

"He Really Struggled with Ted"
—Bob Wright

Jack Welch was pretty open to a deal with Turner but he really struggled with Ted and the perception that we would be buying Ted and his company. Nevertheless I convinced Jack to actually get on a plane with me and go to Atlanta and pitch an offer to Ted. Jack and I flew down to Peachtree-DeKalb Airport and met with Ted at the Ritz-Carlton Hotel in Buckhead. We sort of came in the back door and went upstairs to meet in a suite. We spent about an hour and a half talking and Ted never sat down. He tried to sit down but he was really antsy. I was used to Ted's behavior, but for Jack it was new. I said I really thought we should do this deal but Ted said we weren't offering the right price. I think he wanted $30 a share and we were offering something like $25.50. Ted said he also had some other concerns and asked about whether Jack would want him to be a vice chairman of GE and Jack said, "No." When Ted asked him why, Jack said, "Because I don't want you to be a vice chairman, I want you to run CNN." Jack was very straightforward about it and said he didn't think Ted would add anything to GE at the corporate level and he worried that he would be too difficult to work with.

By the end of the meeting, Ted said, "You know what? I don't think I want to do this."

So I said, "Don't let that be your final answer. We'll talk when we get back." So I called him the next day and he said, "I don't think there's a place for me at GE and Jack didn't offer enough money."

I said, "Well, is it that he didn't give you enough money and there's no place for you or is it there's no place so he didn't give you enough money?"

And Ted said, "Well, it's six of one, half dozen of the other."

———————— A TED STORY ————————

"Jack Welch Wouldn't Be Jack Shit!"
—Tom Brokaw

I went out to spend the weekend with Ted in Montana and Jack Welch had just walked out on him. They had been talking seriously and they came that close. It's a shame but in the end Jack just didn't think he could be in business with Ted. So Ted was fit to be tied and we got in the Land Rover and we're bouncing across the landscape with Chris Francis, the fishing guide, and Gordy Crawford, a major investor in Ted's company, in the back seat. Ted is going on, "That Jack Welch, he wanted me to be vice chairman of this and the honorary chairman of that. He didn't give me the respect I deserve! I built this company from nothing! I'm worth billions of dollars and they want me to be a vice chairman? I'll tell you something, Tom, if it had been for . . . hadn't been for . . . what's the name of that guy who invented the lightbulb?"

I said, "Thomas Edison."

"Yeah, if it hadn't been for Thomas Edison, Jack Welch wouldn't be Jack Shit!"

I thought Crawford and Chris were going to fall out of the truck. Years later, at Jack Welch's retirement party, we ended his tape with me telling that story and I said, "Don't worry, Jack. We all know you really are Jack Shit."

I was discouraged by the NBC discussions but I didn't think that General Electric would want to own that network forever and thought we might have discussions with them again sometime down the road (which, in fact, we did). In any event, striking out with ABC and NBC left me to consider CBS. I should point out here that by the mid-1990s, the Fox network was well established as a fourth broadcast network. But Rupert Murdoch's News Corporation owned them, and while I knew he had coveted CNN for years, Murdoch was not someone with whom I wanted to do business. Seeing the way he used his newspapers to advance his personal political agenda really bothered me. I certainly encouraged our networks to air programming about issues I considered important, like the environment and overpopulation, but Murdoch specifically supported or tore down individual political candidates through his publications, particularly in Europe. We had worked very hard to establish CNN as an impartial outlet with the highest journalistic standards and doing a deal with him would jeopardize everything we'd built.

My conversations at CBS were with Larry Tisch, the billionaire financier who had made his fortune in a wide range of businesses including hotels, tobacco, and insurance. With no background in media, he was in the network business to get a financial return and it looked like he might be willing to sell CBS for about $5 billion. As we analyzed a valuation for CBS, we also entered discussions with King World about acquiring them. The company was founded and run by the King brothers— Roger and Michael—and I knew them from back in the '70s when they sold me rerun rights for *The Little Rascals* on Channel 17. When they started out, *The Little Rascals* was about the only property they had but with hits like *Jeopardy!, Wheel of Fortune,* and *Oprah,* they had grown King World into the most successful syndication company in television. The King brothers were great guys—fun-loving entrepreneurs—and we liked the idea of being part of the same company. They would sell to us in a merger for about $1 billion. Their company was generating tremendous cash flow and I hoped to use those resources to help finance a bigger deal with a network.

We were also in some interesting discussions with Bill Gates of Microsoft.

―――――― A TED STORY ――――――

"A Deal Made in Heaven"
—Bill Gates

(BILL GATES IS CHAIRMAN OF
MICROSOFT CORPORATION.)

The Internet was exploding and it seemed a great place for news. At

Microsoft, we thought we could drive a lot of traffic but we didn't want to start from scratch so the obvious thing to do was to take the only brand that was really specific to news at the time—CNN—and do something with them. Our offer to Ted was that we would invest in Turner at market and create a 50/50 joint venture to manage CNN.com. It was a dream deal. Ted was willing to let us do the technology piece. Neither he nor his key people at the time had really put their minds around that and we had no problem letting them retain editorial control. We were willing to guarantee all the losses of the joint venture so that Turner corporately would have only seen profits.

Ted was eager to do it. We'd have these discussions and Ted would get on the phone and yell, "We should do this! This is great, let's do it!"

But at the time he had these weird control provisions relative to Time Warner and the other cable guys who owned pieces of his company. It kind of drove him crazy—he never really knew how to deal with having sort of a boss. You know, you get up on Monday with a wild idea and then you have to think, "Am I going to get vetoed?" He just didn't like it. And so part of our idea with this deal was that we would dilute those guys down in terms of their control so a lot of that voting stuff wouldn't affect Ted as much anymore. It was just a deal made in heaven.

There was a lot to be said for a deal with Microsoft. They had just invested a billion dollars in Comcast and now they were willing to invest a billion in Turner. We could put that cash to good use and in the meantime, we'd jump-start our online business and take a lead against our competitors. With Gates's billion and the cash that King World and our own companies were generating, we could go after CBS with $2 billion in cash and $3 billion from the banks.

But there were also issues about working with Microsoft that concerned me. Bill Gates and I are good friends now but back then I was just getting to know him and partnerships like this can be tricky. With a proposed joint management of CNN.com, I worried about being in a conflicting position with our partners over strategy or other issues. The CNN management team was particularly nervous. Microsoft had developed a reputation for being aggressive, so everyone's guard was up. The Internet was also new and there were those who thought that CNN.com might someday be worth more than the cable network. They worried that for $1 billion we would be giving to Gates half of something that would soon be worth far more.

While all of this was going on—discussions with Capital Cities/ABC, NBC, CBS, King World, and Microsoft—I continued to speak openly about my frustration with my board, particularly Time Warner. Their ability to veto deals made it hard to get a deal done and it was a cloud that hung over even preliminary discussions I had with potential partners. In the time since they had invested in us, our company had grown substantially, and I had a number of conversations with Jerry Levin and others about buying out their shares at a healthy profit. I spoke openly to them about feeling fenced in and to turn up the pressure I shared my concerns in public. It was my hope that we might orchestrate a transaction whereby Time Warner would exit the company and we could move forward with our strategic plans.

At the height of these discussions, while I was with Jane in Montana, Jerry Levin called and said he wanted to fly out and see me. It sounded important, and it was.

27

Time Warner Merger

In the summer of 1995, Turner Broadcasting was hitting on all cylinders. Our entertainment networks were growing rapidly and CNN was once again enjoying record high ratings. This time, the spike in news viewership was not caused by a war but by the O. J. Simpson saga. This coverage didn't make me as proud as had our telecasts from Baghdad and many advertisers weren't too thrilled with the idea of plugging their products during a double murder trial, but whether I liked it or not it was a huge story and it was gratifying to see people turning to CNN in big numbers to keep up to date. It had taken our company until 1989 to break the $1 billion mark in annual revenues and halfway through 1995—just six years later—we were on track to grow that number to nearly $3.5 billion.

Morale was high. Over the years we had attracted a strong team and I did what I could to keep them excited about coming to work every day. I had always been frugal with the company's resources and we couldn't pay the extravagant salaries of the big media companies in New York and Los Angeles, but we did provide stock options that would prove to be very valuable. Many of our people could have earned bigger paychecks elsewhere but I'd like to think it was the unusual opportunities and the vibrant atmosphere at Turner Broadcasting that motivated them to stay. And because we were growing quickly and launching so many new businesses, opportunities continued to present themselves to our talented and hardworking employees. It became part of our company's culture to take chances on younger, and oftentimes unproven, executives. Convincing people to leave stable companies

to take a chance on a financially shaky
UHF station or a start-up news channel
was not easy and we usually didn't fill positions with classic textbook candidates.
But for young people who wanted hands-on
experience in television news, there was
no better training ground than CNN (a
twenty-three-year-old Katie Couric worked
for us as a desk assistant), and many of
these quickly rose through the ranks to
hold significant positions. In the summer
of 1995 the head of our entertainment division, Scott Sassa, was still in his thirties,
as were all but one of the network presidents reporting to him, the only exception
being a twenty-nine-year-old he had put in
charge of TBS SuperStation.

I continued to focus on the future and
broader strategic issues and let our executives worry about the day-to-day running
of the individual businesses. The company
had now grown too big and complex for
me to keep up with all the details. That
said, each of our managers knew that
there were certain things I expected to be
kept informed about. I had a particular interest in programming and wanted to know
about which series we were acquiring or

movies we planned to produce. This part of the job was enjoyable for me and I still believe that quality programming was an important differentiator for us and I didn't want anything going on our air that I didn't feel good about.

From my early days I understood the importance of careful scheduling and thinking through how a TV audience flowed from one show to the next. Our network presidents didn't run all their lineup changes by me but generally I approved the bigger ones (and every manager of TBS knew that if they planned to move *The Andy Griffith Show* anywhere I needed to hear about it first!). I also intervened whenever it was necessary to keep our different divisions cooperating with each other. Our success relied on the various pieces of the company working together. For example, I bought the Braves to present their games on TBS; the MGM library provided the foundation to launch TNT and was now the backbone of Turner Classic Movies; Headline News would not have worked without the newsgathering capabilities of CNN; and we purchased Hanna-

Barbera specifically to launch the Cartoon Network.

Still, each of these entities had their own management structure and inevitably disputes would arise. An important part of my job was making sure they were resolved quickly and in the best interests of the overall company. The nature of my job called for decisions that weren't always popular (tough decisions seldom are) but I did my best to make them quickly and to keep things moving forward. You'd have to ask them, but I believe that most people enjoyed working with me.

Nineteen ninety-five was shaping up to be another great year but I never stopped looking ahead and when I did I saw plenty to be concerned about. We'd done everything I could think of to acquire a broadcast network but Time Warner continued to block us. I felt like the Republicans in Spain during the Spanish Civil War; I could handle the four columns approaching Madrid from every direction but my real problem was the fifth column—the enemy behind our lines. I knew that we couldn't win the media game if we didn't grow and while a network might be off the table, we still had other strategic holes to fill. We didn't own a large production facility, and while I had not been interested in owning cable systems in the past, as new channels launched and the broadcasters were handed new opportunities by the must-carry rules, I started to think that being part of a company that controlled distribution would make some sense. There were lots of options but no matter what I decided, I'd have to reconfigure our relationship with TCI and Time Warner.

━━━━━━ A TED STORY ━━━━━━

"He Felt Very Vulnerable"
—John Malone

Ted was on the TCI board of directors at that time. We were very close with him and he kept raising the issue that he felt very vulnerable. He decided to go talk to Mike Milken about whether it was feasible for him to raise enough capital to just outright buy a network. I believe it was at that meeting that Mike convinced Ted that he could probably do it, but it would be very

risky and probably foolish. He reminded him that he took one shot with
Kerkorian that damn near put him
over the edge. Ted remembered the
pain of that and I think he came to the
conclusion that with retransmission
consent and with the vertical integra-
tion going on that it was time for him
to think seriously about joining forces
with somebody.

He called me up and talked to me
about it and said, "You know we love
you guys but you're too far right-wing
for me and I think if CNN is going to
be controlled by anybody or go fit with
anybody it needs to fit with somebody
who's in the news business—and because of Time Inc. the most logical
thing might be to do something with
Time Warner."

When Jerry Levin called and said he
wanted to meet with me, I didn't know what
to expect. We'd been having so many different discussions over the past several
months it could have been anything. We
had guests at the Flying D Ranch but I told

him that if he wanted to see me right away he was welcome to fly out.

─────────── A TED STORY ───────────

"I Think We Should Buy"
—Jerry Levin

We had been looking at different ways to get the Time Warner stock up and one of our options was to monetize an asset. I was considering several options at the time and there were many different things we were interested in doing, like investing more in cable. We did start to have conversations about selling our interest in Turner. I believe at that time that Rupert Murdoch had shown interest in CNN, GE was interested in CNN, and I guess I took a cold shower and decided that that asset belonged together with the news operations of Time Warner. At the same time I started to think that TBS and TNT, as ad-supported entertainment channels, would be a nice complement to HBO and we were also in the cable business. So one day I told

Dick Parsons, our president, and Rich Bressler, our CFO, that rather than selling I think we should buy—so let's get a small group together—like one banker and the three of us—and figure out how to do it. We decided that the only way to finance it was with stock but it really was a question of how to convince Ted to go along with it and ultimately to get Malone on board so that he would be supportive.

I deputized myself to fly out to the ranch and Jane Fonda picked me up at the airport. I don't think they had any idea why I was coming, and as a matter of fact, Jane said to me, "Don't mess with my husband," because I think she thought we were going down a completely different road and trying to do something that was antagonistic to Ted's interest. I said, "No, no, no, this is going to be a good meeting—not to worry!"

Interestingly, they were entertaining Gordy Crawford that weekend and at one point Tom Brokaw and his wife showed up. Here I am trying to have a confidential conversation with all these people around, so I took Ted aside and showed him my list of five reasons why this made so much sense and after agreeing with my points he said, "Wait a second, I have to talk to Jane," and he came back and said, "Okay!"

A TED STORY

"I Do Have to Make One Phone Call"
—Tom Brokaw

I think Ted had forgotten that he'd invited us over that weekend and when I arrived with my daughter and my wife, Ted and Jerry Levin came around the corner and Ted said to me, "Hey, we just made a deal! Maybe now we'll buy CBS, or maybe we'll buy NBC and you'll come work for us!" Jerry was stunned and I walked over and said, "Congratulations Jerry. If you'll excuse me, I do have to make one phone call."

I needed to get back to Bill Gates as our discussions with Microsoft were still ongoing. The future certainly would have looked very different if I'd made the deal with Gates instead of Time Warner and I sometimes wonder how things would have turned out. I hated having to call Bill to tell him our deal was off.

—————— A TED STORY ——————

"I Was Just Heartbroken"
—Bill Gates

I was still hoping to do our deal with CNN when Ted called and said, "Maybe it's wrong, but I decided to do it. Jerry came out and talked to me and I've agreed to do a deal with him." I was just heartbroken and I still wonder if I'd just made it a little more concrete to Ted that he had this other solution if he would have done a deal with us instead. I think my personality and Ted's would have worked fine together because we're both long-term conceptual thinkers, willing to bring in a broad set of considerations into any decision. He's a wild optimist and I count myself the same. He's always thinking about how the pieces can come together in a different way. We both love decisions that seem crazy to other people but then they wake up five years later and see why it was obvious when at the time it seemed weird. In the media business, Rupert Murdoch is often thought of as a good long-term thinker, but even Rupert would say that Ted's in a league by himself. Ted's a major wizard in terms of having a whole new way of thinking and doing things.

Anyway, the more I think about that CNN deal not happening, the worse I feel about it.

There was a lot that went into my decision to merge with Time Warner. The timing seemed right for a number of reasons, not the least of which was the fact that I'd never been part of a really big company, and I wanted to see what it would be like to be on top of the mountain looking down.

I was also very proud of what we had built at CNN and I liked the idea of merging with a company with strong journalistic credentials such as those at Time Inc. Jerry would be CEO and I'd be vice chairman, but since I would have responsibility of overseeing the company's cable networks (including HBO), my day-to-day responsibilities wouldn't change much.

From a deal perspective, I thought that our company's stock was trading at about what it was worth but that Time Warner's was significantly undervalued—maybe by as much as 50 percent. I believed we'd be merging into a company with significant upside. A lot of Wall Street analysts thought that Time Inc. and Warner Communications were never properly integrated after their merger and I figured that if we could execute better and get everyone cooperating, we could really get the stock up significantly. Jerry and I were very different personalities but I thought we could make a good team. He was soft-spoken, and I was confident that my enthusiasm and energy would help drive performance and create buzz about our stock.

I did have some anxiety about no longer being CEO but I had already given so much of my autonomy to Time Warner and TCI that I felt this wouldn't be such a radical change. And since I would own about 10 percent of the new company's stock, and other big stakes would be held by supportive partners like TCI and Gordy Crawford—a good friend of mine who had invested on behalf of his company, Capital Research and Management Group—I figured that the ultimate control of this new company would be in friendly hands.

The final reason I agreed to the deal was a simple one. I was flat-out tired. It was now more than thirty years since my father's death and I'd been running the company on my own ever since. Thirty years of long weeks and eighteen-hour days would get to anyone and by this time I was exhausted. I still planned to work hard but I liked the idea of being supported by a larger company. Besides, our assets fit together really well and in Warner Brothers, we finally had the big studio we needed.

——————— A TED STORY ———————

"Our Stories Are Not So Dissimilar"
—Dick Parsons

(DICK PARSONS IS THE RETIRED CEO
OF TIME WARNER. IN 1995, HE SERVED
AS THE COMPANY'S PRESIDENT.)

I was on vacation when I got a call from Jerry, who said, "Get back in the office. Ted's agreed to sell the company." To do the deal we had to get John Malone's blessing, so I rushed back from vacation and Jerry and I flew back out to Montana to pick up Ted and the three of us flew to Denver to see Malone. I was new to Time Warner so the first time I met Ted was when we picked him up at the Bozeman airport. He got on the plane and after introducing himself, he started explaining to me who Ted Turner was— how he was a self-made man, how in the early days of TBS he used to peel the stamps off the incoming mail and reuse them, how he built his empire, why he wanted to merge with Time

Warner, how he wanted to see what it was like to be big and have some muscle, how he and Jerry would be a great team, etc.

That took about a half hour and then he proceeded to explain to me who I was. We'd landed in Denver and our plane was on the tarmac waiting for the car when he said, "Now, you know, our stories are not so dissimilar."

And I said, "What do you mean?"

"Well, take you. You were born black—*bad break!* But you know, you worked hard and you overcame it. I'm white but I had some tough breaks, too, but I did all this work and I overcame it and so it's the same thing."

After nearly falling out of my chair I said, "Well, I guess I see where you're coming from, Ted."

Someone once said that there's supposed to be a little box in everybody's head and when an idea forms before it comes out, it goes in that box and gets checked out for political correctness and appropriateness and timeliness, but Ted doesn't have one. If the idea forms—BOOM—out it comes and he will say things that will just set you back on your heels. But because he's such a fundamentally guileless and genuine guy, he gets away with it.

———————— A TED STORY ————————

"A Pretty Darn Good Marriage"
—John Malone

In all honesty I thought that this was a pretty darn good marriage. Given Ted's creativity and Time Warner's resources I believed they were going to be able to do a lot of great things. I was unhappy that we ended up not being the marriage partner but I also thought that this was probably a smart business decision for Ted. By this time his politics had swung liberal and there was no way our politics can be regarded as liberal; we're libertarian but not liberal.

For Ted the sale brought him prestige and a bigger platform and he felt he was merging with his buddies—people he'd worked with for years. These were the days when Ted and I were spending time together at his ranch and he was asking my advice about how to play his cards and I said, "Look, Jerry Levin owns no stock. He has some options but no stock. On the other hand, Ted, you, me, and Gordy Crawford will be the three largest shareholders of the company and collectively we'll be somewhere like 40 percent of the company. As a practical matter, Ted, you're taking over Time Warner if you play your cards right. I think Jerry's a good guy and I think you'd look hard to find a guy who will work as hard as he will. I see this as him working for you—not you working for him—but you've got to really work the board. You need to make sure the board knows that they will get reelected because of your support and if I were you I would invite the board—the independent directors—down to the ranch and I would really spend some time courting them. Because I think this really turns out to be your company."

That was my advice, and I still think that had the AOL deal not come along it would have been Ted's company.

It took several weeks to agree to the terms of the deal and the negotiations with TCI and our other cable operator-owners were complex, but we worked everything out. Jerry Levin and I made the official announcement in September of '95. The little billboard company that I struggled to hold together had grown into a diversified entity that was being acquired at a value of more than $8 billion. I would now be the largest shareholder of the biggest communications company in the world.

I wish my father could have seen what we'd accomplished with the business he'd left. I'm sure he would have been proud.

28

The New Time Warner

In October of 1995, just after we announced our agreement to merge with Time Warner, the Atlanta Braves made it to the World Series for the third time in five years. After suffering through so many dreadful seasons it was exhilarating to be a consistent contender. After a strike forced the cancellation of the '94 postseason, the 1995 regular season started late and the schedule was shortened to 144 games. The Braves won ninety of theirs, then beat the Colorado Rockies and Cincinnati Reds in the playoffs to face the American League champion Cleveland Indians in the World

Series. The 1995 Indians had an amazing 100–44 record during the regular season and after coming up short in our last three postseason appearances, it looked like the Braves had another uphill battle.

The World Series opened in Atlanta and behind our strong pitching (we had one of the all-time great rotations that year, including John Smoltz, Greg Maddux, and Tom Glavine), the Braves managed to win the first two games, then split the first two in Cleveland to go ahead three games to one. With an opportunity to win it all on the road, we lost game five and flew home to Atlanta with a 3–2 lead and two chances to clinch at home.

Jane and I attended all of the playoff games—both home and away. It was fun but exhausting. Tired as we were and as much as we wanted it to end, it was better to return to Atlanta for a chance to win the championship in front of our home fans. Tom Glavine was our starting pitcher in Game 6 against Dennis Martinez of the Indians. It was a scoreless tie after five and a half innings until David Justice hit a solo homer in the bottom of the sixth. Glavine wound up pitching eight shutout innings and gave up just one hit. Our closer, Mark Wohlers, came on in the ninth and retired three straight Indians. When Marquis Grissom caught that final fly ball we all went wild! The players poured onto the field and the entire crowd—myself included—was jumping up and down, hugging and high-fiving everyone. After nearly twenty years of hard work we were celebrating a World Series championship. When they handed me the trophy I couldn't believe how heavy it was, but I managed to hike it up on my shoulder and the crowd's response was deafening.

It's difficult to compare winning the America's Cup with winning the World Series. In the sailing, I was an actual participant whereas here I was the owner. Both triumphs were thrilling and that night I became the first person ever to win both an America's Cup and a World Series. After buying the team in '77 I told everyone we'd win a championship within five years. It took a lot longer than I had expected but in some ways I think that made it even more satisfying.

Throughout all this excitement, my marriage to Jane was going well. Of all the relationships I'd had in the past, this one was the most intense and fulfilling and we were together most of the time for our first several years. Jane enjoyed spending time with me in Atlanta and at my various properties. She convinced me to exercise more and to eat better and I helped her learn how to fly-fish during our trips to Montana. We spent hours discussing important issues like the environment and world peace and it felt good for me to be with someone who was passionate about so many of the same things that I was. Jane also took an interest in my work and I would use her as a sounding board when I was thinking through important decisions. We got along well with each other's children and we managed to spend a lot more time with them.

Still, I know that being married to me wasn't easy and it was certainly an adjustment for Jane. Probably the hardest part was keeping up with our busy schedule.

—————— A TED STORY ——————

"He Has to Keep Moving"
—Jane Fonda

Given everything that happened to Ted when he was a child—the beatings, the psychological manipulations—like his father asking him to beat him, his mother screaming outside the door, his father coming home drunk at night and telling him stories about women— there was complete toxicity. When he first told me these stories, I wept, and it was just so weird. Here I was crying as he was telling the story and he couldn't understand why I was emotional.

As a result of his upbringing, for Ted there's a fear of abandonment that is deeper than with anyone I've ever known. As a result he needs constant companionship and keeping up with him can be exhausting. It's not just all the constant activity— it's his nervous energy that almost crackles in the air. He can't sit still because if you sit still the demons catch up with you. He has to keep moving.

For him to have survived what he survived more or less intact he had to spend every minute of his life thinking about how to protect himself and that makes it harder for him to open up to other people or to get to know others as whole people. The fact is that the things that allow certain people to become super achievers are the exact opposite qualities that allow them to have successful relationships.

On the business front, things went fairly smoothly between the summer of 1995 and the fall of 1996 as we worked through the details of integrating Turner into Time Warner. As often happens after a merger there were some casualties in the executive ranks. One of the most high-profile departures was that of Michael Fuchs, the longtime head of HBO and recent chairman of Warner Music Group. Michael was a brash guy and he wasn't shy about speaking up about his displeasure with

Jerry Levin and his management of the company. He was particularly upset when he found out that HBO would be reporting to me after the merger, not directly to Jerry as it had in the past.

I don't think it was a case of Michael having issues with me—I'd gotten to know him when he joined the Turner board and we got along fine—but he cared a lot about reporting relationships and his place on the company organization chart. After being rumored to be one of Levin's likely successors, he saw reporting to me as a slap in the face and he resigned. Bob Daly and Terry Semel—the co-chairmen of Warner Brothers, who had their share of clashes with Michael in the past, wound up with responsibility for the music business. As for HBO, we were fortunate that they had a talented number two guy named Jeff Bewkes who was ready to take Michael's place.

─────── A TED STORY ───────

"It's All Too Complicated!"
—Jeff Bewkes

(JEFF BEWKES IS PRESIDENT AND CEO
OF TIME WARNER.)

Ted showed up in my office as the new boss and it was the first time for him that he had a business reporting to him that he didn't create and a guy running it that he didn't put there. So this was all new to him and he started pacing around my office, talking loudly and asking questions like, "How much money do you spend with Bob Wright and Rupert?" He was asking how much we spent advertising HBO on NBC and Fox. I told him the number was about $40 million and he told me I'd have to move all that to TBS and TNT because we shouldn't be spending any money with our competitors.

He then started telling me about how we should make our documentaries with the TBS producers in Atlanta and combine our film production

group with TNT's, etc. Now, I had
grown up in a family with three brothers and was used to a very lively debate around the family dinner table
so having someone raise his voice
and argue with me wasn't anything
new.

When Ted was finally finished I
looked at him and said, "You know,
you must really think I'm an asshole."
That was my opening line. He stopped
pacing and looked at me and said,
"What? Why do you say that?"

I said, "Well, I've been here twenty
years and you come up here and start
telling me we ought to do this we
ought to do that, you don't think I
know that Rupert Murdoch owns Fox
and it competes with us? You don't
think I know that NBC isn't part of our
company? I know that, but I'm trying
to release big shows and big movies
on Saturday night or Sunday night, I
can't, I need a splash on Thursday
on *Seinfeld* or on *Friends.* I need the
young people that are our subscribers.
They're watching *Friends* and *Sein-*

feld—not TNT's forty-third rerun of *The Sands of Iwo Jima!*"

Now that I had his attention we started to debate and at one point I looked at him and said, "You used to sail, right?"

And he said, "Of course I used to sail, what kind of question is that?"

I said, "When you were sailing did you let other people hold the tiller?"

When he said, "No," I said, "Well neither do I and here's how I think it should work. I should get to make these decisions and if you don't like our results you get to fire me."

"Okay, I'll give you three months," he said. And about three months later he told me I was doing all right and we had a great relationship from that point forward.

From there we'd meet just periodically and one time he was in New York and he came in to ask me about my to-do list. I think he came in thinking that HBO was a pretty simple business but he started to realize that it was actually pretty complicated. I was telling him about VOD this and

digital that and all of the other challenges we faced when he fell to the
floor of my office and curled up into a
fetal position with his hands over his
ears. "Please don't tell me more," he
shouted, "it's all too complicated!"

That same night Ted was being interviewed on stage at the Museum of
TV and Radio and there were a lot of
important people there from the media industry and I was sitting in the
audience when he started to tell the
story about our meeting.

"I was meeting with Jeff Bewkes,
who's sitting right there," he said, point-
ing at me in the audience, "and he
was telling me all this new digital stuff
so I just rolled on the floor," and he literally threw himself out of his chair
onto the stage at the Museum of TV
and Radio and reprised his fetal position, covered his ears and yelled, "It's
too hard, too complicated, don't tell
me!"

The audience loved it, and so did I.
To me, he was telling me that he appreciated that what we were trying to
do at HBO was complicated and that

he wasn't going to try to do my job. I remember going back to my staff and telling them that Ted was going to be a great boss, and he was.

Jerry Levin and I worked well together during those first few years. I'd known of his reputation for being pretty astute in the ways of corporate politics but I saw him more as a hardworking, shrewd business-man with whom I'd been collaborating suc-cessfully for the past twenty years.

Now that he was officially my boss we spoke in person or on the phone almost daily—generally updating each other or talk-ing about strategic issues—and for the most part he let me do my job. When we gave our presentations to employees and investors about the virtues of our companies coming together they were well received. People on the Time Warner side, who were used to seeing a more sedate leader like Jerry, seemed to respond well to my energy and enthusiasm. Our fellow employees saw us working as a team and no one could argue that the assets of the two companies didn't make for a powerful combination.

In the months following the merger, we pushed each operating division to find cost savings, and we did everything from laying off nonessential employees to closing entire companies in the case of overlapping operations. These cuts weren't easy and in one case, my own son was a casualty. Now that we were part of a company that owned Warner Brothers, having a second home video division was redundant and when we closed Turner Home Video, my son Teddy was laid off. Prior to this, he and I were having dinner with Jane and some friends at a big restaurant in Atlanta. At one point during our meal, Teddy asked me, "What happens to us after the merger?" He was referring to the Home Video division and I responded, "You're toast."

My hearing has deteriorated over the years and as it has, my speaking voice has gotten louder. Apparently, unbeknownst to any of us, there must have been a reporter near us in that restaurant, since just a day later articles appeared describing this exchange, but making it sound like I was singling out Teddy. Actually, I was just answering his question honestly and when these stories ran, the two of us got a laugh out of it.

I think the story actually helped our terminated employees understand that we were making tough decisions and weren't playing any favorites—even with my own son. (By the way, while all of my kids worked at least some time at the company, and I helped them get jobs there in the first place, once they were hired I never believed in giving them special treatment. Some other businesses are run like family dynasties but as the CEO of a publicly traded company, I didn't think it was appropriate to favor my children.)

As a businessman, I believed in running a lean operation and I accepted these post-merger cost cuts, but it really bothered me when I saw how much money was being spent at the higher corporate levels. Time Warner executives ate in fancy private dining rooms and their offices and boardrooms were full of expensive artwork. When I found out that the value of these paintings ran into the millions, I was upset. At one of our board meetings I said, "So while we're laying off $30,000-a-year employees in Atlanta, we have million-dollar oil paintings hanging on the walls in New York?" The contradiction was plain to everyone and soon the paintings were removed and sold. For months thereafter, dark rectangles on the faded walls served as a reminder of the expensive artwork that used to be there.

I also spoke up whenever I saw a lack of cooperation between divisions. I was used to running a business where everyone worked together, but at Time Warner the corporate culture was different. There, the division CEOs generally ran their individual businesses as they saw fit, but I merged with Time Warner with an understanding that this would change. In particular, I expected our entertainment networks to have access to newer programming being produced at Warner Brothers. Historically, after theatrical movies ran on pay channels like HBO they were then licensed to the broadcast networks, and I wanted TBS and TNT to move into that advanced position.

I knew that by doing this we could grow the ratings of TBS and TNT and increase their overall value. We had done these deals with New Line and Castle Rock on some hit movies like *Dumb and Dumber* and *The Shawshank Redemption* and the results were positive. But the Warner Brothers people had been doing business with the networks for years and didn't like the idea of changing. I thought I'd been clear with them about how this strategy would work and when I found out that a package of movies was instead being sold to CBS, I was furious. I called Bob Daly, co-chairman of Warner Brothers, and explained again that we were now part of the same company—one that I happened to own about 10 percent of—and he needed to get with the program.

Daly didn't like it but I hadn't sold my company to Time Warner so we could continue to do business as usual once the deal was done. Jerry Levin generally supported me and I think he appreciated my speaking. The role of CEO at Time Warner had been weakened so much over the years and the division heads had been allowed to operate so freely that it would have been hard for Jerry to change his behavior suddenly and become more assertive after our merger. I filled that role on occasion instead and it all came naturally to me.

Jerry and I worked well together even though there were times when our differences were apparent. The corporate floor at Time Warner headquarters in New York was a pretty staid environment. Between his secretary's area and his office Jerry had a meeting room. Once I got my own office on the floor and started to spend more time in New York, whenever I wanted to see Jerry I simply walked through the meeting room and right into Jerry's space. This always seemed to surprise him and I never understood why until someone explained to me that he rarely let visitors into his own private office. So, unbeknownst to me, I'd been violating some unspoken corporate protocol.

Despite our differences and the fact that we never became particularly close personally, Jerry would often describe me at public events as his "best friend." After doing this several times I finally asked him, "Jerry, if I'm your best friend, who's your *second* best? I've never even been over to your home for dinner." Looking back with 20/20 hindsight, I can see that the personal differences we experienced when business was good should have warned me about how we'd get along when times got tough.

But there were plenty of issues on which Jerry and I agreed. Shortly before our merger officially closed, in the fall of 1996, the two of us were united in a dispute with Rupert Murdoch's News Corporation. Rupert was launching Fox News Channel and was trying to get distribution on cable and satellite systems. When you roll out a new advertising-supported cable service like Fox News you want to be available in as many households as possible. You also need to be carried in major markets if you want to attract national advertisers, and for a news channel, no market is more important than New York City. It so happened that the bulk of the cable households in New York were owned by Time Warner Cable, and when the system managers balked at carrying Murdoch's channel, war broke out.

I'd never made a secret of my dislike for Murdoch's business practices, and given the poor journalistic standards his newspapers exhibited, the idea of his getting into television news didn't make me happy. From CNN's earliest days I was concerned that someone would come after us with a right-wing network and now it was happening. But when Time Warner Cable originally passed on carrying the Fox News Channel, I had nothing to do with the decision. Back then, there were several new services trying to get launched, and channel slots were scarce. They already carried CNN, Headline News, and NY1 (Time Warner's own local news channel), and they were being actively pitched by MSNBC (the channel that Microsoft launched with NBC after their deal with us didn't materialize). Given all the news programming they already carried they probably wouldn't have added any more but when the Federal Trade Commission approved the Time Warner–Turner merger, Time Warner Cable had to pledge to carry a CNN competitor on at least half their systems. After looking at both Fox News and MSNBC, they decided to take the latter.

It's important to understand that the programming people at Time Warner Cable were tough negotiators and even after our companies merged, it was difficult to get them to carry newer Turner channels like the Cartoon Network and Turner Classic Movies. Once the Time Warner–Fox dispute became public, it was portrayed as if

we were picking on Fox and that the
behind-the-scenes battle was really between Rupert Murdoch and me. While that
wasn't true I figured out that the press attention would give me the opportunity to
explain to people that Rupert had a history
of manipulating his media's coverage to
advance his political purposes. At the
height of this public feud I even went so far
as to challenge him to a boxing match in
Las Vegas. He declined. (By the way, professional wrestling was popular on our entertainment networks at this time and one
of our executives suggested that instead
of boxing Murdoch, I should wrestle him
on a pay-per-view event. But I passed on
this idea. I didn't want to wrestle Rupert, I
joked, I wanted to *hit* him!)

Murdoch didn't respond to me directly;
instead, his media outlets started to go after me. That October, when the Braves
were playing the Yankees in the '96 World
Series on the Fox Broadcasting Network, I
learned that the producers of those games
were instructed not to show me on camera
unless it was unflattering. The first three
games they never put me on the air, and
when they did finally put the camera on

me, with Jane and Jerry Levin during game 4, the announcers didn't say a word. When the Braves went behind 8–6 in the tenth inning, they put me back on to show how upset I was. After that, whenever they showed me they tried to make me look silly, like when I turned my Braves hat into a rally cap—upside down and sideways on my head—or the time I dozed off a little during a game.

Murdoch's *New York Post* also made fun of me. They doctored a picture to show me in a straitjacket with a headline that said, "Is Ted Turner Crazy?" Instead of letting this bother me I decided to have some fun. Shortly thereafter I gave a speech in New York and I told the audience that I was still mad at Rupert and now I was considering shooting him. This was a sophisticated New York crowd and they were startled until they realized I was joking when I added, "I figure that now that his own paper says I'm crazy, I can kill him and get off by reason of insanity!"

The negotiations over Fox News were further complicated when New York mayor Rudolph Giuliani got involved on the side of News Corp. I don't know what kind of deal those two had together but Giuliani pressed the case that Time Warner needed to carry Fox News and even offered up one of the city's channels as a slot they could use. (Local communities have the right to a certain number of public access channels when they allow a cable company to serve their market.)

I stayed out of the way while a deal was worked out in the summer of 1997. Fox wound up being very aggressive with launch fees, ultimately offering to pay Time Warner Cable more than $10 per subscriber to gain carriage in New York. This was an expensive strategy but it certainly proved helpful in gaining national distribution quickly. Before long, Fox News was in millions of homes and, sadly, their ratings eventually surpassed CNN's. While we tried to stay true to our mission of delivering news stories in an unbiased fashion, their strategy of reporting and airing talk shows with a right-wing slant proved to be popular.

Throughout this period I continued to spend time with the divisions that reported to me, and I enjoyed working with Mike Lynne and Bob Shaye at New Line Cinema. They were great entrepreneurs and while they had built their business primarily with smaller budget films, I challenged them to spend more money on bigger projects.

───── A TED STORY ─────

"You Guys Should Make Really, Really Big Movies"
—Michael Lynne

Ted was significantly influencing our decision making going back to 1994 and 1995 when we were doing *The Mask* and *Dumb and Dumber.* We were still committed to modest budget films—I think *Dumb and Dumber* cost $16 million—it's what we had always done. But there was a time when we were down in Atlanta for a management meeting and in the course of talking about the movie business, Ted said, "You know what the problem is? We're not making enough hundred-million-dollar movies." He turned and he looked at Bob and me across the table, and with everyone else in the room, he said, "You guys should make really, really big movies; maybe the most expensive movies that have ever been made!" We all laughed because at that point we probably had never made a movie for more than $35 million.

This was not really an actionable plan but in a funny way this statement stayed in the back of our heads and from time to time Ted would reiterate this point and keep pushing us to stretch and do the kind of big blockbusters that he had in mind. He really believed—maybe a little more than we believed it at that time—that we could deliver at the level of any major that was out there if we had the wherewithal to do it. So when *The Lord of the Rings* came along, the idea and the concept and the potential was so extraordinary that we decided that it was the right thing for us to do.

Disney's Miramax had controlled the rights to *The Lord of the Rings* trilogy, but when director Peter Jackson wanted to shoot the first two movies at the same time,

they balked. When Jackson had brought
the project to New Line, Mike Lynne and
Bob Shaye had a different idea. After seeing a demo tape of how he envisioned mixing real people with hobbits and showing
the new technology he planned to use for
the big crowd scenes, the New Line executives encouraged Jackson to consider
shooting *all three* films at once. Jackson
loved that idea and when the concept was
finally brought to me for approval, I loved it,
too.

Mike and Bob were very creative but they
were also great businesspeople; over the
years they had figured out a way to lower
their risk on movies by getting up-front ad-
vances from international distribution partners. Moving forward with an unproven,
expensive trilogy was a major gamble, but
when Bob and Mike told me that they
wanted to do it I enthusiastically agreed. It
turned out that I was giving a green light
not only to what was by far New Line's most
expensive venture ever, but a project that
would become the most successful trilogy
in movie history. Even after the efficiencies
gained by shooting the three films at once,
the total production expense was more than

$300 million (only slightly less than what three individual *Star Wars* movies might cost), but taken together these movies grossed nearly $3 billion at the worldwide box office and generated an even greater amount in home video and merchandise sales.

When the third of these films won the 2003 Oscar for Best Picture, I was right there, cheering!

———

Through the first three quarters of 1997, Time Warner's stock started climbing. As Jerry and I made our case for how well the two companies—and the two of us—were working together, investors understood. Whether I was encouraging better coop- eration between divisions, raising con- cerns about expensive artwork, or fighting with Murdoch, Wall Street analysts appre- ciated seeing a new level of energy at what Jerry often referred to as "The New Time Warner." We also focused on plans to im- prove the company's performance. One of these was to turn TBS from a superstation to a pure cable network. The details of this conversion are complicated but essentially we were able to move from a situation where we generated revenues from advertising only to one where we collected subscriber fees just as we did with CNN and TNT. In exchange for these fees we provided cable operators the ability to insert local ads, and given TBS's strong ratings, this was valuable inventory. When we netted out the value of that lost inventory from the new revenue we would generate from subscription fees, we would add about $100 million a year to Time Warner's bottom line.

Within the first nine months of 1997, Time Warner stock jumped by about 50 percent. The ramifications of this growth became clear to me when I was flying to New York for business meetings and to receive a special award from the United Nations. Looking through my monthly financial statements I realized that since the start of 1997, the value of my Time Warner stock had increased from roughly $2.2 billion to $3.2 billion. I'd made a billion dollars in just nine months. At that same time, I had been considering ways that I could

make a meaningful statement at the upcoming United Nations event. That's when
it hit me. I would donate a billion dollars to
the United Nations!

29

Billion-Dollar Gift

In addition to being active with Rotary and other civic organizations, my dad was also philanthropic with his own small resources. Not only did he make contributions to causes that he cared about, but I also discovered after I left Brown that while he never paid for my full four years, he did support the tuition of two African-American students at his alma mater, Millsaps College. It made a big impression on me to see someone as hard-charging as my father take the time to quietly help out two young people like this. Sometime during the 1970s—years after my father's passing but before I had made a significant amount of money—I attended a seminar on philanthropy in Washington, D.C. At dinner I was seated next to a man who was quite a bit older than I and we began discussing charitable foundations. He told me that his father had been wealthy and that he had set up a family foundation when he was still a relatively young man. His children at the time were already young adults and he made each of them members of the foundation's board of directors. This man described what a wonderful thing his father had done because it brought his family together. He and his siblings learned about what their father wanted to do with his fortune—what kinds of things he was interested in supporting—and it was fun for them to gather at regular times throughout the year to sit around a boardroom table and decide what good things they wanted to do with his money.

I filed this away in my mind and told myself that if I were ever wealthy enough to have a foundation, this was how I'd do it, setting it up while I'm still relatively young and helping to keep my family together by putting each of my children on the board.

That time came in 1990 when I finally had sufficient resources to create the Turner Foundation, with a board of directors consisting of my five children, Jane Fonda, and myself. My family and I have always taken an interest in protecting the environment so that's where we decided to place our emphasis. Every grant we make is decided by a majority vote of the board and we're all treated equally.

When we first started meeting we had quite a bit of contention—we disagreed about funding this organization or that. But over time, we learned to compromise and respect each other's opinions and it really brought my children together. And since the work we were doing was philanthropic, it made us all feel good about what we were doing. I can also remember the first time my kids outvoted me on one of our grants. They were nervous about how I would react but when I showed a sense of humor and said, "On this board, we're all equals—I'm just another banana in this bunch," they all realized that this was how compromise and cooperation are supposed to work.

Today, the Turner Foundation's executive

director is Mike Finley, a former superintendent of Yellowstone National Park. I've known Mike since the mid-1990s when Jane Fonda and I went to Yellowstone to learn more about their wolf rehabilitation program. I took an instant liking to him and tried for several years to convince him to come work with me, and in 2001, after years working in the Park Service, he agreed to join us. Mike's done a terrific job and, in the years since its creation, the Turner Foundation has invested nearly $300 million in grants and has made a significant impact. I wish I could remember who that man was who first gave me the idea for a family foundation, because I owe him a debt of gratitude.

While the Turner Foundation helped me understand the impact we could have through philanthropic contributions, my earlier experience with the Better World Society opened my eyes to the power of assembling a team of international leaders to address global issues. Had I not experienced these two organizations, I don't think I would have had the confidence to move forward with what I was about to propose to the United Nations.

I rarely plan speeches far in advance and when I do I don't usually write a full script but instead jot down a series of bullet points on the themes I plan to cover. I'm much more comfortable just being spontaneous. So when I was being honored as the 1997 Man of the Year by the United Nations Association, I only left myself about seventy-two hours to consider what I'd say that evening.

The United Nations has long been one of my favorite organizations. It's vitally important for the world to have a place where leaders can get together and try to solve global problems, and I've always believed that as long as countries are talking, they don't go to war with each other. If it hadn't been for the United Nations, I honestly don't think we would have survived the Cold War. When Nikita Khrushchev was angry, the U.N. gave him a forum where he could vent, and it was far better for him to burn off steam by banging his shoe on the podium than by launching nuclear missiles. The United Nations isn't perfect, and it has its flaws like any other organization, but

the ideals it stands for are worth our support, and because of my long-standing
passion for the U.N. I wanted to say something meaningful and memorable that
night.

When I first came up with my billion-
dollar pledge idea on that flight to New York,
it wasn't the first time I'd thought about giving a big sum of money to the U.N. About a
year before, when Boutros Boutros-Ghali
was still secretary-general, I discussed the
idea of my buying the debt of nearly a billion dollars that the United States owed the
United Nations for dues our government
had not yet paid. I thought it was a disgrace
that these payments were in arrears and
wondered if I could purchase a note from
the U.N. at a discount, then turn to the
United States government and ask them to
pay. I could be the "repo man" for the U.N.!
I quickly learned that individuals could not
get involved with collecting U.S. debts. As
it developed, the United States was still
about $1 billion behind in its payments in
1997 and my idea was simply to make a
billion-dollar gift directly to the U.N.

Once we were settled in our hotel room
in New York, I explained my idea to Jane.

Tears formed in her eyes and she told me, "I'm proud to be married to you." I was still nervous and I tossed and turned that night, and then called Taylor Glover, my right-hand man, early the following morning.

He answered the phone, and I said, "Hey, pal, I have an idea. Are you sitting down?"

Taylor answered, "Better than that, I'm lying down."

I apologized for waking him up but went on to explain my idea. While he might have still been groggy this wasn't completely out of left field for Taylor since he'd been involved in my past discussions about U.N. debt payments. Once he understood that my new plan to make a direct gift of a billion dollars, I asked him to start working with our attorneys to figure out how to get this done.

When Taylor said he'd get right on it I said, "Please do, because I'm thinking about announcing it tomorrow night."

There were many issues to resolve, including tax ramifications and questions around my control of Time Warner stock. I thought through that day, and that night I had trouble sleeping. I'd given away lots of money over the years—probably close to $200 million by that point, including gifts to the Turner Foundation, the McCallie School, Brown University, and The Citadel, but never had I made a gift this large. This one would represent close to one third of my entire net worth, but I kept reminding myself that it was really just nine months earnings so it wasn't that big a deal.

As I tossed and turned my phone rang and it was Taylor calling to tell me that I couldn't make a gift directly to the United Nations. Just as an individual can't get involved with issues relating to debts owed by nation-states, the U.N. also cannot accept direct donations from individuals. Part of me was relieved; I thought that maybe this was God's way of telling me that I wasn't supposed to give away all that money!

But I couldn't shake the idea of a billion-dollar gift and when I'm faced with obstacles, I love thinking through ways to get around them. I came up with another approach. Why not create an independent foundation that doesn't give money directly to the U.N. but gives financial support to their causes? This seemed like it might work and when I ran it by my lawyers and financial people, they agreed. We developed a plan in which I would provide the foundation with $100 million a year for ten years. Looking at this in terms of present net value, it was worth something less than a billion in '97 dollars but it was still close and a lot of money. By the end of that next day we had worked out enough of the details that I could go ahead and make the announcement.

Kofi Annan had only been secretary-general since the beginning of that year and we'd already gotten to know each other. He was going to be in the audience that night and I didn't want my announcement to surprise him, so I asked for a meeting in his office that afternoon. When I walked him through my plan, he thought I was kidding; but once he realized I was serious, he was thrilled. He had a tough job and it was a treat for him to get some good news.

My spirits were lifted by Kofi's response and that evening wound up being one of the most exciting of my life. The dinner was a black-tie affair at the Marriott Marquis in

Times Square and the place was packed. People assumed I'd give a standard acceptance speech, so when I instead announced that I'd be giving a billion dollars to U.N.-related causes the audience was stunned. The ovation was tremendous. It gave me an incredible amount of pride to be in a position to make this kind of gift, but I also made a point to thank all the employees at Turner Broadcasting and Time Warner because if it hadn't been for all their hard work, the stock would never have performed so well.

There was a crush of press attention and immediately following the dinner—still wearing my tux—I went on CNN's *Larry King Live* to talk some more about it. When they were getting the graphics ready before the show I looked at the monitor and it said "Breaking News." I joked to Larry, who by then was an old friend, "Yeah, the 'breaking news' is that Ted Turner's broke!"

But when the show began I made it clear that while the amount I was giving away was certainly a lot of money, I was going to be just fine and I was putting other rich people on notice that I would be calling on them to be more generous.

Once I got to be wealthy and started to spend time with other people who were rich, I was amazed at how little some of them gave away. Many people had more money than they knew what to do with, and my point to them was—don't give away the cash you know what to do with, just give all that extra money you *don't* know what to do with. Being generous always made me feel great, and it seemed like every time I gave money away, I somehow made that much more. Now that I was pledging such a large amount, I could lead by example and decided it was time for me to get out in front of the parade.

By making my announcement so quickly there was no time to come up with a name for the new foundation. I later decided that the ideal one would be the most straightforward: the United Nations Foundation. When I ran this by Kofi Annan he said that they believed in us and would give us permission to use their prestigious name.

I knew that running a foundation like this would be a difficult, full-time job and I wanted to find someone who was not only a good leader but who also had strong political connections around the world. During the course of my many visits to Washington to testify on behalf of the SuperStation and various other issues, I had come to know Colorado congressman Tim Wirth. Serving as a member of both the House of Representatives and later, the Senate, Tim spent a lot of time on environmental, population growth, and climate change issues. After leaving the Senate he worked in the State Department as undersecretary for global affairs. He was the perfect guy for the job and I was thrilled when he accepted my offer.

Tim and his team have accomplished a great deal in the years since we created the United Nations Foundation. We've focused our efforts on children's health, energy and the environment, peace, security, and human rights, technology, and women and population, and have supported U.N. projects in 115 countries. A big part of the UNF's success has been its ability to partner with other organizations to tackle these big problems. For example, in trying to fight polio around the world we've joined forces with Rotary International, the Bill and Melinda Gates Foundation, and others to try to bring as many resources and as much coordination to the problem as we can. By partnering we can also spread the range of issues and broaden the number of territories we serve.

I'm particularly proud of the work we've done to fight malaria—a preventable and treatable disease that kills more than one million people every year (one person dies from malaria every thirty seconds). People can lower their risk of infection dramatically by sleeping under mosquito nets; and since a quality bed net costs about $10, this was a solution we could pursue effectively. Things really came together in 2006 when Rick Reilly of *Sports Illustrated* got behind this cause and wrote a column about it. We created a campaign called "Nothing But Nets." Partnering with organizations like *Sports Illustrated,* the NBA, the Mark Gordon Foundation, the United Methodist Church, and the Lutherans, we've raised tremendous awareness and nearly $20 million to support this cause.

Getting back to the issue that first motivated me to consider offering financial support to the U.N., we've also helped convince the United States government to pay its dues. The U.N. itself doesn't have a lobbying function so we created a foundation subsidiary called the Better World Fund to do that work on their behalf. We ran ads in local markets urging people to write their congressman or woman and tell them that great nations pay their debts. The campaign worked!

Thanks to Tim Wirth and his great team, the U.N. Foundation has done innovative work to make the world a better place and has helped strengthen the U.N. in the process. This gives me a lot of satisfaction, as have my efforts to influence other wealthy people to become more active in philanthropy. After announcing my billion-dollar grant I challenged my fellow billionaires to do more. I realized that many of them used their net worth as a way to keep score and they enjoyed seeing where they ranked on lists put out by magazines like *Fortune* and *Forbes*. Understanding how competitive most of these people are, I called on the media outlets to start publishing lists of these people who *gave away* the most. I figured that this would not only motivate people to try to get to the top of the philanthropy list, it could also shame some whose names didn't show up. People aren't born knowing how to give; we're basically pretty selfish creatures and being generous is something we have to learn. In any event, Salon.com was the first to take up the list idea and other media outlets joined in later. While Bill Gates was already giving away a lot of money before we went public with our campaign, he has given me some credit for calling it to his attention, and it was particularly gratifying to see Warren Buffett make his massive pledge to the Gates Foundation in 2006.

——————— A TED STORY ———————

"What an Honor for Me"
—Muhammad Yunus

(WINNER OF THE 2006 NOBEL PEACE PRIZE, MUHAMMAD YUNUS IS THE FOUNDER OF THE GRAMEEN BANK OF BANGLADESH AND A MEMBER OF THE UNITED NATIONS FOUNDATION BOARD OF DIRECTORS.)

I was in Washington attending a meeting when I heard a news item that Ted Turner had donated $1 billion to the United Nations. About an hour later I gave an interview to a journalist, who, among other things, asked me, "What do you think of Ted Turner donating $1 billion to the U.N.?"

Immediately I said, "It's a crazy idea. Why should he give $1 billion to the United Nations?"

And the journalist said, "Why not? What's wrong with it?"

"This will all disappear in meeting the U.N.'s financial gap," I said, "because they will probably pay their salaries with it or something like that. If he wants to get the best mileage out of it he should create a foundation and give the money to the foundation so the money is managed well. That's the best way to do it." So that was the first instantaneous remark I made, without knowing that Ted had already planned to do exactly that.

About six months later I was back in Bangladesh and got a call from him. After he explained that he wanted me to join the U.N. Foundation board I said, "This is unbelievable that you are tracking me down in Bangladesh. What an honor for me." This was in 1998 and was my first contact with Ted Turner. When I first attended a board meeting and met Ted in person I had no idea what to expect. I knew he had lots of money, but when I talked to him he was a very regular kind of a guy—very friendly, warm, and casual.

But as I continued to know him I saw the depth of this person and through his foundation he has created a completely new window for a private initiative to work with the U.N. Although the United Nations Charter says, "We the people," governments took it over and it became a governmental organization. Ted Turner made a difference in a big way by showing that the private sector can play a role in helping the United Nations really become the people's organization.

I've also shared some lighter moments with Ted. I remember one time walking to a meeting with him on the streets of New York, and as we walked and talked he'd stop to pick up little pieces of trash. Along the way, any trash he found he picked it up and he always held on to it until he found a trash can to deposit it. He did this very meticulously and I thought it was very funny. There are so many people in New York City and so much trash, why should one person keep on picking it up? But later on I understood how committed he was in keeping the city clean and also his notion that if everyone did their small part like this, we wouldn't have any litter piling up.

On another occasion we were attending a U.N. Foundation board meeting in Brazil. We were on a field visit visiting an organization that ran an innovative health program for the poor. The organization head was making an open-air presentation to us. It was a beautiful, warm day. Besides the U.N. Foundation board members, several distinguished guests were also in attendance. Of course, the presentations were carefully prepared and the atmosphere around was very serious. We were all listening very carefully and attentively when, suddenly, Ted looked at a tree nearby and became completely withdrawn from the discussions. He started drifting away from us and began playing with a monkey who was jumping on the tree. He even followed him as he moved from tree to tree! I'll never forget that moment. We had all been so serious but when we saw Ted Turner—the chairman of the foundation—chasing that monkey around the trees, we all burst into laughter! Ted loves animals. He could not help it.

As I began to channel more of my energies and resources toward philanthropic causes I had an even greater desire to improve Time Warner's performance and to drive up its stock. The better that Time Warner did, the more I'd be able to give away.

But in the final years of the 1990s, bigger, traditional media companies like Time Warner started to lose the spotlight to newer start-ups that were making their mark online. Having been a leader in the cable industry when it was new, I wasn't sure if I had the energy to do it all over again with the Internet. I felt like I'd made my way all the way to California and before I caught my breath, they wanted me to build the Golden Gate Bridge!

30

Transitions

A few months before my decision to create the United Nations Foundation, Jerry Levin's son was murdered. Losing a child is difficult in any circumstances and this case was particularly tragic. Jonathan Levin was an English teacher at a Bronx high school and he was stabbed and shot by former students who broke into his Manhattan apartment to steal his ATM card for drug money. In keeping with Jewish custom, the funeral was held the day after his body was discovered (it turned out he'd been murdered three days earlier),

and it was clear to everyone in the syna-
gogue that Jerry was devastated.

Given the high-profile nature of the crime
and since so many people saw Jerry in such
rough shape at the funeral, some speculated that he would retire. They couldn't
imagine how he could recover from this kind
of loss and continue to run a big public
company like Time Warner—or if he'd even
want to. I did what I could to be supportive
and I knew from the aftermath of my father's
suicide that while there's always the option
to quit and run, working your way through a
tragedy can sometimes be the best way to
move forward.

Jerry chose to return. Within two weeks
of his son's funeral he was back in the office
with a renewed desire to grow the company,
but to do so in a way that would make a difference and leave a legacy that would have
made his son proud. I respected him for this
decision and later when I announced my
billion-dollar pledge, Jerry described my
philanthropy as being emblematic of the
kind of company that he was trying to build.

Jerry Levin didn't just want Time Warner
to be big, he wanted it to be great, and in

the late 1990s, it seemed like the great new businesses were being created on the Internet. I first started paying attention to the Internet when I heard references to "dot-coms" in sales reports from our cable networks. CNN and our entertainment channels were enjoying tremendous growth in ad sales during the mid- to late 1990s and an increasing percentage of that money came from dot-coms. Some of these new start-ups raised large amounts of capital at high valuations and then spent a lot of that money on traditional media outlets like television, radio, and print. As investors poured their resources into online companies they turned their noses up at the older conglomerates like Time Warner. It was a strange time. I'd had to work hard for years to build Turner Broadcasting into a company that investors would value, and now these online entrepreneurs were raising millions of dollars almost out of thin air. After years of blazing trails, it felt odd to find myself at a company that was considered to be "old media."

Jerry grew increasingly concerned that we were missing out. I never doubted that the Internet was important—plenty of people that I respected assured me that it was—it's just that as someone who never uses a computer, it wasn't something I was engaged in. I thought that we had a lot of growth upside in our core businesses—advertising- and subscriber-supported media—and I was worried that we were taking our eye off more important opportunities like the purchase of a broadcast network (and in that market these were increasingly undervalued).

But in the late 1990s, if you didn't think that most of your future was going online, it was hard to get anyone's attention, including Jerry's. He was obsessed with formulating an Internet strategy for Time Warner that would be, as he described it, "transformational." His passion for new distribution technologies went all the way back to the early 1970s when he pushed to put HBO on a satellite. He was also an early advocate for interactive product. In 1994 he was a strong proponent of the Full Service Network, an expensive and high-profile test run by Time Warner Cable in their Orlando, Florida, system. This offered consumers the ability to shop, play games, and order videos on demand, all through an interactive TV platform. In many ways the technology was ahead of its time but the test was deemed a failure and was shut down after about eighteen months.

Time Warner had also invested a lot of time and money in a project called Pathfinder, a free Web site where they highlighted content from the various magazines. The plan upset people at the individual magazines who didn't like having their sites merged into this larger grouping, and consumers seemed to prefer going to the individual magazine sites directly. Ultimately, this expensive, high-profile effort was viewed by media observers and Wall Street as another failure.

By 1999, Time Warner was taking flak from investors and the press for not being more successful on the Internet—for neither making any bold acquisitions nor creating any successful online businesses of our own. After a run-up in Time Warner stock for the first few years after the Turner merger, our shares were no longer in favor. Feeling increased pressure to do something, Jerry created a group called Time Warner Digital Media, whose charge was to coordinate the online businesses under one management umbrella. This sounded like a reasonable idea but it caused a lot of tension across the company when existing Web operations like Time Inc. magazine sites and CNN.com were essentially pulled out from underneath their companies' management and told to report into a centralized structure. Rich Bressler, who had been CFO of Time Warner, was named CEO of the unit and given the task of trying to pull this all together. In addition to thinking that Rich would do a good job coordinating these efforts, by putting his CFO in charge it seemed clear that Jerry saw mergers and acquisitions as a key part of his plan.

―――――― A TED STORY ――――――

"So We're Going to Put Ourselves Out of Business?"
—Jeff Bewkes

The heads of the various divisions of Time Warner were invited to a dinner at the 21 Club to discuss our Internet strategy. Ted was there, as were Bob Daly and Terry Semel from Warner

Brothers, Joe Collins from Time Warner Cable, Terry McGuirk from Turner, and Don Logan from Time Inc. I was there representing HBO. Jerry Levin had called the meeting and Dick Parsons was also in attendance but the bulk of the evening was a long, fairly formal presentation from Rich Bressler, who was running Time Warner Digital Media. He went through a series of flip charts on an easel, covering everything from internal strategies he was proposing to possible acquisitions of companies that were emerging at the time, like Lycos and AltaVista. It was all fairly awkward as several of the people gathered didn't really know or care a whole lot about the Internet and there weren't many questions asked throughout the presentation.

For his part, Ted remained unusually quiet until the very end. As Jerry was wrapping things up by stressing the importance of the company moving aggressively in all these areas and as people were literally getting ready to get up from their chairs, Ted suddenly spoke up. "So, are you telling us we need to move aggressively to put all our content on the Internet, is that what you're saying?" to which Rich and Jerry agreed.

"So, that would include putting material from our magazines on the Internet free of charge, right?" When he got agreement again, Ted turned to Don Logan and asked, "Don, what are you charging for *Time* magazine?"

Don responded, "What do you mean, the cover price?"

And Ted said, "Yeah, it's like a buck-fifty, right? And for *People* it's something like two dollars, right? So you make millions and millions of dollars from magazine subscriptions now but we're going to put it all online free of charge?" Ted then waited a beat and said, *"So we're going to put ourselves out of business?"*

It was hilarious, and typical Ted Turner. After a three-hour presentation on a topic he's supposed to know nothing about he puts his finger right on the center of the problem.

Driven by Wall Street's "irrational exuberance" around Internet stocks, the general discussions around our digital strategy took us in some strange directions. Based on the high valuations of online companies, it looked like Time Warner wasn't getting nearly the value we deserved for our own properties. One of the most glaring examples was CNN.com. Unlike most online businesses, this one not only had a lot of traffic, it also generated meaningful revenue. If you valued CNN.com like an Internet start-up, it could have been worth as much as the rest of Turner Broadcasting. These valuations may have been irrational but they were also impossible to ignore, and some within Time Warner suggested that to capture this value we should take CNN.com public.

But when you worked that through, you quickly realized it was impractical, since CNN's Web business relied so heavily on the newsgathering and sales infrastructure of the cable network that you couldn't separate the businesses. Given that, some suggested that we should spin off the entire CNN News Group. Driven entirely by

the bizarre behavior of the investors during the dot-com boom, smart people at
Time Warner were seriously considering
taking CNN public simply to take advantage of the potential value of CNN.com.
This would have caused our company tremendous disruption, and fortunately, we
never got too far along with these plans,
but the fact that we even thought about it
says a lot about what crazy times these
dot-com boom years really were.

With this kind of mind-set swirling around
the corporate world in the fall of 1999, Jerry
Levin scheduled a Time Warner management meeting in China, timed to precede
immediately the *Fortune* Global Forum,
which was held that year in Beijing. One of
Fortune's invited guests was Steve Case—
the founder of AOL—and at some point
during the conference, Steve met with
Jerry and mentioned the idea of merging
his company with ours. After his return
from China, Jerry told me about this discussion but he didn't seem overly interested in Case's idea and I assumed this
deal wasn't going anywhere. Based on the
relative value of our two companies at that
time, AOL would actually be in a position

to acquire Time Warner. By the fourth quarter of 1999, despite the fact that our company's revenue was five times AOL's, their market capitalization was nearly twice that of Time Warner's.

This boggled my mind. Time Warner was a company with solid, valuable assets (Time Inc.'s magazines, CNN and our other cable channels, Warner Brothers and our movie libraries, Time Warner Cable, among others) and I couldn't see how they arrived at AOL's value. Investors said they placed a premium on AOL's growth prospects but given my knowledge of the cable industry, I couldn't see AOL growing much more once cable operators rolled out their high-speed Internet services. Why would they give that franchise over to AOL when they could introduce their own services like Road Runner (in which Time Warner already owned a stake)? These were days when lots of wild merger speculations were swirling around and I assumed this was another one of those.

When I found out that spouses weren't invited on that Time Warner management trip to China, I decided not to go. There was no way I could be that far away from Jane for that length of time. Even without a trip to China, our schedules were already hard enough to keep up with. For example, Jane couldn't even be with me the night I announced my pledge to create the U.N. Foundation since she was making a speech of her own to a women's group in Colorado. I had to go straight from the *Larry King Live* set to the airport in New Jersey and fly overnight to meet Jane in Los Angeles so I could spend the weekend with her and her family. This kind of juggling became typical as Jane attempted to maintain her independence while we both tried to keep up with our professional and philanthropic pursuits and at the same time maintain a relationship with each other and our children.

Our travel and crowded schedules took a toll on our relationship and there came a time when we had trouble communicating with each other even when we were together. This was the point when I started to worry about our marriage.

After we split up, some media reports speculated that our marriage ended because I was mad at Jane for becoming a Christian, but that is not correct. The press has portrayed me as being anti-religion but that's not fair, either. They often refer to the time when I said "Christianity is a religion for losers." I've regretted using those words and I apologized for them repeatedly, but in fairness, the statement has been taken completely out of context. What I meant when I made that unfortunate comment was that the teachings of Jesus appealed largely to the downtrodden. While making the rich and powerful nervous, Jesus gave hope to those near the bottom of society: the poor, the sick, and the hungry. I've studied the Bible extensively and have great respect for people of all faiths.

―――――― A TED STORY ――――――

"He Knows I'm Not a Loser"
—President Jimmy Carter

I've discussed religion with Ted as much as I would consider appropriate and Rosalynn and I have talked to Jane extensively about our Christian faith. We've been distressed in the past when Ted has said things like "Christians are losers." He knows I'm a Christian and he knows I'm not a loser, but he says things in the heat of the moment and often underestimates the permanence of what he says. An average college professor can say anything and it's never recorded but I know from being president, forty years after you've said three words about a subject George Will or somebody's going to go back through the ancient files and find that you said this or that. Ted's that way, too, and many people will never forget what he said about Christianity.

My hope is that, eventually, Ted will have a profound religious experience and have an unequivocal awareness that Christ is Savior, and that he can be relaxed with this. He's an agnostic by temperament, and not just about religion. He's a skeptic by nature and when somebody tells Ted something he really feels an innate need to explore the issue and see if it's really true or not. I think this is what's made him an explorer in the finest sense of the word.

It is true that I was upset when I found out about Jane's conversion but it wasn't because she had become Christian. My frustration was because she didn't discuss it with me. This sort of thing doesn't happen to someone overnight and having such an important matter dropped on me out of the blue made me realize just how much our communication had broken down.

--- A TED STORY ---

"I Was Being Led"
—Jane Fonda

There's this thing that has to happen, it's like a softening, a giving up—it's a humbling and opening to the spirit. It's an amazing thing, and because it happened to me late in life, I was very aware of it and conscious of it. Ted can't let that happen. He believes that there's a God but he can't allow himself to have that become an event or an experiential revelation because that opens you up to everything and he can't truly open his soul to the holy spirit, or whatever you want to call it. It's the same reason that he can't go back to the past and heal himself. He can't because he can't really open up because he's too afraid that it will all come in and drown him. His notion of God is a very cerebral one.

I didn't see it as religion at the time. I just felt for about six years that I was being led. When I came to Atlanta, for the first time I met so many great, smart people who were religious and went to church. Ted didn't know it but for all those years when we would go to the endless receptions and parties I was off always in a corner often talking to Nancy McGuirk—Terry's wife— or Rosalynn Carter or Jimmy Carter. I was exploring and Ted had no idea. I would never tell him about these conversations because I knew he would try to talk me out of what I was doing.

For me, being in nature is when I feel the most transcendent and the most presence of God. I hiked a lot with Ted and there's one slope that goes up behind the house on the Flying D, where one spring the bitterroot flowers were beautiful. Bitterroot is the Montana state flower but they only come out at certain moments and on certain kinds of terrain—rocky soil in full sun—and they look like they're lit from the inside. I showed one to Ted and it blew his mind. From then on every time he saw one it would be a big epiphany. If I'd say, "Wait! Stop, Ted look at that. Look at the way the sun is hitting that grove of aspen," he would begin to take the time to really notice. He definitely changed a little with me and became more open to that kind of observation.

We wanted our marriage to work, so when our communication deteriorated significantly we decided to get counseling. I'm a believer in the value of therapy and had myself started seeing a psychiatrist in Atlanta when I sold my company to Time Warner. I knew that would be a difficult transition and having someone to talk to proved to be helpful. I was hopeful that seeing a couples counselor might help Jane and me as well.

―――――― A TED STORY ――――――

"Playing on Different Teams"
—Jane Fonda

I've been in three marriages that didn't work and in each case what begins to happen is you come to the point when you realize something's wrong. You're not at a point where you can say, "I'm going to leave," but it's like you're playing on different teams. About eight and a half or nine years into my marriage with Ted I was starting to play on a different team, and my team was looking out for myself. He was willing to try to work on things and we went to see the counselor. But when we were both talking about the relationship I soon realized I had my own issues to work on. So I started working on me, but he didn't work on him, and that's why I decided to move along.

Ted and I went to the therapist for months but he couldn't let anything in, he couldn't let my words in, in trying to explain what it was that I was looking for. All he knew was that I had changed and I had thrown all these changes at him and he couldn't take it and that's when he started looking for somebody else because he thought "this isn't going to last."

Jane and I were together for ten great years. We both worked on the relationship, but the marriage had run its course, so we decided to finalize our split on January 3, 2000.

We had built the house together at the Flying D Ranch. Jane decorated the place beautifully, and we had a lot of fun out there. There's a big stone fireplace in the living room, and she laid out every single rock on the floor and told the builders how she wanted them arranged. When I first went back there without her after the divorce, Jane had taken all her things. Our closets faced each other's, and when I saw her empty space I sat down on the floor between them and cried. I loved Jane very much and still love her to this day. The house at the Flying D continues to bring back memories. Jane had planted an apple tree near the front door, and a few years ago, the first time it produced apples, I put a few in my briefcase and delivered them to her at her home in Atlanta.

As with other setbacks in my life, I knew I needed to keep moving. I reconnected with an old friend named Frederique D'Arragon, whom I'd met many years before during my sailing career, and she and I began dating. (We stayed together for three years and remain good friends today.)

January 3, 2000, was a Monday. The world was discovering that Y2K had come and gone without a major disaster, and I was in Big Sur, California, trying to relax. Unbeknownst to me, back in New York and Virginia, conversations had resumed between Jerry Levin and Steve Case. Apparently, over the holidays, Jerry had decided that this was the deal he wanted to do. They agreed to terms on Thursday night over dinner at Case's house and on Friday, January 7, Jerry called to tell me that we had a deal. We were merging with AOL.

31

AOL: Phased Out and Fenced In

Time Warner was not good at keeping a lid on confidential news, and when Jerry Levin and Steve Case agreed to terms on the AOL merger, they wanted to make the announcement quickly. This would be a $160 *billion* transaction—the biggest corporate merger ever—and after shaking hands on the deal late on a Thursday night, Jerry and Steve agreed that all the legal and due diligence work had to be completed over the weekend so that the announcement could be made the following Monday morning.

I was used to moving quickly, but that

first full week of the year 2000 was a whirl-wind. On Monday, January 3, my marriage to Jane came to an end. That Friday, Jerry called to tell me the AOL deal was on. I flew to New York for a Sunday board meeting and the announcement would be made the next day. This was a lot to absorb, and it didn't help that I had come down with the flu over the holidays.

I was feeling awful and even though I had my doubts about the merger, I reluctantly supported it. The Internet continued to be the rage and while I wasn't swept up in it myself, Jerry was a smart guy and was convinced that this deal would not only validate Time Warner's value, it would also transform the company. I was concerned about AOL using their inflated stock to make the purchase, but the premium they were paying for Time Warner—roughly 60 percent—was very high.

All this sounded good, but before committing to vote my shares I felt obligated to get some outside advice before Sunday's board meeting, and for this I turned to the four smartest men I knew, whom I had worked with in the past, and who understood the situation. These were Mike

Milken, John Malone, Gordy Crawford, and Taylor Glover. In each case, when I discussed the deal with them individually, they recommended that I should vote for it.

───────── A TED STORY ─────────

"It Was All Thrown Together So Quickly"
—Taylor Glover

I was away in England and I got a call from Rich Bressler, who told me they wanted Ted to sign a document voting his shares in favor of the deal. They put enormous pressure on getting this thing signed immediately and when I spoke to Ted, he'd say things like, "Well, eleven of the other twelve directors can't be wrong." He'd pose questions to me in a rhetorical way and when I'd say, "Yes," in response, that was affirmation for him. But I was on vacation in Europe having trouble keeping a phone connection, not sitting with Ted face-to-face. I don't think I ever saw a document relating to the terms of the deal and I'm not even sure I saw the one he signed voting

his shares over. It was all thrown together so quickly it was incredible.

A TED STORY

"A Completely Different Account"
—Gordy Crawford

I can tell you exactly when I heard
about the Time Warner–AOL merger.
My company was having a three-day
retreat right here in Los Angeles, at
Shutters Hotel. I was on a break Sunday night when I got a call from my
son, who works at Warner Brothers.
He said the word running all through
the Warner grapevine was that Time
Warner was merging with AOL. I said,
"Well, I haven't heard anything and I
think that's something that the Time
Warner guys would mention to me."

It turned out that Jerry Levin had
called me at home, leaving a message on my voice mail that he had an
important thing he wanted to talk to
me about but he didn't know where I
was. So I heard the rumor of it from

my son on Sunday night before it was announced on Monday morning, but Ted had to commit before the public announcement of the transaction. I don't know why Ted thinks we had that discussion but we couldn't have because I didn't know anything about the deal.

In fact, I was involved in putting Jerry Levin together with Jerry Yang in a potential transaction with Yahoo. Those discussions had been going on since the prior summer and they went right down to the wire. It turned out Jerry Levin was doing parallel negotiations with Jerry and Yahoo, unbeknownst to Steve Case at AOL. The negotiations with Yahoo broke down in late December when, basically, Jerry Yang decided he didn't want to do anything. Anyhow, Ted had to commit long before he and I ever talked. I don't know if he talked to Milken and Malone and he probably did talk to Taylor about it, but I never got involved in it until it was an announced merger and Ted had long ago signed his shares.

In fairness to Ted, in the subsequent weeks after the deal, he and I spoke about it and I was fairly supportive. Basically I was just wrong. I didn't know all the shenanigans going on within the company and because I was an old media guy, I missed the whole fundamental vulnerability of the dial-up model. So certainly after the deal was announced and done, Ted would be accurate saying that I talked positively about it.

A TED STORY

"This Gave You a Chance"
—Michael Milken

We obviously talked about it, but I would say it maybe a little differently. There was a whole series of conversations but I do think the issue that was a little different here was that the opportunity to get value was substantially better by taking that deal. The decision about whether to hold or not *after* the deal was a different story.

Every single media company today sells below what it sold back then, not just Time Warner; but this gave you a chance. The AOL–Time Warner deal was creating a value substantially more than Time Warner was worth. The question was obviously if you didn't sell, what was going to happen. That's a whole different story.

―――――――――

―――― A TED STORY ――――

"What Are You Calling Me For?"
—John Malone

Ted's memory is different than mine. My memory is by the time he got to me I asked, "Have you agreed to support it?" and he said, "Yes."

So I laughed and said, "What are you calling me for?"

And he said, "No, in all seriousness, what do you think of the deal?"

I told him that on paper I thought it looked like a pretty good deal. The government had made me give my Time Warner votes up and so even if

I didn't like it there was nothing I could do about it. But at that point, I did believe that financially the deal would work.

The Time Warner board meeting was held at 2:00 on Sunday afternoon. When I arrived, a ten-page document was handed to me that committed me to vote for the deal, and to pledge that I would not reverse that decision during the time it took to close, which was expected to be as long as twelve months. There wasn't time to even read the document and I didn't have an attorney with me, but I assured Jerry and the board that if the board voted in favor of the deal, I'd sign the agreement.

The board session lasted almost seven hours. With big deals like this one, it's customary for the board to listen to lengthy presentations and hear recommendations from investment bankers, and in this case, the people from Morgan Stanley made a forceful case for why this was a great deal for Time Warner shareholders. According to the transaction's supporters, this would be the ultimate combination. They said that Time Warner, with all its valuable "old media" assets, would be "turbo-charged" by this merger with AOL, one of the fastest growing and most well-respected "new media" companies.

Everyone agreed that this would put AOL Time Warner out in front of our competitors. We'd be the biggest, most diversified, and most formidable company in the media industry. So when we voted, we were unanimous and I signed the document voting my shares irrevocably. AOL's board approved the deal that same day. All that was left was the announcement and I went back to my hotel to rest.

News of the deal began to trickle out Sunday night, and by the time we gathered for the press conference—in the auditorium of the Equitable Center—the crowd was tremendous. Years earlier, when I held another New York press conference to announce my bid for CBS, that seemed like a really big deal. We also got a lot of notice in 1995, when Jerry and I announced the merger of Turner and Time Warner. But January 10, 2000, was on a different level altogether. The world was hyped up over the Internet and here was a deal that seemed to validate all that hysteria. It was the biggest transaction in corporate history and the media crush was unprecedented.

For me, the announcement was unique for different reasons. In every deal I'd done in the past I was a principal, but in this case I wasn't involved in the final negotiations and only found out three days earlier that a deal had even been struck. Instead of being the only person or one of two making the announcement, on this day I shared the stage with five other men. The lead players were Jerry Levin and Steve Case and they spoke first while I sat in a chair alongside Dick Parsons, AOL's Bob Pittman, and their CFO, Mike Kelly. I didn't know Case and Pittman very well and had just met Kelly that morning. For the first time, the deal I was helping to announce truly wasn't my deal. But I had agreed to support it and my responsibility was to be an upbeat cheerleader for the new company.

After Steve and Jerry made their comments, it was my turn to take the podium, and I didn't hold back. "Shortly before 9:00 P.M. last night," I said, "I had the honor and privilege of signing these papers that irrevocably cast a vote—the first vote taken—a vote for my 100 million shares, more or less, for this merger. I did it with as much or more excitement and enthusiasm as I did when I first made love some forty-two years ago!" I got a laugh but I also made the point that I was excited about the deal and would support it to the best of my ability. (Days later, during a Turner Broadcasting executive committee meeting in Atlanta, one of our executives said that they all did the math and were surprised that I was nineteen years old when the earlier event in question occurred. "It's true," I confessed. "It took me nineteen years before my first time, but it was just a few minutes before my second—I was a fast learner!")

It was an exciting moment. The press coverage was extensive and largely favorable. The merger was hailed as "a deal for the new millennium," and Time Warner's stock rose about 40 percent that day. The shares I owned personally were now worth about $10 billion.

Little did I know that it would all be down-hill from here.

Shortly after the announcement, it became clear that many within Time Warner did not share Jerry's enthusiasm for the deal. On that Friday after Jerry and Steve shook hands, lawyers for Time Warner seques-tered members of top management and briefed them on the merger. Not only were they shocked, many were frustrated and insulted to find that the deal was fully ne-gotiated and this was the first they'd heard of it. Jerry had worked so quickly and se-cretly that even Time Warner's own CFO had been kept in the dark. Like me, when they first heard the terms they had trouble accepting the idea that AOL was acquiring Time Warner and it was hard to think that we would be called AOL Time Warner, not Time Warner AOL. Many at Time Warner who had business dealings with AOL viewed their people as arrogant, brash, and generally hard to work with. That the merger would drive Time Warner's stock to new highs was not enough to gain their enthusiasm. Merging companies is challenging in the best of circumstances, and with so many Time Warner people questioning the deal the task here would be particularly difficult.

Just a few months later, Internet stocks started to plummet. During a three-week period starting in late March the Nasdaq index lost almost one third of its value. AOL's stock fell, too, and since this was the currency they were using to buy our company, the deal looked worse by the day. Several factors contributed to the technology stock sell-off, but a big reason for the downturn was a realization that many of these companies simply were not good businesses.

In the late 1990s, the goal for many dot-com start-ups was to raise money and spend it aggressively to grow market share as quickly as possible. But with many of these companies, their cash burn rates were so great and their revenue so low that they began to run out of money, and just as advertising had been the first thing they spent cash on when they had it, it was the first thing they cut as they ran out. Since so many of AOL's advertising customers were other dot-com companies, the downturn put a big strain on the business. As we approached the June shareholder vote on the merger Steve and Jerry continued to assure investors that AOL was different. They would survive this downturn, and once the company was combined with Time Warner's content, ad sales, and cross-promotional capabilities, this new merged company's growth would resume.

At this same time, unbeknownst to me, Jerry and Steve had formulated a new management structure for the company. That May, on the day when they planned to send out a press release announcing these changes, I was out at my Vermejo Park Ranch in New Mexico. The phone rang and it was Jerry. He said, "I'm restructuring the company. I'm splitting it in two parts and I'm going to give Pittman half and Parsons the other half. The cable networks will report to Pittman. You will continue to be vice chairman of the overall company."

I was stunned. I said, "Jerry, I've got a contract that still has a year and a half to run and it stipulates that I'll be in charge of the networks."

"Well, if you read your contract," he answered, "you'll see that we can change your responsibilities as long as we pay you your salary for the rest of your term and we're perfectly willing to do that if needed."

I tried to stay calm and I said, "Jerry, in my entire career I've never heard of abrogating someone's contract." Jerry tried to convince me that I would play an important role as vice chairman but when I asked him what my duties would be, it was clear that there weren't any. Shortly after hanging up, I got a fax of the press release announcing the new management structure.

For the first time in my life, I'd been fired.

——— A TED STORY ———

"In His Mind I Fired Him"
—Jerry Levin

I was trying to build a bigger company with more Internet activity and this was something that Ted was not interested in, just as he wasn't interested in the start-up of The WB Network, which he looked at as taking resources away or being competitive with what he was doing. So I had to figure out how to make this work in terms of management. I started to put in place a structure to run a new, bigger company with a lot of pressure because of the profile of AOL and Time Warner and the desire to really go forward on the Internet.

I was trying to get everybody into a different position and I couldn't expect Ted to work for Bob Pittman or even Steve Case. But because of the force of his personality I genuinely wanted him attached to AOL Time Warner. The intention was that he would be a cheerleader and inspirer. He could go off and do other things and not have to worry about the day-to-day. This was important to me but it was hard to get that point of view across. I was concerned about the conversation and tried to articulate it with some feeling. I couldn't say to him, "You know, when people build a business and they're the fiery entrepreneur, once it gets institutionalized they're probably better off stepping away—and of course, maybe it's better if you decide to step away." But during the call, he never said, "You're firing me." He just kind of took it and then went on this public bandstand that he had been fired.

He thought we took his balls off and that started the obvious deterioration— much to my regret—of our relationship because he was offended. In his mind I fired him. Now he, like everybody else, was very supportive of the transaction because obviously the stock was up and was worth a lot of money and it looked good and got a lot of attention. And then when the bubble burst and the stock started to go down that's when the relationship really deteriorated. I don't say this meanspiritedly at all because I think Ted is one of the most fabulous individuals of the past century, but he does like to target someone as the devil. That was Murdoch for a while, and I had also been the devil several times before in our relationship so I've just accepted that. I think that's what happened. I became the symbol of all of his problems. And if it helps him to know that I'm the proximate cause of a number of things and now I'm out of the way, that's okay, too. I hope and I believe he's actually better off now because he was not constructed to be a part of institutions like AOL Time Warner or Time Warner. He's better off doing what he's meant to do, which is to perfect the planet.

Remember, I had known and worked with Ted for a long period of time—since the early 1970s. I was the one who introduced him that night when he pledged a billion dollars to start the U.N. Foundation and it was one of the greatest evenings of my life. Just working together on CNN was so meaningful to me, and seeing his relationship with Jane was the most fascinating thing. We had a long history together and we really haven't spoken in years, which I really regret. I take whatever responsibility but it's just a shame. I have everlasting regret that we don't talk.

——————— A TED STORY ———————

"I Think You've Been Screwed"
—John Malone

I went down and visited Ted in New Mexico. Jane had left by then and her stuff was being hauled out of the ranch. I took a helicopter there and took Ted for a ride to see his property from the air, which he had never done. The first morning I was there Ted gets a fax announcing some details of the AOL deal and it says that Bob Pittman is going to be running the Turner networks. And Ted walks out of his little office there with this thing and he shows it to me and he says, "How can they do this? I have a contract."

And I said, "Well, I don't know what your lawyers will tell you but all you can get is money damages and they're still going to pay you. I think you've been screwed, Ted."

He was ashen-faced. He said, "How could Jerry Levin do this to me? He was supposed to be my best friend in the world."

I called Levin after that to find out

how he could have stabbed Ted in the back. Jerry's public posture was it was a requirement of the deal but then he privately said they were having problems with Ted and his personal conduct. But whatever the justification or lack thereof they did it to him. They absolutely screwed him. They reneged on a commitment that they should never have reneged on. That's the way I look at it because I didn't see that Pittman was even half the guy as Ted in terms of running the Turner networks. Levin screwed him and there's no way you can tell me otherwise. I know how badly Steve Case wanted that deal. If Jerry had said, "Absolutely not, Ted's got a contract," or something, there's no way Case would have said, "Bullshit."

It didn't ring true. I think it was a deliberate move to cut Ted's balls off and the fact that they didn't disclose that to him when they got him to sign an agreement to support the deal but only afterward, I just think it was pretty low, frankly, and that's what I told him. I said, "You've been stabbed in the back by a guy you thought was your friend and it's pretty ugly, Ted."

To breach an understanding and a relationship of many years and even to do it in the face of damaging the very business that you're acquiring, the whole thing just stank. I really lost my enthusiasm for that management team at that point.

I was in shock. Jerry was taking away my responsibilities but my contract gave him that option, as long as my salary was paid out through the end of the term. My pay at the time was about $1 million a year, but that didn't matter much to Jerry or Steve. They wanted me out and if it cost the company $1.5 million, that was fine with them. I found it hard to take that they were laying off 40,000 employees to cut costs but had no problem paying me my seven-figure salary to do nothing. I had worked at the same company my entire career and had been in charge of the Turner businesses for nearly forty years and now it was over.

AOL and Time Warner shareholders

formally approved the merger the following month. Jerry and Steve were determined to keep pressing forward through the regulatory approval process but, of course, I had lost my enthusiasm for the deal. I was worried about the future of the company. It seemed increasingly obvious that Time Warner was hitching its wagon to a lame horse but having been pushed to the sidelines after pledging my shares, there wasn't a lot I could do about it. When I was in Atlanta or New York I continued to go to my office but I didn't have anything to do. Bob Pittman was friendly but he didn't ask for my advice. Jerry and Steve continued to invite me to periodic meetings with the division heads but fairly soon it became clear that these were nothing more than update sessions and the company's important strategic decisions were being made in meetings to which I wasn't invited.

It's hard to know how I would have felt if the company had been doing well, but standing on the sidelines while our stock and my personal fortune cratered was hard to take. Less than a year from the merger announcement, AOL's stock was down by half. The dot-com bubble had burst and a downturn in the ad market was hurting Time Warner businesses across the board. Companies like Time Warner and Turner Broadcasting had weathered many ups and downs in the ad market over the years, but in this case, for AOL, the situation was extreme. Their stock price was driven by very ambitious sales targets, which had relied heavily on selling ads to other dot-com companies, which, by this point, were dropping like flies. AOL Time Warner was in a precarious position and Jerry and Steve refused to show any concern publicly and continued to stick with their aggressive growth projections. The regulators finally approved the merger in January 2001.

In March of that year, Bob Pittman brought Jamie Kellner, who had been in charge of The WB Network, to Atlanta to also run Turner Broadcasting, replacing Terry McGuirk. I wasn't consulted on this decision and while I didn't have issues with Jamie, I was not a supporter of The WB because I didn't see any way that it would ever make money. (And it didn't—several years later it merged with UPN to form The CW.)

It was a really rough time. Psychiatrists will tell you that the two most traumatic things that can happen to a man are going through a divorce and losing his job, and these two things were happening to me at the same time. And I couldn't sell my stock as the company's value plummeted. I was like Humphrey Bogart in *The Treasure of the Sierra Madre,* watching all that gold dust slipping through his fingers.

In that same summer, when things looked like they couldn't get any worse, I was hit by another tragedy—the loss of one of my grandchildren. My youngest child, Jennie, and her husband, Peek, had a daughter named Maddox who was diagnosed with Hurler's syndrome. This is a very rare genetic disorder and sufferers have an enzyme deficiency that limits their body's ability to break down chains of sugar molecules. This causes waste materials to gather in connective tissues and vital organs, including the heart and the brain. In addition to causing physical deformities and mental retardation, it inevitably leads to premature death. Jennie and Peek showed great courage throughout their ordeal, and Maddox passed away in August 2001, three months shy of her third birthday. To see my daughter go through this with her child, and watch someone so innocent suffer and die so young, was brutally hard on everyone in the family.

For me, it brought back sad memories of my sister, Mary Jean, another innocent child who was taken from us. It was a terrible time for our family and with the other problems that I faced, it was almost too much. I developed anxiety that was worse than anything I'd experienced before. When I lost my sister and my father I was able to channel my energies into work and my sailing career. But I was now retired from competitive sports and my hands were tied behind my back as the company I built went in a nosedive.

Nearly all of my life I've slept like a log, but now I was tossing and turning almost every night. Eventually, I came up with a technique that helped. After spending my days dealing with all the things that were going wrong, at night I'd put my head on the pillow and try to think about the things

I was thankful for, especially my family. In my mind, almost like a slide show, I'd picture my children and their families and think of each of their names. I'd start with the oldest, Laura, and picture her, then her husband, then their kids. Then I'd go to Teddy, the next oldest, and do the same with him and his family. Once I'd worked through Rhett, Beau, Jennie and their children, I'd go back in the reverse direction. Picturing my family helped calm me and cleared my head of worries as I slowly drifted off to sleep.

But even on days following a decent night's rest, I found myself sad, frustrated, and perhaps more than at any other time in my life, worried. How much lower could the stock go? For the first year after the deal's announcement, as a company "insider," security laws prevented me from selling stock. That term was now over but there was a concern that stock sales by a high-profile person and a member of the company's board of directors (I had not yet given up my seat) might trigger even more concerns and increased selling. The stock had fallen so far by the summer of 2001 (shares traded below $40 in August) that part of me thought that it couldn't possibly go any lower. But what if it did? To finance my philanthropy and land purchases I had taken on about $250 million in debt. When I was worth $7 to $10 billion I was okay but now that the stock was dropping, I had to be concerned. I started to have thoughts about having to sell my properties, even considering which ones would go first.

At the end of August I flew to Brisbane, Australia, for our fifth summer Goodwill Games. Coming on the heels of my granddaughter's funeral, it was a sad flight. The Games themselves provided a welcome distraction, but even this international sporting event was bittersweet for me. I continued to believe that gathering the world's athletes for peaceful competition was a great idea, but the Goodwill Games were still losing money, and I expected that the new regime at Turner Broadcasting would pull the plug on them and that these games would be the last.

I left Australia following the closing ceremonies. As I made that long flight back to Atlanta I tried to rest, but wound up spending much of the flight reflecting on all that had happened over the past twenty months. I continued to be concerned, but on that evening of September 9, 2001, I tried to convince myself that things could only get better.

32

Stepping Away

On the morning of September 11, 2001, I was in my CNN Center office with my television tuned to CNN and the sound turned down. I was jet-lagged and tired after my flight home from Australia but I remember speaking briefly to my old friend NBA commissioner David Stern first thing that day. We had executives getting ready to fly to New York to meet with NBA representatives about a possible new rights agreement, and I wanted to check in with him before that meeting. Sometime after that call CNN began showing images of smoke coming out of one of the World Trade Center towers. The initial reports said it might have been a small plane accident. I was having trouble understanding how a crash like that could happen in downtown Manhattan when I saw on my monitor another plane go into the second tower and instantly thought, "We're at war." It felt like I was watching Pearl Harbor, live.

I immediately went downstairs to the CNN studios to offer what support and encouragement I could. At one point, I looked up at a monitor displaying Headline News and it was still running its usual loop of various news stories. I ran into Walter Isaacson—who had replaced Tom Johnson as CEO of CNN in July—and suggested he should put the regular CNN feed on Headline News as well. He agreed and the change was made minutes later. As tragic as those events were, it was gratifying once again to see CNN performing at such a high level at such a critical moment. But this was a different experience for me than our coverage of the Gulf War. I don't know if any decisions were discussed that were similar to the ones we made to let our crews stay in Baghdad, but if they were, my input wasn't requested. CNN didn't report to me anymore and it was a strange feeling to be on the outside looking in at this company that I'd helped create. (Months later, when the U.S. war effort began in Afghanistan, I volunteered to go over as a military correspondent. I figured this would be another unique experience and without day-to-day responsibilities I could certainly spare the time. CNN management politely declined my offer.)

Jerry was in Europe on September 11 and was greatly affected by the day's events. The tragedy brought back reminders of his son's murder, and once he was able to fly back to New York, he returned to his job that much more adamant about AOL Time Warner making a difference. He was quoted referring to the company as a "ministry" and said that, post-9/11, our journalistic mission was more critical than ever. I had always been in favor of using the company's media for the common good but the Time Warner mind-set seemed to be at odds with the culture at AOL. Not only had they never considered their company to be a journalistic enterprise, their primary focus had always been on growing the business and making their numbers. With the country moving into a recession, the company struggling, and the 9/11 tragedy so fresh in everyone's minds, this was a tense and difficult time at AOL Time Warner.

After months of portraying our company as nearly invincible, in late September Jerry and Steve confessed to investors that they weren't going to make the numbers for the third quarter. The market responded in a predictable way, driving the stock down to a new low of $30 per share.

As AOL Time Warner's problems intensified, I felt like I was increasingly being kept at arm's length. When I requested updates or reports on corporate issues, I rarely got what I asked for. I didn't appreciate being treated this way. I might have been stripped of my operating role but I was still vice chairman, the largest individual shareholder, and a member of the board and I deserved to be kept in the loop. I continued with my years-old practice of being away from the office for days at a time. Earlier in my career, when I was delegating to trusted people who worked with me, this worked well; they did their jobs without daily interference and I would be out at one of my properties clearing my head and thinking about strategic issues. But now that I was no longer in charge, I think my absences worked against me as it became easier for Jerry to shut me out.

I tried a few times to discuss this with Steve Case but I got the feeling that he didn't really know what was going on either. It seemed ironic that Case and I—the two founders of the company—were being ignored. The situation was unacceptable and something needed to be done.

─────── A TED STORY ───────

"Let's Get a Meeting with Case"
—Taylor Glover

Both Ted and I had the perception that Jerry Levin had built a wall insulating Ted from the company and people on the inside were telling me that the same thing was happening to Steve Case. Given the fact that AOL had acquired Time Warner, you'd have thought that Case would have this monumental role but he really didn't; Jerry still controlled everything. I suggested to Ted that we meet with Case to discuss our concerns with him and he agreed.

We set up a time to meet before the November 2001 board meeting in Dulles, Virginia. The plan was for me to go a half hour early and talk with Case privately about our perception of what was happening to Ted and to him. Ted would join us in progress, after I'd had a chance to lay this all out. Just prior to the meeting, I was surprised to learn that Steve was bringing his fellow "AOL" board members to the meeting, including Ken Novak and Miles Gilburne, but I decided to tell the entire group the same things I had planned to say to Steve privately.

I told them that in the first few weeks after the merger, Ted remained involved and informed—there was no wall around him. "Then a row of bricks went up," I said. "Then another row was added, then another, and another, and pretty soon Ted couldn't see over that wall anymore. He could try to jump and pull himself up to try to see over it but eventually it got too high." I looked at Case and said, "Ted's been totally shut out and we think the same thing is happening to you."

My perception at the start of the meeting was that Steve looked very stiff and didn't seem particularly interested. He was probably wondering why he was meeting with somebody like me in the first place. But as I described this situation he leaned forward in his chair and all but acknowledged that this was happening to him. He didn't say it in words but his body language said, "Okay, we're all in the same camp here," and you could sense around the table a collective desire to go after Jerry.

The meeting was cordial and constructive but before we could get into any further discussion on our next steps Ted burst through the door and the tone changed immediately. Ted had a fire in his eyes like I'd never seen before and to my surprise he started screaming at Case. He said,

"You don't have any money in this damn deal! What are you worth, anyway? And what are *you* worth, Novak?" He instantly put everybody on the defensive but he made an important point. A lot of the people on the AOL side had cashed out a great deal of their stock while Ted had held on to his and was riding it into the ground.

The meeting didn't go quite the way we had planned but it was productive. We helped Steve Case understand more clearly what was happening to him and to Ted. He and the other AOL directors also saw firsthand how irate Ted had become. If it came time to count noses around the table, Ted would be on their side. Case already controlled half the board. All he needed was Ted and one or two others and Jerry was history.

I knew that Taylor had planned for the meeting to go differently but the more I thought about the events of the prior two years the harder it was to contain myself.

Getting fired was tough enough, and now I had to stand on the sidelines and watch the people who pushed me out run the company nearly into the ground. At this point, I realized I could no longer reserve all my anger for Jerry Levin. It was clear if AOL hadn't merged with us, they would be in far worse shape. Instead, just prior to the dot-com bubble bursting, they acquired Time Warner with their inflated stock, effectively slowing their own descent while dragging us down with them in the process. I wasn't happy and it was time for these guys to see it for themselves.

In the board meeting the next day I was more restrained, but when it was explained that our earnings were coming in well below the projections we had given Wall Street it was time for me to voice my disappointment to the full group of directors. Jerry was sitting right next to me and after trying to be supportive of him for so long I didn't know if I'd have the courage to speak up, but I did.

"I'm not happy," I said. The room got very quiet. "I'm not happy with these results and I'm very disappointed with the senior management of this company." I got a little louder and more adamant as I went along, reminding my fellow directors that our stock price had been cut in half since that summer and saying that it was time that we as a board stepped up and did something about it. When I finished, no one else said a word. The meeting adjourned just a few minutes later.

No discussion followed my comments, but no one defended Jerry, either, and he must have realized that the handwriting was on the wall. In the following days he worked out a deal with Fay Vincent, a longtime director and head of the board's governance committee. Jerry announced his resignation in December, explaining that he would officially leave the company in May of 2002. Dick Parsons would succeed him as CEO and Bob Pittman would be COO, marking one of the first times in the nearly two years since the deal was announced that a Time Warner person won out over someone from AOL for a key executive position. Steve Case would remain in his role as the company's chairman.

Amid these transitions some people

speculated that I might try to take over as the company's chairman or CEO. I considered this briefly—along with just about every scenario I could think of to help the business—but returning to a management role simply wasn't desirable. Running AOL Time Warner would have meant significant changes in my lifestyle. I'd have to move to New York and spending time at my properties would no longer be an option. I might have convinced myself to make these sacrifices if I thought I had the answers to the company's problems but I didn't. We had made a fundamentally bad move by merging with AOL, and I didn't know how to turn the ship around any more than anybody else did. It was a relief to have Jerry gone and his replacement had the full support of the board. Dick Parsons is a good guy and the last thing he needed was Ted Turner going on some other quixotic adventure to try to regain power in the company. The best thing I could do now was to give Dick my support and hope that he could at least get things stabilized.

Dick moved quickly to assure Wall Street that he would be transparent and realistic when it came to reporting on the company's performance. In March of 2002 he made it clear that our first quarter results would fall well short of projections and when these disappointing numbers were announced in late April, the stock dipped below $20. Realizing that my days of having a meaningful say at the company were over and with philanthropic and other commitments, I decided to start liquidating some stock. In May I sold 10 million shares of AOL at about $18.50 a share. This netted me almost $190 million and while it was a relief to pay off most of my bank debt, it hurt to know that just a year earlier these same shares were trading closer to $50.

The price kept falling as we headed into the summer and by early July it fell below $13. Then, just as things couldn't get any worse, *The Washington Post* ran a story describing accounting irregularities on the AOL side of the company. The piece accused management of artificially inflating revenue numbers to meet the company's aggressive sales targets. When analyzing dot-com companies, Wall Street focused almost entirely on revenue growth and keeping these numbers high was vital to maintaining a healthy stock price. The *Post* article accused AOL management of maneuvers that wouldn't necessarily change the bottom line, but would present a misleading revenue picture. For example, they described AOL winning legal disputes with other companies and instead of taking cash as their settlement, they would "sell" them AOL advertising inventory of equivalent value. They'd then record this dollar amount as ad revenue, thus artificially boosting their top-line numbers.

Coincidentally or not, Bob Pittman resigned the day the story broke, and shortly thereafter, the Securities and Exchange Commission announced a full investigation of the company. On this news, the stock hit an all-time low of $8.70. It had been hard enough watching what I felt to be mismanagement of the company, but when I first heard of these allegations, my disappointment reached new levels. Throughout my career, I had run the company aggressively but I always demanded that we be honest. At Turner Broadcasting, we worked hard and overcame huge obstacles, but we always played by the rules. From my upbringing with my dad to the military schools I attended, honor and integrity were paramount with me. To be associated now with a company accused of dishonest behaviors left me disappointed and angry.

Meanwhile, over the past two and a half years my net worth had gone from nearly $10 billion down to about $2 billion. To put this in perspective, I lost nearly $8 billion in roughly thirty months. This means that, on average, my net worth dropped by about $67 million *per week,* or nearly $10 million *per day, every day,* for two and a half years. Losing that much money so quickly might have been a record, but it obviously wasn't the kind I was hoping to set.

But what could I do about it? No one wants to sell at a low and when the stock fell below $9.00 it was hard to imagine things getting any worse. The company was being punished for not making its numbers and the SEC investigation hung over us like a cloud, but when you looked simply at the asset value of the Time Warner side of the company, the stock was clearly worth more than where it was currently trading. Wall Street realized this, too, and buyers slowly returned to the stock as we moved toward the end of the year, eventually heading back into the low teens.

As time passed I could see few reasons to hang around. Shortly after the start of 2003, Walter Isaacson resigned from his position as CNN's chief executive. When the decision was made on his replacement I wasn't even consulted. I didn't necessarily have an issue with their selection of Jim Walton—he's a good guy and a longtime CNN employee who worked his way up through the ranks—but watching this move get made without any of my input really hurt and drove home the fact that they were paying me $1 million a year to do nothing (my salary practically amounted to hush money). It was time for me to move on.

But as I contemplated this move, something still didn't feel right. I had lost all this money, been fired from my job, and now I was going to resign from the company, while the mastermind of this disastrous merger—Steve Case—was still the company's chairman? I didn't think it was good for the company. Dick Parsons was running the company day to day but Case's presence as chairman was enough to bring out a lot of bitterness and resentment in many of our executives and employees. While I never got to know him very well, I was in some ways sympathetic to Steve. His brother had recently passed away from brain cancer. I knew how painful a loss like this could be and I felt sorry for him. Like me, he was an entrepreneur who had built his company, not a corporate executive who had businesses handed to him. Still, I was a major shareholder and believed it was in the best interest of the company for him to be replaced as chairman.

―――――――― A TED STORY ――――――――

"Steve Case Had to Go"
—Gordy Crawford

When everything was crumbling at AOL and the stock was collapsing I would increasingly talk to the friends I developed over the years, at Turner and particularly at Warner Brothers. These guys had had their personal fortunes wiped out. The stock had collapsed and they were furious—but nobody had laid a glove on Steve Case, who was the architect of all this. He may say he never knew it was going on—which I always found hard to believe—but even if he didn't, it was definitely his kind of cowboy culture that he set up that allowed it all to happen. The guys at Warner Brothers would tell me how Steve would come out to the West Coast as chairman of the company and have a meeting at Warner Brothers and they all had to sit around the room, kow-towing to the chairman who had brought this calamity upon them.

It was just horrible for the culture of the firm, so I thought, "We've got to get rid of Steve Case." I called Ted and I called John Malone because they were the two other significant holders of Time Warner stock and I said let's get together and talk about what we want to do. Everyone agreed, so Ted and I both flew out to Malone's and we had a meeting in John's office that lasted most of a morning. We talked about a wide range of things

that needed to be done at Time Warner, but the one piece of actual business that came out of the meeting
was that Steve Case had to go. John
said, "He's got to go but I'm not doing
it," and Ted said, "I'm not doing it."

"Okay guys," I said, "I'll do it." So
my next trip back to New York I went
in and did my usual thing, seeing two
or three Time Warner people, going
over the numbers with CFO Wayne
Pace, and then I saw Steve Case. I
told Case about the meeting with
John and Ted and said, "I want you to
resign."

"No," he said, "no way, I'm not going. That's fine you feel that way, but
I'm not going anywhere."

I said, "Well, you know we may
have to vote against you. We're probably not going to do a proxy fight but
we're definitely going to vote against
you when it's time for the annual
meeting and I'm going to encourage
other investors to do the same." As I
recall I actually ended up making half
a dozen calls to other large investors

and proposed that. Over the next three or four months there was more noise and people talking about Steve leaving and that's when he finally decided not to run again.

Steve announced his resignation from the company in the middle of January, and shortly thereafter I decided to do the same. We would both remain on the board but would officially step away from our management positions at the directors meeting in May.

If you included my time mowing grass around my father's billboards, I'd been working for the company for about fifty years. Knowing it was coming to an end, I was in a somber mood as I approached that May board meeting. Dick Parsons was assuming Case's role as chairman and when it came time to recognize our resignations, he went on for several minutes about Steve's contributions to the company, his founding of AOL, and so forth, but I didn't get much more than a quick mention. I don't think I was snubbed intentionally. There had been so many other high-level changes and departures that mine was considered to be just one of the latest, but this company had been my life. Moving on was a momentous thing for me and I left that meeting a little bit sad.

As I've said, I try to move forward from setbacks as quickly as possible. I also know that things don't always work out the way you want them to and I've always tried to have a Plan B. In 2000, when I realized I was being pushed aside, I purchased a small office building in Atlanta, just a few blocks from CNN Center. Given its location adjacent to Centennial Park, it looked like it could be a good investment, and I wanted to have a place to go if and when I was either forced out or resigned from AOL Time Warner. I had the place furnished so I wouldn't have to wait for movers when the time came to leave my office in CNN Center.

Immediately after announcing my resignation, my assistant, Debbie Masterson, and I moved to the Turner Building (which was suitably located on Luckie Street—at this point I needed all the luck I could get!). My office window looked out at the CNN Center. I was now on the outside but it was refreshing for me to be in my new location as I was turning this page in my life.

Even though I was nearly sixty-five I had no plans to retire. Part of my Plan B was to be sure that if I left the company I had a business to work on in addition to my philanthropy. Around the same time I bought the Luckie Street property, George McKerrow, Jr., the founder of LongHorn Steakhouses, came to me with a concept for a new restaurant chain. He wanted to create a place that served great, fresh food in a casual, western-themed environment and he suggested that we include bison on the menu. I liked the idea a lot. By the year 2000 the various bison herds on my properties numbered about forty thousand. I loved these animals and while it took me a while to warm to the idea of serving them as food, I realized that helping consumers develop a taste for bison would not only increase the value of my herd, it would be in the best long-term interests of the bison. Bison meat is a lot healthier and leaner than beef. With so much less fat it can be a little tricky to cook but I knew that once people tasted bison prepared properly they would love it, and once bison ranchers realized they had a viable market, they'd want to raise more. The best way to ensure that bison would increase was to get more people to eat them!

George and I agreed to go into business together and we decided to name our restaurants Ted's Montana Grill. Our first location opened in January 2002 in Columbus, Ohio, and after all that had transpired over the past couple of years it was exciting to be creating something new. I've relearned that it's almost as much fun to be running a small company as a big one. The same challenges are there and succeeding with restaurants is really tough. Entry barriers are low (anyone with $500 and a kitchen can open one) and consumers' tastes are fickle, but my partner and his team have done a great job. Within our first five years we opened more than fifty restaurants, created about three thousand new jobs, and had a lot of fun and excitement. It's been a new challenge for me and we're almost breaking even!

In December of 2003, Taylor Glover and I
were driving to a planning meeting for Ted's
Montana Grill when Debbie Masterson
called me with the news that Jimmy Brown
had died. He was seventy-nine years old
and had been ill for some time but his passing was still a surprise and a shock. Sitting
there in the car, tears streamed down my
face as and, instinctively, I started to sing
"The Three Bells," a song I used to sing to
Jimmy. The words go like this:

From a village hidden deep in the valley
One rainy morning dark and gray
A soul winged its way to heaven
Jimmy Brown had passed away

Just a lonely bell was ringing in the little
   valley town
'Twas farewell that it was singing to our
   good friend Jimmy Brown
And the little congregation prayed for
   guidance from above
"Lead us not into temptation, may his
   soul find the salvation
Of thy great eternal love"

Jimmy had been critically important to me and my family and the only constant in my life over the past fifty years. When he first went to work for my dad, he was like a big brother to me. We sailed together, fished together, and most of all spent hours with each other as good friends. Jimmy was the first to get to my father after hearing the gunshot that took his life. Then, after having had such a major impact on me, Jimmy played a key role in helping raise my children. While I was busy sailing and Janie was home with five young kids, Jimmy was part of the glue that kept it all together.

Jimmy used to tell me that when he was a small boy growing up, he'd look through the windows at the country club at the fancy black-tie parties and wish to himself that someday he could wear a tuxedo and go to a party like that. When he turned seventy, my kids and I decided to throw him a formal birthday party at the Capital City Club in Atlanta. Jimmy got his wish, and not only did he attend a black-tie dinner, it was in his honor. It was a wonderful evening, the very least we could do for someone who'd done so much for all of us.

My entire family was there for his funeral and Jane Fonda flew in as well. He had a huge impact on her just as he had on everyone he'd ever met. It was a beautiful event, held at the church at Avalon in Florida. As Jimmy had requested, we had a New Orleans–style procession with musicians and a horse-drawn casket.

My family and I loved Jimmy a great deal and to this day I still feel his loss tremendously.

When I resigned as vice chairman of AOL Time Warner, I considered leaving the board at the same time. I decided against it because I still loved the company, I still owned a significant amount of its stock, and I hoped that I might have some influence if I continued to be involved as a director. I was also concerned that there wasn't anyone on the board with any experience in journalism or the media business. The other directors were all smart, accomplished people but they'd all achieved their success in other fields. Perhaps I was spoiled by the old Turner Broadcasting board. That group was unusual, with all of the members holding key positions in the cable industry. I had suggested that they consider people like Tom Johnson or Tom Brokaw to be directors (the former having recently retired from CNN and the latter preparing to leave NBC) but my advice wasn't heeded.

Going to these board meetings became a painful chore for me. After so many years of enjoying tremendous growth, working with an AOL Time Warner board that was trying to get things stabilized, shedding assets and laying people off, was hard. Slowly loosening my ties to Time Warner (the "AOL" part of the name was dropped in late 2003), I continued to sell my shares. In February 2003, a month after my announced resignation as vice chairman, I began to sell more stock and by May of 2003, I was down to about 7 million shares—a significant stake but well down from the nearly 100 million that I had once owned.

I kept up with the media business by reading the industry trade magazines and the usual board materials the company sent to its directors, but increasingly the bulk of my time and energy was focused on my philanthropy and helping Ted's Montana Grill get going. I was moving forward but still wrestled with occasional bouts of anxiety and frustration.

Even with my hard-charging lifestyle I've managed to take care of myself and have enjoyed reasonably good health. But in late 2004, shortly after my sixty-fourth birthday, I started having trouble with fibrillation in my heart. The first time it happened my heart started racing and I didn't know what was wrong. In hindsight, the best thing I could have done would have been to simply lie down until it passed, but the symptoms scared me so I raced to the emergency room to make sure everything was okay. After trying different procedures for two years I had two catheter ablations that so far seem to have taken care of the problem. I had to slow down for a few weeks and I slept more than usual, but then, when I was starting to feel better, I broke a bone in my shoulder skiing in Montana and needed surgery.

Over a stretch of about six months I was seeing so many doctors that I started to refer to myself as the "Phantom of the Hospital." I tried to keep my sense of humor (whenever I walked down the hospital hall-ways I enjoyed sticking my head in other people's rooms and ask, "Hey, what are you in here for?"), but my health problems did slow me down and since my affiliation with Time Warner continued to cause me a fair amount of stress I decided that I'd had enough. I made the announcement that our annual shareholder meeting in May would be my last. It was nice that the event was held in Atlanta. They played a flattering video of my career and gave me a warm send-off. That August, with Time Warner stock back up above $16.00, I sold my final 7 million shares.

When I took over my dad's billboard com-pany, I was determined to make it a suc-cess. I managed to do that and was fortunate enough to have a great time and make a lot of money in the process. Along the way I also began to realize there were a lot of problems in the world that needed solving. I started to focus on these, and these efforts gave me an even greater sense of satisfaction than I'd achieved in business.

I was sixty-seven years old when I stepped away from Time Warner. I had been through a lot but I still felt I had plenty of time and energy left and I was determined to put it to good use.

33

Onward and Upward

Over the years, I've visited more than sixty countries in every part of the world. In addition to making a lot of friends I've also seen firsthand the desperate challenges facing so many people. It's been eye-opening for me and I've discovered that the more people you meet, the more you learn, and the more you learn, the more you want to help, and the more you help, the better you feel.

Stepping away from my business career wasn't easy, and the circumstances of my departure left me with lingering sadness, but being free from those responsibilities has allowed me to concentrate my energies to work on solutions to the world's more pressing problems. Instead of worrying about overnight Nielsen ratings for the Turner cable networks I spend more time reading magazines like *The Economist* and books about the future of the planet. Early in my career I didn't have much money, but I did have cable networks, and I tried to air positive, informative programs with partners like the National Geographic Society, Audubon, Cousteau, and the National Wildlife Federation. These days I have some money but no networks, so I'm putting my resources and energies toward tackling the important issues. Today, the three problems that concern me the most are the threat of nuclear annihilation, climate change, and the continuing growth of the world's population.

I first became concerned about population in the late 1970s and early 1980s when I met and read books by Paul Ehrlich and Lester Brown. They opened my eyes to the fact that the world's population is growing rapidly and the rate of increase over the past century has been truly alarming. From the dawn of mankind, it took several million years for the world's population to grow to one billion people and we passed this milestone around the year 1800. It took only 130 years to double that number, and by the time I was born, in 1938, the world's population had moved just beyond the 2 billion mark. It then took just thirty years to add the third billion, fourteen years for the fourth (1974), and thirteen more years to reach 5 billion, in 1987. We added the sixth billion in eleven years and trends suggest that we'll pass 7 billion sometime around 2009. It's not inconceivable that the world's human population could quadruple in my lifetime (I'll turn eighty-three in 2021, the year we're projected to reach 8 billion).

These are staggering facts and we have to be concerned about the demands that this level of human growth is putting on the planet. The amount of food, medicine, and energy we consume, the volume of waste we produce, and the toxins we put into our air and our water continue to increase as we add more people. At the same time, per capita consumption, especially in developed countries like the United States, is increasing as our population grows. Take automobiles. According to the U.S. Department of Energy, in 1938, the year I was born, there were roughly 230 motor vehicles per 1,000 Americans. That number has more than tripled to about 775 per 1,000 people today. Not only are we driving more cars longer distances, we're building bigger houses, eating more, and buying more consumer goods. This is all a result of a growth-driven capitalistic society and while a lot of good comes from that (I've certainly benefited from the capitalist system), we have to take a hard look at the consequences.

There's no one easy solution to the population explosion. Human beings are hardwired to procreate. We enjoy sex and we love the offspring we produce. Before I became concerned about population I had five children myself, and I love each one of them dearly. (Fortunately, my kids still laugh when I joke that if I'd known better at the time I would have tried to have fewer kids, but now it's too late to send any of them back!) Nevertheless, I'm convinced that the world would be better off if we limit the number of children we have to just two per family. A lot of the growth in population has occurred in underdeveloped countries and I'm encouraged by efforts there to educate and empower women to make smarter decisions when it comes to their relationships and their own reproductive rights. I understand that some religions view family planning as a sin but I'm concerned that our world is now in a dire situation where not making efforts to keep family sizes down is increasingly irresponsible.

Another thing that keeps me up at night is the possibility of nuclear war. During the Cold War, we Americans came to view the Soviets as the enemy but my firsthand exposure to their citizens and to a leader like Mikhail Gorbachev helped me realize that they didn't want a nuclear war any more than we did. I assumed that once the Cold War ended the United States and Russia would scrap their nuclear weapons and the threat of "mutually assured destruction" would go away once and for all. It wasn't until I saw a *60 Minutes* piece in late 2000 that I realized the threat is equally great or greater now as it was during the

Cold War. Today, the United States and Russia each still continue to have thousands of nuclear warheads aimed at each other and on hair-trigger alert. We don't think that one side will launch a strike against the other, but what if there's an accident or a mistake? It's not like we haven't made mistakes in the past. In 1979, a military engineer in Nebraska loaded a simulated attack into our warning system by accident, and in 1983, the Soviets' detection system showed five nuclear missiles launched against their country by the United States. The incidents were resolved but we might not always be this lucky. It only takes about thirty minutes for U.S.- and Russian-based nuclear missiles to reach their targets across the globe. Once a missile is airborne, the warning time for the other side is incredibly short, and once the country launches a response, the world as we know it would be wiped out in an afternoon's time. This is to say nothing about other nuclear powers like the U.K., France, China, India, Pakistan, and Israel. Some of these countries have histories of conflict with their neighbors that go back centuries and they are obviously capable of mistakes just as we and the Russians are.

It became clear to me that when it came to the threat of nuclear annihilation the world still had plenty to be concerned about and I wanted to do something about it. By the year 2000 I was encouraged by the success we were having with the U.N. Foundation and decided to fund the creation of another foundation to study and remedy the nuclear threat in an independent way, free from the whims of annual government funding. I had no firsthand experience dealing with these issues and knew we needed an expert. Tim Wirth told me there was only one person for this job—his fellow former senator, Sam Nunn of Georgia.

As a centrist Democrat, Sam has earned respect on both sides of the aisle and around the world. While serving in the Senate he did a superb job as chairman of the Armed Services Committee and became an expert on nuclear issues. In the early 1990s, he worked with Republican senator Richard Lugar on the Cooperative Threat Reduction program, commonly known as the Nunn-Lugar Act. After the

Cold War ended, the United States and the rest of the world clearly had an interest in seeing Russia's vast nuclear arsenal dismantled in a safe, effective way. But this is an expensive proposition and, if done incorrectly, could lead to dangerous materials winding up in the wrong hands. Through Nunn-Lugar, the United States has supplied funding and other assistance to contribute to these efforts, and by 2007, fifteen years after the program's start, more than seven thousand nuclear warheads have been deactivated along with the destruction of hundreds of missiles, launchers, and bombers.

I had met Sam before but didn't know him well when I invited him to have breakfast. When I explained my idea he grasped it immediately and joined in. We agreed that Sam and I would be co-chairmen of the effort and that he would be CEO. With someone with Sam's experience at the helm, I committed $250 million toward the creation of the Nuclear Threat Initiative. Since taking over, Sam has engaged NTI in a multipronged effort to try to make the world a safer place. He's worked to convince the U.S. and Russian governments that gradual bilateral disarmament would be in each country's best interests. Effectively, we're asking nothing more than for those nations to live up to the Nuclear Non-Proliferation Treaty that we all signed in 1968. I carry a copy of this treaty's Article Six in my wallet. Its language is clear and unambiguous: "Each of the parties to this treaty undertakes to pursue negotiations in good faith on effective measures relating to the cessation of the nuclear arms race at an early date and to nuclear disarmament, and on a treaty on general and complete disarmament under strict and effective international control."

NTI has also concentrated on trying to minimize the threat of nuclear terrorism. With the proper materials, in particular weapons-grade uranium, it's not very hard to create a nuclear weapon, and in the hands of a terrorist, the damage that just one of these could create would be devastating. But enriching uranium to a weapons-grade level is not easy, and it's more likely that a terrorist organization would try to buy or steal these materials from a country that has already produced them for their own military.

A real danger we face today is that there is a great deal of enriched radioactive material around the world that is simply not accounted for, especially in the eastern states of the former Soviet Union. To call attention to this problem, NTI funded the production of a film called *The Last Best Chance*. We put a lot of effort into making this film both dramatic and realistic (incidentally, this movie gave Senator Fred Thompson a chance to play the president of the United States years before he ran for the actual office), showing how terrorists could get their hands on these nuclear materials and how dangerous that would be. The show premiered on HBO and we now offer it for free on NTI's Web site, in hopes that more people will see it and begin to understand the importance of collecting and safeguarding these materials.

To help prevent a disaster, a superpower like the United States needs to play a leading role, but not a dictatorial one, and I'm increasingly concerned about the way we project ourselves to the rest of the world. I don't believe that other countries are predisposed to dislike the United States simply because of our wealth. Whether you're talking about a person or a country, it's okay to be rich and it's okay to be power-ful, just as long as you're humble and co-operative. But if you combine being rich and powerful with being arrogant and un-cooperative, people won't cut you much slack, and I'm afraid that that's the kind of international stance we've taken in recent years.

I tried to make this point a couple of years ago during a Q&A session following a speech. I was critical of the time when our president said to the rest of the world, "You're either with us or against us." I fol-lowed that comment by asking, rhetori-cally, "Well, what if you haven't made up your mind yet?" I took a lot of heat for say-ing that. "Ted Turner can't decide if he's for the terrorists or against them," was the sarcastic line some of my critics took, but that missed my point.

Of course I'm against terrorism, but I'm also against war if it's in any way avoid-able. What I meant by my comments was that an individual or country could support the abolition of terrorism but also disagree with the ways a country chooses to fight it. I really don't see the wisdom of spending

billions of dollars to bomb a country like
Iraq, then spending billions of dollars repair-
ing the damage we've done, all to remove
one crazy dictator from power. There's no
denying Saddam Hussein was a brutally
cruel leader but he never posed a credible
threat to the United States. Had we been
more patient I believe he could have been
removed from power through different
means and without the loss of so many
American and Iraqi lives, and without leaving so many U.S. troops there in such difficult circumstances.

We also need to realize that the old
models of warfare simply don't apply anymore. In the old days, when two countries
went to war, they lined up their armies on
the battlefield and whichever side inflicted
more casualties on the other was the vic-
tor. But in recent times we've seen from
Vietnam and now Iraq that we're fighting
very different wars against a very different
kind of enemy. Nearly sixty thousand American servicemen and women lost their
lives fighting in Vietnam, but more than 3
million North Vietnamese were killed, and
they were the victors. It's nearly impossible to wage a military battle against an

enemy that's willing to make that kind of sacrifice. Taking on Islamic fundamentalists we face a similar challenge. Not only are they willing to tolerate casualties, they believe that dying for their cause will send them directly to a heaven where they'll be surrounded by beautiful women! The truth is, it's easy to start wars, but very hard to stop them, and I worry that our militant posture around the world weakens our position of leadership and hurts our efforts at diplomacy. I believe that if you go around looking for enemies, you'll find them, but if you go out looking for friends, you'll find them, too. The United States has so much to offer other countries besides our military might. Instead of sending bombs and missiles to Iraq we'd have been better served sending doctors, nurses, and teachers.

Since the United States government is still far from friendly with countries like Iran and North Korea, when they say they are pursuing uranium enrichment programs to produce nuclear energy, not weapons, it creates a dilemma for everyone involved. If a country sincerely wants to pursue nuclear power and therefore needs a steady supply of enriched uranium, they need to create their own enrichment capabilities. Of course, once these are in place, outsiders will become suspicious and tensions will arise. At NTI, we're working on a creative but practical solution to this problem.

Instead of building enrichment capabilities, what if a country could buy uranium that has been enriched to a level suitable for nuclear power, but beneath that which is required for making weapons? In 2006, through Sam Nunn's leadership and with the generous financial support of Warren Buffett, NTI announced that it would contribute $50 million to the creation of a nuclear fuel bank. The gift would be made to the International Atomic Energy Agency, which would then be responsible for establishing and maintaining this operation. We made our pledge with the stipulation that one or more of the IAEA's 144 member states would contribute an additional $100 million in funding or an equivalent value of low enriched uranium to begin the bank's creation. We believe that responsibility for creating a bank like this ultimately resides with world governments but we made this pledge hoping to generate some activity. To date, no one has taken us up on this challenge but we've stimulated a lot of conversations on this subject and we hope to see some action very soon.

—————— A TED STORY ——————

"Ted Is Unabashed"
—Senator Sam Nunn

One of the great things about Ted is that he's transparent. He doesn't have a hidden agenda or hidden policies. I've heard him say several times if it weren't for the First Amendment he'd be in jail or worse! He can be outrageous and he can be absolutely brilliant. Ted is unabashed, unafraid, and certainly persistent and spontaneous, with a lot of wisdom and with the ability to get to the core issues. He's displayed all of those during the course of our deliberations.

We had a meeting once at Harvard's Kennedy School with a bunch of experts from Harvard—not just the Kennedy School but from around the campus—to talk with us about the nuclear challenges. I think we started about 10:00 and Ted flew up that morning. I had given him a background paper on the meeting and some of the subjects we were going to talk about.

Ted didn't say anything for about the first hour and then we got on a particular subject and he interrupted and said something to the effect of, "Damn. I'm supposed to know all about this—Sam gave me a memo on this but I spent the whole weekend with my former wife Jane Fonda and we had a wonderful time—and by the way, I got permission from all of my girlfriends." He said, "I was leaving her this morning and I was going to read that paper on the airplane but Jane told me, 'Here's a book you've got to read by this psychiatrist because it will address some of your problems.'"

Ted is saying this to a group of intellectuals sitting around the table who don't know him at all. "Jane, as you probably know, thinks I'm crazy," he said, "but reading this book on the way up here when I should have been reading that paper, I came to the conclusion that this psychiatrist is the one who's crazy!"

And then he stopped and we got back on the subject. By making these comments, Ted relaxed everybody and there were no more stiff necks around the table after that and we got down to the real issues after that in a much more meaningful way. Ted joined in the discussion and grasped the issues very well.

When Senator Nunn speaks about the nuclear threat, he often includes this story, which he describes as a "parable of hope." In 1993, after the Soviet Union had collapsed, our two countries signed the U.S.-Russian Highly Enriched Uranium (or HEU) Agreement. Through this deal, five hundred tons of enriched uranium taken directly from former Soviet nuclear weapons is being blended down to low enriched uranium, for use in American nuclear power plants. Shipments of this material began in 1995 and are expected to continue to 2013. Now, here's something remarkable to consider: In the United States, 20 percent of all our electricity comes from nuclear power plants, and 50 percent of the nuclear fuel used in the United States comes here via Russia as a result of this HEU agreement. That means that roughly one in every ten lightbulbs in the United States is powered by material taken from Soviet missiles that not long ago were pointed directly at us. These kinds of innovative, peaceful, and cooperative efforts continue to fill me with hope about the future.

In addition to the nuclear threat, our team at NTI is also concerned about biological outbreaks. Whether these occur naturally or are caused by the intentional use of harmful agents, they pose a significant global health and security risk. In an effort to help governments and nongovernment agencies around the world prevent, detect, and respond to these threats we established the Global Health and Security Initiative (GHSI). We were very pleased in January 2008 when Google. org chose to give one of its earliest grants to GHSI. It's great to see successful companies like Google being so aggressive and creative in their philanthropic efforts and I was gratified to see them recognize and reward our work at NTI.

I'm also pleased to see people turning their attention to global climate change. I've been speaking out on this subject for years and it hasn't been easy. I've known Al Gore since the 1970s when he was a junior congressman and I was in Washington trying to get the SuperStation off the ground. These many years later it's been gratifying for me to see the success he's had with *An Inconvenient Truth* and watching folks from across the political spectrum take an interest in what has become one of the most serious challenges that our planet has ever faced. Solving these problems will require the effort and cooperation of individuals, corporations, and governments around the world.

The potential impact of climate change is varied and complex, but some of the solutions are fairly straightforward. First of all, we need to change our own personal habits. Energy consumption and CO_2 emissions in countries like China and India are increasing at rapid rates but before the United States can lecture others on being more efficient, we need to set a better example ourselves. Americans have become spoiled by luxuries like air-conditioning, SUVs, and big homes, and it's time we reconsidered the wisdom of driving a four-thousand-pound vehicle to take a two-hundred-pound person to buy a quarter-pound hamburger.

Despite the success that Al Gore and others have had in spreading the message about climate change, plenty of skeptics remain. My hope is that while we might respectfully disagree, we can reach a consensus that there will be many other benefits to lessening our consumption of fossil fuels. For one thing, we could make strides toward cleaning up our air. I still spend a lot of my time in Atlanta and in the past twenty years, asthma cases there have doubled. All you need to do is look at the traffic and smog to understand why. The United States could also lessen its dependence on other nations for so much of its energy, a goal we can all support, regardless of our political affiliation.

One of the reasons I'm optimistic about

our chances in fighting climate change and improving the environment is that doing it will create one of the greatest business opportunities in history. The whole world is going to have to overhaul its entire energy system—a massive undertaking. The alternative energy market is like the early days of cable, but on a much bigger scale. If I were a young person starting out in business today, this is where I'd be placing my efforts. Just like thirty-five years ago when I decided to make a career in television, today there are hundreds of hungry, eager entrepreneurs out to make their fortunes by solving the energy issues.

Over the past several years I've asked Taylor Glover and his team to analyze various alternative energy businesses looking for investment opportunities. We've considered windmill farms on some of my properties but after extensive testing of the wind patterns decided that these would not be economical with today's tax policies. The more we looked into it, the more we felt that solar power offered the greatest opportunities. In 2006 we created a holding company called Turner Renewable Energy and made our first investment in a company called DT Solar. Run by smart entrepreneurs, DT Solar installs solar units for commercial properties and they have quickly built a solid business with excellent growth prospects, and in 2007 we merged the company with First Solar at a price that gave us a healthy return. There are lots of visionary companies like these around the world and many of them will be big winners as they help the world work its way out of an outdated fossil energy system.

A combination of things will have to happen if we're going to combat the global climate crisis, but most of all we need good leadership. Political leaders have to make this issue a priority. They need to use their bully pulpits to speak to the problems and set policies designed to address them. Business leaders have to change the way they run their companies, not only in response to financial and marketplace incentives but also in cases where these adjustments might hurt their bottom line but are simply the right thing to do. The political leadership we're starting to see— particularly in state and local governments— encourages me, as do the steps that major, influential corporations like Wal-Mart and General Electric are taking to run their companies in a more environmentally responsible fashion.

Even my former rival Rupert Murdoch is leading the charge at News Corporation to lessen their carbon footprint, including at their newspaper printing presses, which is no easy task. I was so pleased to hear of Rupert's initiative that I sent him a note and invited him for lunch at Ted's Montana Grill in New York. Who would have thought that after all these years an environmental gesture would give us the excuse to get together and bury the hatchet, but that's exactly what we did. (Rupert and I actually had a good time together. We reminisced a little and since this was shortly after his acquisition of *The Wall Street Journal* and launch of Fox Business Network, I asked him about his plans in that area. After being pushed aside at Time Warner, I was disappointed when they shut down CNNfn, our financial news channel. I always thought we should have kept it going or at least tried to find a buyer. I said to Rupert, "If we'd kept CNNfn on the air, you probably would have paid $100 million for it today, wouldn't you?" And he said, "At least, Ted. Probably more like two or three times that amount." He proved my case and killed my appetite at the same time!)

I like to think that most of the world's problems can be solved, but it won't happen overnight, and that in itself poses a challenge. We live in a society of instant gratification and short attention spans, and these attitudes carry through to our government and business leaders. The brief terms in office that our elected officials serve accentuate the problem. It's difficult to take on hundred-year problems when you're worried about a two-, four-, or even six-year election cycle. Voters want immediate results and politicians want to keep their jobs, so hunkering down to make tough, long-term decisions is not an easy task.

Sometimes these problems can seem overwhelming, and when they do I remind myself of a conversation I had many years ago with Jacques Cousteau. I asked him if he ever got discouraged or worried that the problems he was working on were insurmountable. He looked at me and he said, "Ted, it could be that these problems can't be solved, but what can men of good conscience do but keep trying until the very end?"

Encouraged by Captain Cousteau's words, I intend to keep trying and I really think we can turn things around if we all put our minds to it. When people ask me what condition I think the world is in, I answer with a baseball analogy. It's the seventh inning and we're down two runs. We're behind right now but we still have a chance to win. To pull it out, we need to prevent the other team from scoring again, and then we must score three runs ourselves. But just like late in a ballgame, we've run out of time to waste. We need to stop doing dumb things and to start doing smart ones, and we have to stay optimistic.

We owe it to the 3 million years that our ancestors have been here to make sure we protect our future for the next 3 million years. We have it within us to eliminate illiteracy, disease, poverty, and pain and suffering. It's been estimated that worldwide poverty could be alleviated for just $100 billion a year. If we use just 10 percent of the global military budget, we'd be there. Human beings were responsible for the Holocaust and creating nuclear weapons, but we're also the ones who produced the *Mona Lisa* and Beethoven's Fifth Symphony. In short, we're just as capable of doing great things as we are destructive ones. We're a step away from catastrophe but we're also a step away from paradise. I know we can do it, but we have to work together and we need to get going—right now.

As I approach my seventieth birthday, I'm thankful for the incredibly exciting life I've been fortunate enough to live. Of all my accomplishments, I'm most proud of my children. Laura lives with her family in Atlanta. In addition to raising her children Laura is an active philanthropist who sits on many non-profit boards and chairs the Captain Planet Foundation. Teddy is back in Charleston where he's the founder and manager of a full-service boatyard. Rhett is also in Atlanta where he runs his own documentary film production company. Beau works for Turner Enterprises and in addition to chairing the Turner Endangered Species Fund, he's responsible for the operation of our ranch outfitting business. My youngest daughter, Jennie, is an accomplished film-maker and today breeds horses at her family farm in Kentucky. All five of my children sit on the board of the Turner Foundation and I see them and my eleven grandkids more these days than ever. I do wish I had been able to make my marriages work but it gives me tremendous pleasure to see my kids having grown up to become such good, caring, and productive adults.

In terms of my career, I'm particularly proud of creating CNN and I'm hopeful that the spread of global news will continue to be a force for good and that CNN will resist the temptation to be dragged down by the increased tabloidization of today's popular journalism. I've also taken great pleasure from my philanthropy. Announcing my billion-dollar pledge for the U.N. Foundation was a thrill and seeing all the good that's been done with that money has been incredibly gratifying. Watching other wealthy people like Bill and Melinda Gates and Warren Buffett contributing so much of their resources to charity and having the chance to work with them on some of our projects has been a lot of fun, too.

Looking back, like anybody else, if I had to live my life over there are things I would do differently, but it's been a remarkable ride and I have very few regrets. I'm particularly thankful for my father's advice to set my goals so high that I can't possibly achieve them during my lifetime. That inspiration keeps me energized and eager to keep working hard every day, not only on philanthropy but on new business ventures as well. As I complete this, my first book, I intend to accomplish enough in the next several years to warrant a sequel!

I've often considered and joked about what I might want written on my tombstone. At one point, when I felt like I couldn't get out of the way of the press, "You Can't Interview Me Here" was a leading candidate. In the middle of my career I considered, "Here Lies Ted Turner. He Never Owned a Broadcast Network." These days, I'm leaning toward "I Have Nothing More to Say."

Appendix

Many years ago, I tried to codify the series of things I thought that we as human beings should all try to do to make the world a better place. Originally, there were ten items on this list, but rather than be presumptuous and call them "commandments," and knowing that I had no right telling other people what do (and since I've not been able to live up to all of these consistently myself), I decided to describe these as "voluntary initiatives."

In 2008, I added an eleventh item, to address global climate change. I carry this list in my pocket at all times and share it with others whenever possible.

Eleven Voluntary Initiatives
by Ted Turner

1. I promise to care for Planet Earth and all living things thereon, especially my fellow human beings.
2. I promise to treat all persons every-where with dignity, respect, and friendli-ness.
3. I promise to have no more than one or two children.
4. I promise to use my best efforts to help save what is left of our natural world in its undisturbed state, and to restore de-graded areas.
5. I promise to use as little of our nonre-newable resources as possible.
6. I promise to minimize my use of toxic chemicals, pesticides, and other poi-sons, and to encourage others to do the same.
7. I promise to contribute to those less fortunate, to help them become self-sufficient and enjoy the benefits of a

decent life including clean air and water, adequate food, health care, housing, education, and individual rights.

8. I reject the use of force, in particular military force, and I support the United Nations arbitration of international disputes.

9. I support the total elimination of all nuclear, chemical, and biological weapons, and ultimately the elimination of all weapons of mass destruction.

10. I support the United Nations and its efforts to improve the condition of the planet.

11. I support renewable energy and feel we should move rapidly to contain greenhouse gases.

Acknowledgments

This book wouldn't have happened without a lot of help from many people. I thank Mort Janklow, my agent, for his enthusiastic support and for introducing me to a great team at Hachette Book Group and Grand Central Publishing. Among others there, I thank David Young, Jamie Raab, and Rick Wolff for everything they contributed to making this book the best it could be. I also appreciate the ongoing support of my two right hands—Debbie Masterson and Taylor Glover—for their friendship, support, and everything they do to keep me on track on a daily basis. My friend

Elizabeth Dewberry also lent her literary expertise to provide me with tremendous help when it came to reviewing draft manuscripts. I appreciate the contributions of everyone who took the time to share their own "Ted Stories" with us, and, last but not least, I thank Bill Burke for all his hard work and dedication to this project.

Index

Page 4, bottom, courtesy of Janice Crystal. Page 5, top, courtesy of Turner Broadcasting System, Inc.; center, photographer unknown; bottom, courtesy of Turner Broadcasting System, Inc. Page 6, top, courtesy of Turner Broadcasting System, Inc. Page 7, top, courtesy of United Nations Foundation; center, courtesy of Turner Broadcasting System, Inc.; bottom, courtesy of Ted's Montana Grill. Page 8, top and center, courtesy of Shearon Glover; bottom, *DenverBryan.com.*